$16-95 A85

APPROACHES TO TRAINING AND DEVELOPMENT

DUGAN LAIRD

APPROACHES TO TRAINING AND DEVELOPMENT
Second Edition

with special material
by Peter R. Schleger

**ADDISON-WESLEY
PUBLISHING COMPANY, INC.**
Reading, Massachusetts · Menlo Park, California
Don Mills, Ontario · Wokingham, England
Amsterdam · Sydney · Singapore · Tokyo
Mexico City · Bogotá · Santiago · San Juan

Copyright © 1985 by Addison-Wesley Publishing Company, Inc.

Library of Congress Cataloging in Publication Data

Laird, Dugan.
    Approaches to training and development.

    Bibliography: p.
    Includes index.
    1. Employees, Training of. I. Title.
HF5549.5.T7L33 1985   658.3'124   84-24480
ISBN 0-201-04498-6

Cover design by Gary Fujiwara
Set in 10 point Souvenir Light by TC Systems, Shippensburg, PA
ABCDEFGHIJ-AL-865

HOW IS THIS BOOK ORGANIZED? MORE COMMONLY CALLED THE TABLE OF CONTENTS

REMEMBERING
DUGAN LAIRD

Dugan once told me that, as he looked back at the questions he had answered, his reactions to suggestions made by students, the statements he had given in heated discussion or upon quiet reflection, the regrets he had were always for things he *hadn't* said, rather than for things he had said. For those who knew of his quick wit, his sharp and sometimes startling directness on a subject, this might sound surprising. His point was simple: "If I've made myself clear that I agree or disagree, when they ask my opinion or want an answer or seek advice, then they will go away knowing my agreement or disagreement. On the other hand, if I fail to respond because I am in disagreement and want to protect either them or my goodwill, they might well leave with an impression that will mislead them for the rest of their training life." Such was his approach to the training and development of those who sat at his feet or traveled with him.

This book is what Dugan Laird really believed and knew about training. It is good "Duganese." He put a lot of energy into writing this edition, then agonized over what he'd put in and left out. The revision not only brought it up to date; it also, as he would have said, *rounded it out.* Dugan was determined that this book say what he wanted it to say, as his editor will attest. He won all the arguments, whether he was coining a phrase or playing with grammar. Every once in a while, someone comes along who not only knows something, but also knows how to write and tell others about it. We're fortunate that with all those who know and can't tell, and all those who are telling but don't know much, there is a book that reflects—in understandable terms—what a very knowledgeable trainer knew about a subject on which he spent his lifetime working.

MARTIN M. BROADWELL

Decatur, Georgia
February 1985

APPROACHES TO TRAINING AND DEVELOPMENT

WHY THIS BOOK?

REFLECTIONS ON A REVISION

Revising an old manuscript, I have discovered, can be either exhilarating or gruesome. At its worst, the process must be like giving artifical respiration to the very, very dead. At its best, it's like attending commencement exercises for a favorite offspring—and discovering to your glee and surprise that the youngster has a great deal of sense and is part of an expanding and maturing university.

Fortunately, revising *Approaches to Training and Development* has been one of those happy, "commencement" kinds of experience. First of all, training and development is alive and well and growing. In fact, it has grown to be a part of a much larger arena than envisioned when this book first appeared in 1978. The competency study Pat McLagan did for the American Society for Training and Development (ASTD) in 1983 identified the huge number of roles and skills needed for what many now call Human Resources Development.

In fact, HRD is a beguiling concept; it tempts one to retitle the book to cover that larger spectrum. But the book really deals with the training and development function, so the title remains the same . . . as does the abbreviation T & D for the people we are and the things we do.

One of the comforting things in reviewing the first edition was that what was a boast in 1978 is a bromide today:

> "Indeed, it just may be that for the first time since training departments got born, we have more questions than answers. That's just great, too! For too many years, training people were perceived as answers in search of questions. They had the answer—training! Training would cure careless workmanship; training was what you needed when old-timers ran out of motivation; training took care of bad attitudes.

> Today's professional training and development specialists first determine exactly what the problem is. Then they ask, 'What's causing it?' Only after accumulating hard data to answer those questions do they prescribe training—and then only when training is the appropriate solution. So naturally there are more and more serious questions to ask."

Fortunately we have also enriched our supply of answers. Men like Ned Herrmann have probed deeply into whole brain creativity; Neurological Programming continues to open up the possibility of identifying the internal thought processes of others; we see a new intelligence (even artificial intelligence!) in applying computer technology; scholars like Gardner, Skinner, Rogers, and Knowles continue to enrich learning theory; psychology has learned more about value systems and their impact on developing human behavior; studies of the quality of work life and quality circle activities alter and improve the interface between humans and organizations. It is indeed a human resource development era!

Some answers are definite. Some are tentative. Many are still theoretical. Nearly all are situational, because the magnificent uniqueness of the individual human being becomes more and more evident every day.

This book is quite frankly a mixture of many kinds of answers . . . a deliberate strategy to force each of you to compare your own basic beliefs and practices with approaches taken by other people. And we need as many approaches as we can find—not only because life is complex and situational, but because we are also now blessed with more and more questions. The more we learn, the more we know we don't know.

What great good news! It means that HRD and T & D are growing and can continue to grow . . . in the number of practitioners; in scope, influence, and impact on a growing number of trusting and appreciative clients. People whose training programs were once tolerated are now sought after to help with team building and organizational renewal as well as to train individuals for a job. That means that you and I can continue to grow too.

This book pictures what T & D really is and how it operates, answers typical questions about what we do and why and how—offering answers that are more thoughtful than one can improvise in the heat of a workshop or while pressured to leave for the airport. I have tried to be complete enough to be lucid, brief enough to be digestible, solid enough to be believable—but heretical enough to be provocative. Above all, I hope that this book will be a useful needle, jolting readers into creative action, yet sedating them against that inevitable pain which always accompanies caring about growth in others or in organizations.

In the 33 years I've been closely involved with a dozen T & D departments, and associated as consultant to about 100 more, I've seen many approaches. Most of those approaches contain something worth sharing. Thus this book and this title.

ACKNOWLEDGMENTS

This book is also written as a way of thanking those who continue to lead our profession—people like Geary Rummler, Pat McLagan, Bob Mager, Forrest Belcher, Martin Broadwell, and Paul Chaddock.

Over the years lots of people forced me to have ideas and to share them: Wally Hanson, the original editor of *Training;* John Murphy and his Training Research Forum; Dr. Len Nadler; T. Lee of United Air Lines, and his protégé John. J. Heavey, who recruited more fine T & D people than anyone else I ever met, who supported me when there was no earthly way to do so, and who aggravated me so constantly that I just had to keep finding new approaches.

There are special thanks due to folks who force me to have ideas of my own. At the moment many of these people are in The Woodlands Group, a gang of irreverent believers like their leader Forrest Belcher: Boyce Appel, Don Beck, Geoff Bellman, Joe Hayes, Ned Herrmann, Peggy Hutcheson, Larry Lottier, Frank Basler, Pat McLagan, Mac McCullough, Carlene Reinhart, and Mavis Wilson.

And special thanks to Peter R. Schleger for special duty: research and content for the computer and videotape sections. Thanks too to Ted Nelsen and to Ruth House, who came to the rescue at crucial moments, and to Debbie Ward and—well, it's beginning to sound like the Academy Awards. Best I quit!

Except to thank again a wonderful sister, Bernadette Laird Geist, who always tolerates and encourages and nearly always applauds.

HOW TO READ THIS BOOK

Well, it contains a lot of basic ideas to answer questions which newcomers honestly ask—and which old-timers often ought to be asking. So one might read from cover to cover.

But there are two problems with that. First, the book reflects many approaches—too many to incorporate into a single training system. So small training departments will need to sort out the useful parts. Then too, the book uses what I call a "spiral system" of organization. It zooms around concepts, defining and describing them the first time they just naturally come up in the conversation. It zeroes in on them later, developing them in detail when they're central to the analysis. I hope this proves useful, and that the repetition will be balanced by clarity and unity.

The book might also be read by checking chapter titles, then reading just the parts which seem interesting or relevant or momentarily useful.

That gets to another method: to keep the book on the shelf and read it when problems arise. That strikes me as a smart thing to do with any book—provided, of course, that you've underlined the things you liked, added some items of your own to the lists and charts, and written words of protest beside ideas which didn't digest very well the first time you read them!

Well, there are a few ideas about making the book useful. Here's hoping that if you've spent the money to have a copy, you'll find some added, personal ways to put the book to work for you and your staff.

WHY HAVE A TRAINING AND DEVELOPMENT DEPARTMENT?

HOW ORGANIZATIONS DO THEIR WORK

Imagine yourself in the line at a cafeteria. You come to the coffee urn and turn the spigot. Out comes some coffee. Presumably when the liquid went into the machine, it was water—not coffee. When the coffee grounds were put into the machine, they weren't in consumable, drinkable form. The water and the coffee are material "inputs" to the system called a coffee machine; the "output" is drinkable coffee.

But some person had to add the water and the coffee grounds. These people are also inputs.

Furthermore, the machine will work properly only if these materials are added in the proper amount, in the proper place, and in the proper sequence. There is a technology for the machine and for making the coffee. That technology is a third vital "input" to the system.

And after the machine is turned on, it takes a little time for the water to heat and the coffee to percolate; time is also an "input."

So we have identified four necessary inputs to every system: material, people, technology, and time.

When you reach the end of the line, a cash register "outputs" an itemized bill for your meal—but it can do so only if the cashier "inputs" the prices. Later, during dessert, you decide you'd like another cup of coffee, so you signal an attendant, who brings that second cup to your table. The attendant provides an "output" in the same sense as the coffee machine or the cashier, but this output is different: it's a service rather than a product.

In that cafeteria, in rooms you can't see, there are people who cause recipes and menus to be created, who add up the bills to see how business is going and that all funds are accounted for. These are the people who select the outputs, procure the materials, select the people, and establish the standards. These people are called "managers." They go by familiar names like President, or Chief Executive Officer, or General Manager; there will be subsystems with managers for Sales, Manufacturing, Research and Development; there may even be someone called a Training and Development Manager.

Every system, to survive, must have an output. The cafeteria must produce food; its coffee machine must make coffee; its cashier must collect money; the CEO must see that the cafeteria shows a profit. Likewise, the Sales Manager must produce advertisements and campaigns which produce customers. What does the Training and Development Department produce?

PREPARING PEOPLE TO DO THEIR JOBS

The Training and Development Department (or somebody called the "trainer") is a familiar subgroup in most organizations. Why? Because the people of any organization are like the water put into the coffee machine: for their output to be acceptable, they must change from what they were when they reported for work. At that time they neither knew what a proper output looked like nor the technology by which to achieve it. They must be prepared to do their jobs. That's the big reason for a Training Department!

One way of looking at it is to envision Training as the subsystem that acquaints the people with the material and the technology. It helps them learn how to use the material in an approved fashion that allows the organization to reach its desired output.

Able people may grow to a point where they are ready for responsibilities beyond their initial assignment. When this happens, the organization can profitably help them develop new, larger capabilities. That's why it's a "Training and *Development* Department."

Furthermore, the organization itself may grow and develop. The cafeteria might acquire other cafeterias, or open a cafe with an ambience exotic enough to permit the sale of some foreign cuisine. It might set up a catering service, delivering food to industrial or institutional clients. It might even select totally different outputs, by founding an Institute of Haute Cuisine or buying an existing firm totally unrelated to food. After all, ours is the era of the creative conglomerate.

The point is this: Training and Development has grown concerned not only with helping individuals adequately fill their positions, but also with helping whole organizations and subdepartments grow and develop. Thus the sign on the door has changed from "Training and Development" to titles reflecting missions like "Employee Development," "Organization Development," or "Human Resource Development."

This trend makes it wise for us to look a bit more closely at the interrelationship of the four inputs: people, technology, materials, and time.

Training and Development, though primarily concerned with people, is also concerned with technology, the precise way an organization does business. That technology might be the way a flight attendant greets a passenger on an airliner, or the way an egg is fried; it might be the recipe that makes one soft drink distinctly different from all other soft drinks. It might be the design that makes one automobile more attractive or more efficient than its competitors. It might include the procedures for mixing and bottling the drink, or for assembling the automobile. The point is this: To get the desired final output, an organization requires work. That work is divided up among positions; and positions are divided into tasks—and tasks are assigned to people.

And there we have our second input: people! To perform their assigned tasks properly, all workers need to master and apply the unique technology governing their tasks. So here's where training enters the picture.

Civilization has not yet found the way to conceive and maintain a peopleless organization. Nor has it found a magic potion which injects technology and skill into people. Training is concerned with the meeting between two inputs to organizational effectiveness: people and technology. Since organizations can rarely secure people who are, at the time of employment, total masters of their unique requirements, organizations need a subsystem called "training" to help them master the technology of their tasks. Training changes uninformed employees to informed employees; training changes unskilled or semiskilled workers into employees who can do their assigned tasks in the way the organization wants them done . . . into workers who do things "the right way."

This "right way" is called a standard—and one major function of training is to produce people who do their work "at standard." In fact, one simple way to envision how training contributes is to look at the steps by which people get in control of their positions:

Step 1.   Define the right (or standard) way for performing all the tasks needed by the organization.

Step 2.   Secure people to perform these tasks.

Step 3.   Find out how much of the task they can already perform. (What is their "inventory" of the necessary technology?)

Step 4.   Train them in the difference . . . in what they cannot already do.

Step 5.   Test them to make certain they can perform their assigned tasks to minimum entry-level standards.

Step 6.   Give them the material and the time with which to perform their tasks.

From that six-step process, we can also identify the two remaining inputs: time and material. People can't be miracle workers, creating something from nothing. So we give them materials like fabric from which they can cut dresses . . . like parts which they can assemble into machines . . . like parts of a broken machine which they can analyze and repair. In all these cases, management usually makes some statement about quality; it specifies what the finished product must look like. By stating how many units should be repaired in an hour, or how many dresses sewn in a day, management also sets quantity standards. The job of the training department is to "output" people who can meet those standards, both in quality and quantity.

This description may imply that all training is done after people are hired but *before* they are assigned to their jobs. That's obviously not true. Just look at the rosters of training programs and you'll discover the names of lots of old-timers. What are they doing there?

One legitimate reason for old-timers in training programs is that the organization has changed its technology. And the odds are heavily in favor of its doing so! Some studies maintain that 90 percent of all the scientists who ever lived are alive at this very moment. Other studies show that the so-called "blue collar workers" will learn six brand new technologies in careers from their late teens to their mid-sixties. Another study points out that of all the knowledge taught in high schools today, only 25 percent was known and accepted at the end of World War II in 1945. Every day we can read about how our Age of Technology impacts on every aspect of human enterprise.

Information is probably our most explosive technology. Computers are symbolic of that development: The United States had 10,000 business computers in 1960, 10 million in 1980. New technology will affect over 45 million jobs in the next 20 years (*Careers Tomorrow*, p. 133). We will need 53,000 new computer technicians by 1995 (*Time,* June 25, 1984, p. 54). The home computer is a hot spot in our marketplace.

Robots are a reality: in 1981 3,000 were at work in U.S. factories; today General Motors has 138 welding robots and 19 painting robots at just its Orion Township plant (*The Seattle Times,* July 14, 1984). General Electric planned 47 robots in 1980, expects as many as 1,000 over the next ten years. U.S. robot population increased about 30 percent in 1981 alone, and there is a potential market for as many as 200,000 (*Careers Tomorrow,* pp. 30, 46). Humans must design, build, and repair that robotic workforce. Those of us who now do work to be taken over by robots will need to find new skills . . . or else retire and develop new ways to spend all our spare time.

Maybe we can find new careers. Some strange, beguiling professions are on the horizon: erotic boutique manager, armed courier, or exotic welder. More predictable (and currently more respectable) are bionic-electronic technician, energy technician, holographic inspector, hazardous waste manager, and industrial laser process technician. *Careers Tomorrow* nonetheless comments: "No new industry will make more of an impact on America and the industrial world in the next 20 years than the gene-splicing business." (p. 13)

Such expanding and explosive technology is bound to affect the way an organization achieves its output. It will have particular impact on the technology by which we Training and Development specialists produce our output: new behavior in human beings.

The Training and Development Journal (June 1984), quotes *The Futurist* and lists these new jobs, all relevant to the Training and Development function:

> Artificial intelligence technician;
> Certified alcoholism counselor;
> Executive rehabilitation counselor;
> Benefits analyst;
> Career consultant;
> Color consultant;
> Community psychologist;
> Hotline counselor;
> Image consultant;
> Leisure consultant;
> Relocation counselor;
> Retirement counselor; and
> Wellness consultant.   (p. 11)

Whenever the technology changes, an organization will have incumbent workers who no longer know how to do their jobs the new, right way. When people do not know how to do their job the right way, there is a training need.

People do not usually know how to do their "next job" properly. Thus transfers, or the promotions implied in some career-planning designs, imply potential education needs. Some organizations have training departments which help prepare for the future.

But sometimes we find people in training programs even when the technology hasn't changed, or even when they aren't preparing for new responsibilities.

WHEN PEOPLE CAN DO THEIR JOBS PROPERLY, BUT DON'T . . . WHAT THEN?

That raises the question, "What about people who have been doing their present jobs properly—but no longer do so?" It's certainly true that these people are not meeting the established standards of performance—but will training do them any good?

Not really.

You see, they already know how to do their work; they've shown that in their previous satisfactory performance. Thus the reason for their present non-performance can't possibly be that they don't know how. And training is a remedy for people who do not know how—not for people who do know how but for one reason or another are no longer doing it.

These other problems are performance problems—but they are not truly training problems, and training is not an appropriate solution. Of course, good training departments don't ignore these other performance problems. The smart training and development officer never says, "Sorry, we can't help you!" when managers report old-timers who no longer perform properly.

Training

The function once known as "training" has had to expand its own technology. It has had to locate and implement non-training solutions for all those performance problems which are not caused by not knowing how. Later on we can look at these "other problems and other solutions" in detail. For now, let's just summarize our answer to the question "Why have a training department?" this way:

1. Organizations get outputs because people perform tasks to a desired standard.

2. Before people can perform their tasks properly, they must master the special technology used by their organization. This means acquisition of knowledge and skill. Sometimes this acquisition is needed when the employee is new to the organization; sometimes it is needed because the organization changes its technology; sometimes it is necessary if an individual is to change places within the organization—either by lateral transfer or by promotion.

3. Training is the acquisition of the technology which permits employees to perform to standard.

Thus training may be defined as an experience, a discipline, or a regimen which causes people to acquire new, predetermined behaviors. Whenever employees need new (the accent is on the word "new"!) behaviors, then we need a training department.

But as we have already noted, training departments do more than merely fill the gaps in peoples' repertoires for doing assigned tasks; training specialists nowadays get involved in developing people for "the next job," for retirement, and for their roles in society outside the employing organization.

That brings us to the word "education," a timely concept in our era when "lifelong learning" is a current or imminent reality. If we humans adjust to the technological explosion, then lifelong learning will indeed be a major activity in these next decades when machines and robots will perform more of the tiresome tasks we've been doing . . . and when we will be working fewer hours. One of the nice things we might do in those new free hours is pursue our education.

Not all training specialists distinguish among "training," "education," and "development." They use the three words interchangeably to describe what they do for their organizations. But for those who distinguish, as does Dr. Leonard Nadler in his *Developing Human Resources,* training is what we've described: "Those activities which are designed to improve human performance on the job the employee is presently doing or is being hired to do." (p. 40) Education is those human resource development activities which "are designed to improve the overall competence of the employee in a specified direction and beyond the job now held." (p. 60) To Dr. Nadler, development is concerned with preparing the employees so they can "move with the organization as it develops, changes, and grows." (p. 88)

Education

Let's apply these definitions to familiar activities. We can quickly identify some "leadership" and "pre-supervisory" and "personal development" programs as educational activities. People who have been identified as "promotable" often attend such workshops to enhance their capacity for leadership . . . to receive special orientation in organization goals, policies, or procedures. The "sensitivity training" or T-group syndrome is sometimes used as a vehicle for such education. Assessment centers and career-planning systems often reveal lapses in people's capabilities for future assignments. Education is needed. In these cases, the word is apt, paralleling the Latin origin of "e-ducing," going out from something that is already there. The identified capabilities are used as a basis for an expanded repertoire of skills in the individual. Why increase this repertoire, or inventory? So these individuals can make larger contributions to the organization in their next positions . . . positions for which they are presumably bound. Such activities are legitimately called "education."

Development

The development activity often takes the form of university enrollments for top executives. They can thus acquire new horizons, new technologies, new viewpoints. They can lead the entire organization to newly *developed* goals, postures, and environments. This is perceived as a way to maintain growth and development for the entire organization, not just for the individual. Yet that's misleading, since the sponsors of such "developmental" activities feel that the organization will grow to meet the future precisely because the individual leaders will grow in their insights about the future . . . in their capacity to implement change when the future has become the reality of the present.

Certain sociologists believe such development will be desperately needed—and soon! They point out that mankind faces tremendous social changes—changes equal to those which accompanied the shift from feudal to modern society in the Industrial Revolution. They point to the post-industrial society now being born (*The New Yorker,* Jan. 5, 1976). The blue-collar worker we mentioned earlier in this chapter is actually a myth. As Tom Wolfe said in *New West* (August 30, 1976), these skilled workers all wear shirts "like Joe Namath's or Johnny Bench's" and earn an annual income higher than most British newspaper columnists. And for the first time, say the sociologists, mankind is aware of these changes as they are taking place.

To a great degree, this is exactly what happens in miniscule when training and development officers use "organization development." They affectionately call this process "OD." It's a change program where change is observed as it happens. It involves launching and managing change in the organizational society. OD is very definitely within the purview of the training and development department.

However, in OD they focus on the organization first—and on the interrelationships of people and units within the organization, on structures and communications—not on the growth of the individual. To be sure, individuals will change—and hopefully in larger, "growthful" directions. Thus cause and effect are inextricably linked: people develop because an organization develops; the organization develops because people grow to new dimensions!

Why have such an OD program? Quite possibly because too many resources (human and material, time and technological) are being invested or squandered in ways which do not produce the desired output. Or perhaps they produce the desired output—but at too great a cost in time, material, or human values. Organization development may question the real "success" of organizations which meet all their goals in ways that make all the human resources feel miserable or unfulfilled in the process . . . miserable about the condition of their work lives. They agree with Hamlet: "Something is rotten in the state of Denmark!"

How can things get that rotten? There are lots of reasons. For instance, such a thorough organization reappraisal may be necessary because individuals or subgroups have consistently invested their talent, energy, and resources to achieve personal or departmental goals rather than the objectives established for the entire organization. Such reappraisals might be needed simply because communications go sour: key messages are never sent, or they get distorted, or they get lost. Perhaps feelings are never shared: they get "all bottled up" and only the content of doing business is shared. Everything is tasks, tasks, tasks!

Organization development programs use the human beings within the organization as resources in a problem-solving effort which might reassign or reorganize the subgroups, restructure the communications channels or media, reshape individual responsibilities, behavioral modes, or communicative style. It might, in fact, examine every facet of the inter-human and systemic structure in order to find a better way—a way which would permit the human energy to cooperatively produce desired outputs in order to reach organizational goals in ways which prove satisfying and fulfilling to all participant members of the organization.

SUMMARY

Nowadays, training departments seek to be ever more relevant to organization goals, to solve performance problems throughout the entire organization—and to do so in a variety of ways. Thus they are concerned with things other than just training. They seek other solutions to other types of human performance problems.

As a result their titles are changing. One hears of Human Performance Directors, of Managers of Organization Development, Vice President of Education and Training, Director of Development, Director of Human Resources Development. That last one, Human Resources Development, has a nice ring to it. With its acronym, HRD, it's growing increasingly popular—and is somewhat suspiciously accepted by outsiders who may be asking, "Just how pompous can these characters get?"

True, the new titles and much of the jargon of the training and development technology are still smug and pompous. But they reflect a refreshing answer to the question, "Why have a Training Department?" Refreshing because it reveals an expansion . . . a new relevance and new accountabilities.

In 1983, The American Society for Training and Development, under the leadership of Patricia A. McLagan, completed its "Models For Excellence," a competency study. It listed 15 distinct roles and 31 specific competencies required for total performance by a Training and Development professional. A look at those roles and competencies reveals the breadth and depth of a thorough answer to our question, "Why have a Training and Development Department?"

The roles include needs analyst, program designer, task analyst, theoretician, instructional writer, media specialist, instructor, group facilitator, individual Development Counselor, transfer agent, program administrator, evaluator, marketer, strategist, and manager of Training and Development.

The competencies vary from understanding of adult learning to computer competence, from questioning skills to presentation skills, from futuring skills to library skills, and from cost-benefit analysis skills to group process skills. (pp. 4, 6)

Despite the new, larger charter of the training departments all around us, this book will call the person who leads the development of an organization's "human inputs" the T & D officer. Staff members who assist the growth of people will be known as T & D specialists. "T & D," of course, means training and development.

Of course there are lots of organizations in which one person is the entire operation . . . the director who decides what training will happen and when and where and how. Such a person designs the visuals and creates the lesson plan, leads the learning experiences and handles the follow-up. This happens again and again in the single office, the single shop, the local plant, or the branch office. This is a true T & D officer/specialist, all rolled into one!

Then there are other organizations so large and so complex that the T & D department is specialized, just like all the other departments. There are the decision makers with lofty titles; there are the media specialists who put lettering onto visual aids; there are instructional technologists, and there are instructors; there are programmers who put learning systems onto computers for "assisted instruction."

This book will try to examine principles and practices for all these situations. It will examine ideas that have been used with common effectiveness in T & D departments from the most Spartan to the most sophisticated. No matter how big or how small the T & D operation, they all have in common that one

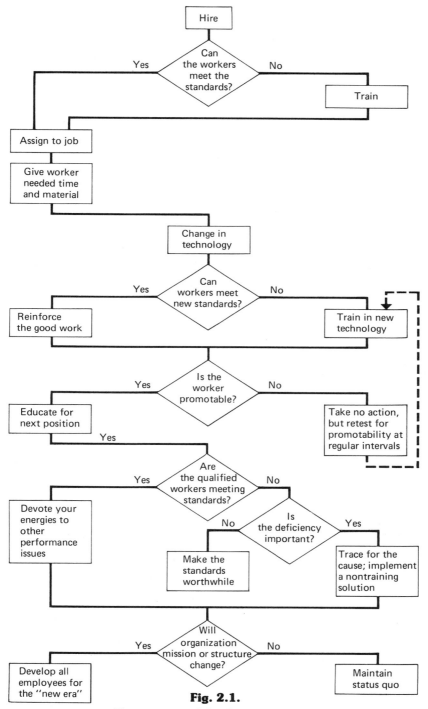

Fig. 2.1.

The training and development process.

important goal: to keep the human resources performing at or above the established standards.

To summarize the training and development process of human resource development, how about the graphic approach in Fig. 2.1?

Why have a T & D department?

Because organizations, in order to get their desired output, need someone who is clearly responsible for:

- Training people to do their present tasks properly,
- Educating certain employees so they can assume greater responsibilities in the future, and
- Developing people and entire organizations for futures . . . sometimes for undefined and undefinable futures.

Why? Because someone must be responsible for human growth if the status quo is to be maintained satisfactorily—and if the future is to be met. Because someone must help people make tomorrow a successful "today."

CHAPTER **3**

WHAT DO
T & D
OFFICERS DO?

When we think of schizophrenics, we think of personalities that are split two ways. Can the human personality be split four ways? Well, some T & D officers might tell us that their professional personality is split four ways: they must perform as administrator, consultant, designer of learning experiences, and instructor.

That four-way split properly identifies the several separate facets of the T & D function. When T & D officers work alone as the total training department for their organization, they must indeed be expert in all four activities. When they head a larger staff, they must provide for and manage all four functions.

Let's look at each of the four roles in detail.

AS ADMINISTRATORS

As administrator of the training function, the T & D officer must do all the things any other manager achieves. This means planning, organizing, directing, and controlling the ongoing function. Thus T & D officers set policy for developing the human resources of the organization. They then see that that policy is carried out through systems and programs . . . possibly through a T & D staff, and assuredly with the active involvement of line management.

What are the policy decisions the T & D officer must make?

First, someone must decide what training will be done. That means there must be a definition of what training is, and a set of criteria on which validated training needs will be prioritized. The real training needs lie in the operating departments, which the T & D officer may refer to as "clients." But there are times when there is more work to be done than there are available resources to do it. Someone must then decide where the energy and funds will actually be expended. This decision is simplified and expedited when there is a policy statement about which criteria have priority: dollar impact? . . . costs of doing the training? . . . the number of people to be trained? . . . pressure from competition? . . . political clout of the requester? . . . government edict? A policy clarifying such priorities needs organizational sanction, but must originate with the T & D officer.

It may be painful to say "no" to requests for help, but that is less apt to happen if the T & D officer is a good planner, foreseeing problems before they arise; when one must say "no," it is less painful if a clearcut policy is available to explain why.

Naturally then, this T & D officer must have ready access to organizational goals, problems, and strategies. To know what new products, programs, technologies, or approaches the organization is contemplating is to be a pro-active rather than a belated solver of human performance problems. To be pro-active is to be a preventer of human performance problems rather than a mere "firefighter" who handles problems after they have already become full-blown conflagrations.

At other times the T & D officer will become aware of performance problems which remain invisible to an operating management that is somehow "blinded" to the failure of its own staff to meet desired performance standards. Does the T & D officer take the initiative in revealing this problem? Or does the organization have to wait until the potential client grows painfully aware of the situation? Someone must make a policy statement to answer that question—and that "someone" is the T & D officer.

Just as changing technology alters the products and procedures used "out in the shop," there is a steadily expanding technology by which training and development are achieved. There are new media, such as videotape and computer assisted instruction; there are new classroom or workshop methods like Guided Fantasy and Fishbowling; there are new approaches to instruction like Andragogy and Learner-Controlled Instruction. Which of these will the organization use? Which will it discourage . . . because of budget constraints or organizational norms? For example, sensitivity training is "off-limits" in some organizations because it requires or develops a degree of self-disclosure with which the organization is still uncomfortable. The T & D officer is the person who must ultimately decide the "limits" of instructional methods.

Someone must also set scheduling policy: setting the dates and locations for programs, determining the length of the training day, deciding whether enrollments should involve trainees from many departments and locations or from homogeneous groupings. Someone must ask, "In what programs does the synergism of exchanging departmental technology and values exceed the faster mastery and potential team building possible when the rosters include learners from the same discipline or location?" Scheduling involves asking, "Should the shop be shut down in order for every participant to achieve the expected learnings?" The answers to such questions are sometimes hard to find and even harder to "sell." Someone must find them and someone must sell them—and that someone is the T & D officer.

How will participants be selected for training? On what priority? How is their immediate manager or supervisor expected to brief them on the reasons they are being trained? How will that manager/supervisor review the learning objectives with them before the training? Who will tell them the quality and quantity standards they are expected to achieve when they return to their work after the training? The content of these vital messages, the mechanisms for sending them and the policies governing them must be established and communicated by someone. That someone is the T & D officer.

The word "communicated" is critically important. T & D officers are not only responsible for setting policy: they are responsible for communicating that policy to all other parts of the management structure. How can the T & D department expect compliance if clients do not know the criteria for determining training needs, for enrollments, or for achievements? How can the line managers make effective use of their investment in training processes if they are not given guidelines?

A written statement of training policy is a vitally important document for several reasons:

- First, it serves as a day-to-day reference in making those innumerable "subdecisions" which arise for managers in both the T & D and client departments.
- Next, it provides a useful checkpoint for renewing and redirecting the training activity from time to time.
- It can be a useful planning document.

- It becomes a valid checklist when the T & D officer evaluates the contributions and performance of his or her department.
- Above all, a written statement of T & D policy helps all members of the T & D department function in ticklish moments! Perhaps the issue of "Why?" or "Why not?" or "What shall we do?" hangs heavy over a discussion with a line client. The written policy can explain, clarify, and solidify organizational values. Even if it doesn't provide the precise detailed answers needed at the moment, it can give guidance and suggest actions.

A word about "ticklish moments": they can be very valuable. We need to learn from mistakes and from crisis. The ticklish moments when we use a formal policy statement for guidance are cues to ask ourselves why the crisis occurred and if it was a useful crisis. This is also a time to ask if we need an amended or expanded policy statement. If the same "tickle" comes up again and again, it is a catalyst to improved statements—and improved *policy*—in the future!

If there's a definite policy, why are there ticklish moments? Possibly because the T & D officer involved too few line clients when first creating the policy. This raises another policy issue decided by the T & D officer: which clients? . . . and how often should they be consulted when policy is being reformulated?

As administrators, T & D officers not only set policy: they manage an ongoing function. This happens whether they have a staff or whether they are the entire department in just one person. But if we define management as "getting work done through other people," then T & D officers are just like all other managers. They must plan, delegate, motivate, monitor, control, and evaluate. Their T & D department is, after all, simply one of the suborganizations within the larger organization which it serves.

This means that T & D officers establish budgets and monitor adherence to those budgets. In doing this they may control decisions about learning methods and media. For example: it may be necessary to use a printed book as the medium for programmed instruction because budgets won't permit the expense or development time (up to 350 hours of staff time for every hour of learning time!) to put the program on the computer.

T & D budgets must provide facilities where learning can happen, where it can be designed and places to meet with clients to discuss performance problems, possible programs, learning objectives, evaluation criteria, and procedures for implementing any activity resulting from the consultation. To plan these places properly (especially learning rooms!) T & D officers must know something about methods and media.

Managing the ongoing function in most organizations implies that T & D officers select and manage some staff, with course designers, instructors, consultants, media specialists, or psychologists and clerical support. To give that staff a sense of belonging, security, and recognition, T & D officers must provide environments that accommodate activities ranging from confrontation through quiet meditation, yet also offer efficient access to materials, files, and a reference library.

To build staff, T & D officers need skill in selecting personnel. They want a balance of temperament, experience, and special expertise. The 1983 ASTD study, "Models for Excellence," identifies 31 competencies, a long list involving this wide range:

Career development knowledge	Counseling skill
Data reduction skill	Feedback skill
Industry understanding	Library skills
Model building skills	Negotiation skill
Presentation skill	Questioning skill
Records management skill	Relationship versatility
Objectives preparation skill	Research skill
Delegation skill	Writing skill
Cost-benefit analysis skill	Futuring skill

It even lists "Competency identification skill!" (p. 6)

A policy statement should explain whether T & D is a "career" placement, a "launching pad" for careers elswhere in the organization, or "temporary duty" from which one returns to other assignments. It may well be "All of the above." In fact, that's an excellent answer provided all staff members clearly know their mode at the time they enter the department. This variety of placement allows some to specialize deeply in a chosen career, becoming expert in a wide array of competencies like those listed in the ASTD study. Yet it also permits others to have some time in the people development business as a way to develop themselves, either for wider "education" about the human resource business, or for use of that knowledge when they manage people in other parts of the organization.

If T & D officers preach the gospel of the ever-developing employee to clients (and they'd better preach it!), it's vital that they practice this gospel on their own staff . . . imperative to give periodic upgrading so all T & D specialists can acquire new skill and expertise. Growth should be the norm of the T & D department! This means that time and dollars must be budgeted so staff can attend conferences, workshops, seminars, and developmental activities within the department.

And then there's evaluation. Someone must see that evaluation mechanisms are built into all phases of the change program. This means that there must be measurement before the evaluation. This means that programs will be tested and revised before final implementation. It means that completed programs will be evaluated. But on what criteria? Cost effectiveness? Perceptions? Achievement of learning goals? Changes in employees' on-the-job performance? Changes in operating indices? Some of the above? All of the above? Someone must decide—and make a statement on the decision.

Administratively, the T & D officer must do lots of planning and organizing, must translate the abstractions of policy into workable day-to-day decisions of control and implementation. Those decisions must improve people-performance at all levels, and in all departments.

AS CONSULTANTS TO THE ORGANIZATION

In their role as consultant to the organization, T & D officers help managers of "client" departments solve human performance problems. That isn't always easy.

For one thing, when people have problems, the real nature of the problems is often hard to discover. It gets absorbed inside the people who aren't performing properly. For another thing, the manager whose department is distressed doesn't always find it easy to admit that a problem exists. Such admissions can be very threatening. Thus the consultative skills of the T & D officer involve knowing what questions to ask, when to ask them, how to create an environment in which facts—including the facts of feelings!—become the basis of decisions. This implies that the clients' feelings must be expressed and facilitated . . . must be a part of the consultant's probe and part of the decision. That is correct. After all, feelings are a part of the reality of the whole performance problem being probed.

If the problem is properly identified, the T & D officer may need to bow out of the problem-solving process. Why? Well, the problem may not stem from human behavior at all. To precisely the degree that T & D officers have high credibility, they will be asked to solve all kinds of problems. But if sales have slumped because products are no longer competitive, or if manufacturing levels are low because one plant was lost in a flood, the T & D officer is not the person best qualified to help solve the problem. T & D officers are useful in solving human performance problems. When they go beyond that, they are exceeding their expertise and their charter.

This does not mean that T & D officers bow out of problems when training is not the solution—only when the problem doesn't stem from human performance. Most organizations expect a full range of human performance improvement services from the T & D department.

Performance problems—all of them!—are the legitimate and obligatory concern of the T & D officer, but not all human performance problems can be solved by training.

We have already noted that when people know how to do their job, but aren't doing it, then training is not a useful solution. After all, there is no sense in sending workers to class to learn what they already know! If they aren't doing what they know how to do, then there must be some cause. T & D officers are responsible for helping management discover that cause—and for working with managers to implement effective solutions.

Now managers in client departments are apt to think that training is what their people need. The T & D officer is responsible for helping them see the fallacy in that viewpoint; the T & D officer is ultimately responsible for distinguishing training from non-training needs. As they watch T & D officers make this analysis, line managers can grow in their insight about how training contributes toward people's contribution to organization goals.

If training won't work, what will? One possibility to explore is changing the consequences for satisfactory performance. Many times employees cease to do their work the "right way" because there is no positive consequence for doing so. Sometimes doing the job properly is actually punished by the system. In one case, salespeople who exceeded quotas (in other words, the overachievers!) actually had their territory divided up among new salespersons. Clerks who take the time to do thorough jobs may be abused verbally by irritated customers—or even by supervisors who "chew" them for keeping people waiting!

All the training in the world won't produce behavior that perfectly fits the realities of the workplace. Discovering these inconsistencies between goals and rewards is the common task of the T & D specialist and the manager who has the problem in the performance of subordinates. It is one facet of the consultancy of the T & D department.

Another thing is the establishment of proper feedback systems. To the degree that workers get continuous quantitative feedback about their achievements, they will tend to maintain good performance levels. This is a very different thing from management coming around and saying, "Well done, thou good and faithful servant!" Admittedly that is a desirable behavior by managers and superviors—but the feedback that consistently motivates and maintains performance is apt to be a simple numerical tally by the workers themselves.

If workers have specific checkpoints about the quality, and are allowed to count their accomplishments, the quality can be monitored along with the quantity. Thus feedback becomes a motivator, a monitor, and a controller all at one time. Installing effective feedback mechanisms has become part of the technology of the T & D staff, an important tool in solving performance problems. It is yet another "solution" the T & D officer may offer to managers of employees who aren't performing their tasks properly.

At other times jobs don't get done because they are basically undoable. That can happen when jobs are too complex, or when they are too simple. The twentieth-century trend toward specialization and work simplification has proved to be a mixed blessing. On the positive side, it has eliminated some tasks which were superhuman in their expectations. Some work was so complex, varied, or exacting that no single person could be expected to master the entire technology—much less apply it on an hourly basis! Other work was so taxing to the body that no physique could bear the strain. Some tasks required discriminations so fine that neither the eye nor the mind of the worker could perform them correctly or continuously. Work simplification has helped eliminate such excesses, but it has brought with it a trend toward specialization which has also endangered some jobs. It has so oversimplified them that they've become stupid . . . degrading to the performer. Modern business, industry, and bureaucracy is infested with such jobs. They deprive the worker of a sense of variety, dignity, accomplishment.

Thus we hear of "job enrichment," and of job engineering as an important solution to human performance problems. Effectively "engineered" jobs not only get the work done, they get it done in quantities and varieties which match the humanity of the doer. T & D officers can perform more effectively if they can spot problems caused by jobs which are unperformably complex or simple . . . if they can help management re-engineer positions so workers find the work at least bearable—hopefully challenging and fulfilling.

But there are other performance problems when the incumbents know how to do the job (so training isn't required or useful) and when the consequences are appropriate and feedback is provided and the job is well engineered. Still, tasks aren't being completed properly in the necessary quantities and the organization, or unit's, goals are not being met. How can that happen?

It often happens because the organization, or organizational unit, is itself confused about goals and prerogatives. The entire unit may need to be redirected and renewed. If personal tensions are high and trust levels are low; if decisions are slow or absent; if there is more energy expended on personal and subgroup goals than on the mission of the entire organization, then organization development (OD) seems indicated. T & D officers who substitute training or feedback systems as a remedy in such situations inevitably end up with "egg on their face." They have, in effect, prescribed an aspirin as a cure for cancer!

Thus the consultant role of the T & D officer is not merely to find places where training is an appropriate remedy. Rather it is to find all the performance problems, to analyze each, and to recommend an appropriate solution. That solution may be any one, or a combination of training, contingency management, feedback systems, job engineering or organization development. After the recommendation, the T & D officer is responsible for providing, assisting in the implementation of, and evaluating whatever solution is adopted.

As consultants, therefore, T & D officers need to know how to ask questions—and what questions to ask.

Several types of questions come immediately to mind. When consultants want to uncover the feelings surrounding (and sometimes obscuring) a given situation, they want to use open questions. Open questions can't be answered "yes" or "no," or with specific data like "seventeen years," or "The first-line supervisor is responsible for that." Open questions are "How do you feel?" or "What do you think about . . . ?" or "How would you describe . . . ?" or "What is your analysis of . . . ?"

After the feelings are out in the open, the consultant is ready to ask some directive questions. These are such questions as "How long has the problem been evident?" "Who has responsibility for . . . ?" "What is the published performance standard?" "Who sets that standard?" "What actual baselines are you now getting?"

Of course there are questions to avoid—loaded questions like "Don't you think that . . . ?" or "Wouldn't you agree that . . . ?" Indeed, any question which starts with the word "But" is probably a loaded question—one which will put the client on the defensive and obscure the real feelings and the real facts. With such unproductive loaded questions, the client ends up feeling more entrapped than consulted.

Once clients have revealed their feelings, and stated the facts as they see them, the consultant can summarize with reflective questions which achieve the desired basis for action. Reflective questions tend to sound like "You feel, then, that . . . ?" "Is this how you see the situation?" These reflections provide two things: a double check that the consultant understands the problem from the client's viewpoint, and a probable expansion of the area of agreement. In their reflective summaries, T & D specialists, wearing their consultant robes, are careful to reflect back only what they did in fact hear from the client—and to include the feelings as well as the facts.

It is not easy to summarize the consultant activity of the T & D officer because it involves at least 11 of the 15 roles identified in the ASTD competency study. Besides being Manager of Training and Development this officer will probably also be Evaluator, Group Facilitator, Instructor, Marketer, Individual Development Counselor, Needs Analyst, Program Administrator, Strategist, Theoretician, and Transfer Agent. (p. 4)

The role requires skill in:

- Getting at real facts about performance problems;

- Uncovering and responding to feelings, which must also be listed among the facts of the problem;

- Matching appropriate, effective solutions to specific problems rather than invariably recommending a pet remedy such as training or OD or a pet method like roleplays; and

- Locating specialists who have skill in training, feedback, contingency management, job engineering and organization development.

Effective T & D officers are no longer solutions looking for a problem! They are true consultants for the performance problems in the organization which they serve.

AS DESIGNERS OF LEARNING EXPERIENCES

When the T & D staff is tiny then nearly every member (even the T & D officer) will be involved in designing training programs, creating lesson plans and learning materials . . . will be writing roleplays and case studies . . . will be formulating outlines or simulations.

When the T & D department has a fairly large staff, the director may be only an observer or advisor in the selection of learning/teaching methods. But even then that officer must know enough to effectively counsel the staff members who *do* make the decisions . . . must possess wide knowledge of learning methods and some idea of when each is apt to be productive. There is such explosive expansion in the knowledge about how people learn that many T & D officere find they must hurry just to fall slightly behind the times!

Most modern organizations require the use of a sizable number of instructional methods. Why? The objectives are so varied that a limited inventory of learning approaches is invalid. Then too, physical distribution of the trainee population may require that some programs be administered to individuals, others to large groups. For individuals, programmed instruction or auto-instructional and highly mediated programs are useful. Certain objectives may be learnable only in the group mode. Examples would include interpersonal skills, team-building, and manipulation of sophisticated heavy equipment. Team-building skills don't come very easily in programs where the learner interacts only with the printed page, a computer, a teaching machine, or even just one instructor. Handling a heavy piece of machinery can't be mastered from the printed page.

Some training works best when the learners are sharply removed from the workplace, able to introspect, analyze, and synthesize without the pressures or interruptions that go along with the office or the shop. Other learnings are just plain impossible away from the real-world environment. If overcoming distractions is one of the learning objectives, what better place to face distractions than the busy office or the noisy shop? Such learnings should not be scheduled at Valhalla on the Hudson or Cozy Nook in the Poconos or Ocean Beach by the blue Pacific.

There are three distinct domains of behavior in which trainees must be asked to grow:

1. *Cognitive* or mental skills may actually be best acquired through reading, lectures, or demonstrations. But the word "demonstration" implies some step-by-step process or skill which the learner must acquire and then perform back on the job—and we can pretty well rule out reading or lecture as the total learning experience!

2. *Psychomotor skills* involve using the arms, the legs, the torso. For the mind to direct reliable performance by these parts of the body, some practice or drill seems mandatory. Psychomotor growth often relies heavily on Job Instruction Training, JIT, in which instructors "tell and show" the task one step at a time, with learners "doing and reviewing" that step as soon as possible.

3. In the *affective domain* learners are expected to grow in the realm of emotions or feelings. Such new awareness or control of emotional energy can hardly result from a lecture or reading assignment . . . no matter how inspiring. (Not that inspiration is impossible; it's just never been an effective method of producing lasting on-the-job changes in affective behavior.) New research in the use of music and metaphor, controlled environments and right brain/left brain dominance studies offer new excitement in creating affective growth. (They also offer still more evidence that T & D officers always have something new to learn!)

Professional designers of learning experiences know when to use which method, how to effect necessary compromises between the most desirable method and the one the budget can afford—or the environment accept. They provide for try-out when skill is demanded, for participation when current emotional or intellectual biases would block acceptance of new ideas or new technology. They can arrange furniture so it is conducive to proper communication and to an environment which properly stimulates and controls the things trainees say and do. Even if T & D officers don't get directly involved in such designs, they need to counsel their staff members who do get so involved. Thus they need a knowledge of training methods—and there is such an expanding technology in this area that many T & D officers find they must hurry just to fall slightly behind the times!

Effective leadership from the chief T & D officer is critical. There is the everpresent pitfall of faddism in training methodology. There is no absolutely foolproof certain theory about how adults learn; there *is* a great deal of exciting experimentation with new methods. Therefore a brilliant success with one method can cause T & D specialists to become addicted to that method. They soon ardently advocate using it for all learning objectives in all learning environments . . . even when it is terribly inappropriate. Experienced T & D specialists can name as many fads as they have years in service: in the middle 1950s there was a fever of enthusiasm for the case method; in the early 1960s there was the mad rush to present everything in programmed instruction; T-groups and sensitivity training quickly captured the spotlight, and got mistakenly used in all types of training programs; the early 1970s saw a burst of interest in open classrooms.

Now, all those methods are good for certain objectives, certain trainee populations, and in certain environments. But none of them is good in itself! The effective T & D officer is able to counsel staff members in the proper selection . . . to the proper match of learning objectives, trainee population, and organizational environment.

To counsel wisely, T & D officers also need to be well informed about current learning theory. This isn't easy to do. For one reason, the knowledge explosion has hit the field of learning theory just as it has hit other fields of human inquiry. Perhaps a bit more! The research of behaviorists like B. F. Skinner, the work of an adragogist like Malcolm Knowles (who studies *adult* learning), the findings of facilitative psychiatrists like Carl Rogers, and the tough-minded opinions of men like Donald Campbell and Robert Coles—they sometimes conflict, and they very rarely match! Yet for consistent training policy and for effective adaptation into individual training programs, the T & D officer needs a grasp of all these concepts. Conscientious T & D specialists develop a personal theory of how people learn, and expand it as new research and theories become available.

As designers or as managers of the design process, T & D officers need knowledge, experience, and a value system of learning/teaching methods. Nowadays, methodology will probably reflect a unique blend of several theories about how people (adults in particular!) learn and change their on-the-job performance.

AS INSTRUCTORS

The instructor is the ultimate "delivery agent" of the learning system. Instructors therefore manage the critical dynamic process: acquisition of new behaviors by the learner.

This implies skill in bringing to life all the content and all the methods called for in the "lesson plan." It implies skill in two-way communication. It implies flexibility, spontaneity, empathy, compassion—almost everything except feeding multitudes with "but five loaves and two fishes."

The truth is that in recent years our perception of the effective instructor has changed sharply. We are less and less concerned with platform skills; we are more and more concerned with skills in facilitating learning in others. This means that instructor-training workshops don't stress oratorical skills or count the "ers" and "uhs" or practice gestures. Rather, the emphasis is on questioning and listening, on getting feedback and positive reinforcement into the learning experience. Involvement, rather than favorable impression, becomes the focus.

Some people feel this change is seen most clearly in organizational training. Others contend that elementary and secondary schools have similarly altered their image of good teaching. There is even some slight evidence that colleges and universities are beginning to challenge the conventional role that all an instructor does is share knowledge. There is a joke about the definition of a professor: a teacher whose notes are transferred from the professor's notebook to the student's notepad without passing through the heads of either! The assumption is that if the ideas pass through the learner's head, they've done some good. More cogent is the question: "If they have passed through the learner's head, did that intrusion make a real difference in the way the student approaches life?"

The point is that instruction is both a science and an art—and the T & D function must provide people who have mastered instructional skills sufficiently to ensure that behavior change does indeed take place in the learners assigned to them.

Recent years have placed heavy emphasis on the importance of learners doing something other than listening and watching while in class. Indeed, the central question is: "Do they ever actually learn anything at all by merely listening and watching?" The answer tends to be: "No—at least not much that carries over with them into improved on-the-job performance." So recent instructor-training programs (and most instructional design) have moved toward participative types of learning experience. The word "experience" is not accidental; it implies that learners must experience something during the learning if their performance is to be significantly and permanently altered after the training ends.

So it is that B. F. Skinner says in *About Behaviorism,* "To acquire behavior, the student must engage in behavior." That arch-advocate of facilitative learning, Dr. Carl Rogers, points out in *Freedom to Learn,* "Learning is facilitated when the learner participates responsibly in the learning process . . . Significant learning is acquired through doing."

These sound like harmonious viewpoints—and indeed they are. Skinner and Rogers actually agree on more than the principle of participation. Rogers points out that external threats present barriers to significant learnings; Skinner says that only when the love and affection of the teacher has failed to work to produce new behaviors is aversive reinforcement necessary.

Although most theorists agree that external threats must be kept at a minimum, especially in adult learning systems, men like Lionel Tiger and Robin Fox point out in *The Imperial Animal* that "Young adults learn best under conditions of stress," and that the optimal conditions for learning are sharply different between children and adults.

Malcolm Knowles, whose life study is andragogy, the science of adult learning, insists that adults will learn best when they can invest their own valued experience in the learning effort.

All these theories point toward participative learning designs—but with what degree of stress, responsibility, aversive consequences, control? Teachers who conduct organizational learning experiences face just those questions— and must make decisions. It's up to the T & D officer to provide them with effective counseling when such decisions stare them in the face.

SUMMARY

That's the four-faced nature of the T & D officer's position: administrator, consultant, designer, and instructor. It's a big job—and a changing job. As organizations face new problems, the T & D officer, or the staff of T & D specialists, must be ready to face new situations and to offer new solutions. Fortunately the technology of adult learning and of organizational behavior is expanding as rapidly as relevant experience is acquired by T & D departments.

How do the four roles function to make continuous, integrated contributions to the organization? A graphic answer would probably look something like Figs. 3.1 and 3.2. Fig. 3.1 shows the T & D officer's key responsibilities; Fig. 3.2 lists the critical skills.

ADMINISTRATOR	CONSULTANT	DESIGNER	INSTRUCTOR

Sets policy:
Scope of services:
  Training
  Education
  Development
  Feedback systems
  Contingency management
  Job engineering
  Organization development
Scope of useful methods
Scheduling
Participant selection
Participation norms
Evaluation criteria
Communicates policy
Sets program objectives
Establishes budget
Monitors expenditures
Sets facilities standards
Provides facilities
Selects staff
Manages staff
Develops staff
Evaluates T & D effort
	Analyzes performance
	problems
	Recommends solutions:
	  Training
	  Education
	  Development
	  Feedback systems
	  Contingency management
	  Job engineering
	  Organization development
	Establishes program goals
	(with client-managers)
	Evaluates programs
	Assists with programs (?)
	Counsels designers
		Selects methods
		Selects media
		Synthesizes methods
		and media into an
		integrated program
		Provides outlines and
		materials to implement
		the program
		Evaluates tryout
		Redesigns programs as
		tryout data indicate
			Delivers learning design
			Analyzes and responds to
			individual learner needs
			Adapts design to meet
			learner needs
			Provides ongoing feedback and
			evaluation to facilitate learning
			Counsels learners
			Provides feedback to designers
			about strengths and weaknesses
			of designs

←——— Counsels client-managers ———→

←——— Counsels designers ———→

Fig. 3.1.

The T & D officer's key areas of responsibility.

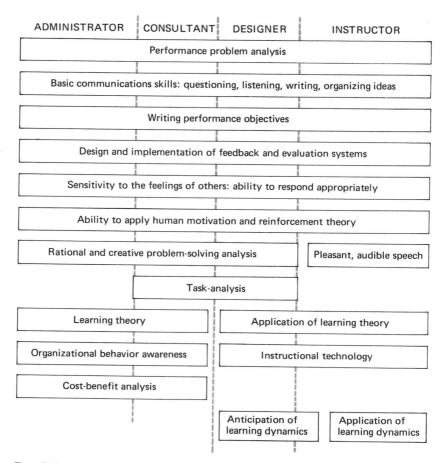

Fig. 3.2.

The critical skills needed by the T & D officer.

CHAPTER 4

WHERE IS THE T & D DEPARTMENT LOCATED?

NEW TRENDS IN ORGANIZATIONAL PLACEMENT

As civilization moves toward increased emphasis on human rights, so organizations are moving toward sharper focus on developing the human potential. Thus the traditional concept of "training and development" has expanded to include concern for "Human Resources Development."

In many organizations the title of T & D officer has given way to Manager, Director, or Vice President of Human Resources. Such a title usually brings responsibility for more than just training and development; it may include such functions as employment, recruitment, compensation and benefits, employee communications, job engineering—and of course, organizational analysis and development. In such cases T & D is naturally a subunit of the Human Resources department. But that still leaves the question, "Where is the Human Resources activity located?"

LINE AND STAFF CONSIDERATIONS

The line/staff dichotomy is blurring nowadays, and has grown rather unpopular with organization theorists. Yet the division still exists as a practical reality in most organizations, and we must regard it as a real issue in placing the T & D function.

Assume for just a moment that your organization has never had a specialized training and development department. It has just decided to install such a group, and has asked your opinion: "Where should we locate this new department on our organization chart? Who should be responsible for what part of the T & D activity?"

This is where a policy statement would come in mighty handy. However, there is no such statement: it's up to you to decide. On what basis do you make your decision? Two basic issues come to mind:

1. Is training and development a line function or a staff function?

2. How do you guarantee sufficient authority for your T & D officer to meet the responsibilities implied in the title?

It's a cliché that training is a line responsibility. Yet in actual practice, training has been placed on the "staff" side of most organizations. Just look at the organization charts. To whom does the T & D officer report? Such placement often brings an immediate stigma . . . the mark of Cain: "They're just staff people, you know!"

In *Developing Human Resources*, Nadler says that although training is a line responsibility, education is not. Any kind of employee development is, by its very nature, a support function. In itself, it doesn't result in products like automobiles or clothing; it doesn't in itself cause customers to buy, or users to be satisfied with a service. T & D supports and enables those results. Yet if T & D is to be relevant to the main outputs of the organization, it must have proximity to the line operation. It must "talk their language" and share the line (or production) values. There is a constant give-and-take between the T & D specialists and their line clients.

If we examine the processes of a typical training program, we can see the precise nature of this interchange. To do so clarifies the reasons why T & D people and line people must work harmoniously in a common activity within which there are inherent differences in viewpoints, values, and expertise.

Often training activity starts with a line manager saying to the T & D officer, "I have a training problem." Astute T & D officers overcome their instinctive reaction: "You *may* have a training problem—but at the moment we don't know that for sure. Besides, *I'm* the one who decides when we have training problems. After all, my expertise is to determine when training will work and when it won't."

Of course, such arrogance is unpardonable. Yet there are times when the T & D officer must face the issue that line managers sometimes expect training to be a panacea for all their people problems. Thus nearly all T & D officers must eventually deny a highly motivated customer the very product the customer is so anxious to buy.

It's at these moments that professional T & D officers use effective consultative questions. They respond to the manager who mistakenly wants training with words more like these: "I'm glad you came to talk it over. What, exactly, are your people doing that they shouldn't be doing?" And then, "What aren't your people doing that they should be doing?"

In this way the proper mental processes are launched. Let's examine the ensuing steps to see what responsibilities and what resources both elements (line and staff) can offer to effective performance problem-solving.

Phase A: Analysis	Line contributions and responsibilities	Staff contributions and responsibilities
1. Discover a problem	The line may initiate the analysis with a request for help. By monitoring management reports and operating indices or through surveys, the T & D officer may initiate the analysis. In any event, the client manager must eventually agree that there is a painful situation. The line has thus taken a very necessary first step: "ownership" of the problem.	Monitoring the operation, or data gathered in periodic surveys and interviews, may permit the initiative to originate in the T & D department. Must use special tact and skill in presenting the "bad news" to a client who isn't yet aware of a performance problem—or who is generally insensitive to performance problems. May find it difficult to persuade the client that training is not the best solution.
2. Performance standards	Must "sign off" that the standards are correct and reasonable. If standards don't already exist, participates as the final authority in their documentation.	Can be party to the analysis of existing printed standards. If no standards exist, can facilitate their creation and documentation by suggesting quantities (units, percentages, dollars, milestones, or timelapse) and vocabulary to describe actions and processes.
3. Identify the deficiency	Must ultimately admit that a problem exists . . . that it "has a hurt," but may find this admission more painful than the performance problem itself.	Able to offer larger and more objective perspective . . . a fresh viewpoint. Skills in consultative questioning help clients admit and define the exact nature and scope of the performance problem. May suggest the verbs which define observable actions, and the adverbs to identify satisfactory performance.

Phase A: Analysis	Line contributions and responsibilities	Staff contributions and responsibilities
		Should insist on measurement of the scope of the problem. This is establishing baselines. Doing so will tell how serious the problem really is . . . how widespread.
4. Cost the deficiency	May resist this step, saying it's impossible to put a price on the task.	Knows the technology of putting price tags on the units of performance.
	Can, when persuaded to do so, lead analysts to hard data about costs of units, time, and products—as well as to hidden costs.	Knows the formula for estimating training costs, and can thus make an accurate cost-benefit analysis.
5. Identify causes of the deficiency	May have dangerous and misleading preconceptions.	Should prevent jumping to conclusions by offering several possible causes.
	May find this a traumatic experience, hard to do in front of "outsiders."	Must avoid preconceptions by client and self.
	May tend to "jump to cause" to get quick remedy or to escape culpability.	May be seen as an enemy of progress by insisting on long-range solution, lacking energy for "quick fix" of symptoms.
	May urge quick solution. Is not truly interested in causes.	May need to accept both quick and long-range solutions.
6. Design and select solutions	May jump to first option, as "I told you all along that a little training would fix everything!"	Must be "the pro" at this stage; is the only party with the expertise.
	Has no real basis for performance analysis and may feel threatened by such new solutions as contingency management, feedback, or feedback mechanisms.	Requires patience in deterring client from jumping to first possible solution.
		May be in awkward spot—a training specialist refusing to prescribe own product.
	May need help in seeing why evaluation criteria need to be established so soon.	May need to accept some short-range solution as a way to get to the long-range solution.
		Sould insist that evaluation critera be established at this point.

Phase B: Solving the Problem

7. Decide to go ahead with the best solution	Lacks perspective; can't put this problem into proper perspective for the entire organization.	Has perspective to assign proper priority to this problem and to this project.
	Must be the one to say "Yes" if T & D department offers its resources for continuing the activity.	Can only recommend; does not "own" the problem.
		Can assist client with identifying and prioritizing key variables in the decision.

Phase B: Solving the Problem	Line contributions and responsibilities	Staff contributions and responsibilities
8. *Establish behavioral (performance) objectives*	Not trained in this technology. Can check validity only. Can supply the numbers and quantities. Has first-hand knowledge of the current inventories of the workers who will become the trainees. If necessary to eliminate some objectives, can make the decision.	Owns this technology and is thus responsible. Knows that if standards have been well defined much of this work is already complete. Can check reasonableness, observability, and measurability of the expected behavioral outcomes. Can query for variable conditions which might require flexibility in applying standards.
9. *Design the program*	Has neither skill nor reason for participating here. May be able to offer answers to questions about suitability of some methods in the physical and social environment where training will occur.	Must do this step. Can check to see that all methods suit physical and social climate where training will happen. (Should adapt, not drop, a method just because it's new to the society where training will happen.) Should insist on establishing the evaluation mechanism at this time.
10. *Select trainers*	Not trained in what to look for; tends to pick the person who does the work best. Can prevent selection of local trainers who would cost the program its credibility. Can recommend local trainers who would have instant credibility with learners. May have regular trainers on own staff. Will hopefully accept some responsibility for conducting the training.	Should explore possibility of using trainers from client organization to give full credibility to the program and the behaviors it teaches. Should look for instructional and communicative skills when picking trainers from client organization. Should encourage active role for management in all sessions.
11. *Upgrade trainers*	Has little energy or expertise for this task, but must comprehend its importance. Can learn, at this phase, the value of having qualified instructors as permanent resources within the department.	A must! Unless client has staff of qualified instructors, local trainers must learn how to teach. If qualified instructors are available, they must learn course content. If "outside" trainers are used, they must learn course content, climate, and norms for the client organization and probable inventory of student population. Some standard program for upgrading line trainers should be part of the permanent resources of the T & D department!

Phase B: **Solving the** **Problem**	*Line contributions and responsibilities*	*Staff contributions and responsibilities*
12. *Select trainees*	Must be accountable for this activity. Must get help in communicating the enrollment so it's not seen as punitive—yet so it is seen as an accountability to learn to do the job as taught in the program . . . and to apply this on the job afterwards. Needs to reallocate or reschedule workload to accommodate the training.	Must refuse to do this. Can assist by seeing that only those who perform the task are enrolled. Can assist (insist?) in seeing that trainees know what is expected of them in the training and later when they apply the learnings on the job. Should stress reasons for the enrollment and accountability for meeting the learning objectives and applying the learnings on the job.
13. *Conduct the training*	Not often skilled in how to teach—so will need help in carrying out assigned roles in presenting the program. Can be an effective way to educate good workers for positions of greater responsibility. If training is done by those in client organization, it gains credibility. Active participation (at a minimum, attendance) by all line managers gives credibility and urgency to the training. Make excellent members of "teaching teams" composed of trainers from both the line-client and the T & D departments!	If staff instructors do the teaching, they may lack awareness of the norms and "no-no's" in the client climate. Can lack credibility since they don't work for management in the client organization. However, if that climate is extremely suspicious, the mantle of the "objective outsider" can be converted to an asset. Can offer sensitivity and insights about the learning dynamics— things to which client trainers are sometimes blind.

Phase C: Evaluation

	Line contributions and responsibilities	*Staff contributions and responsibilities*
14. *Measurement*	Has access to the data sources which establish pre/post baselines. Unskilled in designing the measurement instruments. May have to be convinced of the vital importance of this activity.	Must insist that this be done during and after the training. Provides feedback at all phases of training so measurement of group and individual trainees contributes to the learning itself.
15. *Evaluation*	Must "sign off" on how well the program solved the problem. Not trained in analysis or interpreting symptomatic data. Will need help from the T & D specialists. Can provide confirmation of the evidence revealed by the measurement. Can confirm (and must be party to) conclusions drawn from the data about the effectiveness of the program.	Can help identify and quantify symptoms of success and failure. Can design instruments for the measurement—but must do so as early as steps 3, 8, and 9! Can manage statistical processes needed to make sound judgments about the effectiveness of the program. (May need to check a tendency to let the evaluation become an exercise in statistics rather than a realistic appraisal of how conditions have or haven't changed for the client with the problem!)

Phase C: Evaluation	Line contributions and responsibilities	Staff contributions and responsibilities
	Can identify remaining problems and/or new performance deficiencies.	Can retrain or reprocess the existing (new) levels and/or new problems to see if training will help. If not, helps find other solutions.

A COOPERATIVE EFFORT

It might be interesting to examine all the entries in the preceding table to see how many actions involve cooperation and collaboration between the T & D officer and the client manager. Few are totally assignable to one side of that line/staff boundary! There is an incredible amount of give-and-take, mutual effort required to solve performance problems.

And the reason always boils down to this: the line knows its own operation best (including its problems and resources) and the staff sees larger perspectives as it brings its special technology to the solution of performance problems.

Thus a common placement is for the T & D function to be headquartered in a staff location, with "functional" responsibility for training line employees. When such arrangements are installed, a staff of "professionals" inhabits the central T & D department, and "on-the-job trainers" answer to local management within the line operation.

One danger of this system is that the line trainers may become second-class citizens. They do the routine work, teaching from outlines prepared by the "supertrainers" from the central staff. Indeed, staff instructors are often better paid; they have organizational rather than local visibility; they attend outside seminars and grow in professionalism. The local trainers are all too often given little upgrading, so their instructional skills deteriorate.

Yet the so-called second-class trainers are often perceived as doing the real training work in the real world of the organization. They're out there "on the firing line" and they know "where the real action is." Staff trainers get called things like "eggheads" and "ivory-tower theoreticians."

As long as the rivalry between line and staff trainers can be kept affectionate and collaborative, it presents little real danger to an organization. Furthermore, there are definite ways to overcome the dangers which do exist.

One excellent method is to use teaching teams composed of T & D specialists and line instructors. In small organizations, as with a one-person T & D department, the T & D line-manager team offers both local credibility and instructional expertise. The cross-pollination from such teams is obvious; line trainers are exposed to the technology and larger perspective of staff special-

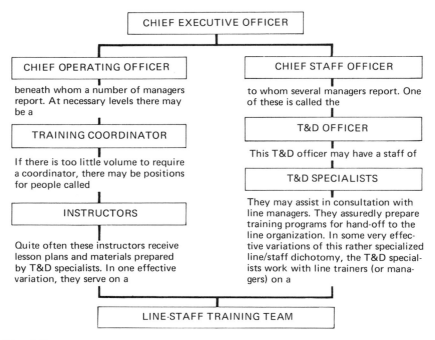

Fig. 4.1.

A productive, traditional system.

ists; T & D specialists get first-hand data and experience in operating shops and offices (Fig. 4.1).

Unfortunately, team-teaching is expensive: two leaders instead of one. Nor is it always appropriate to the methods needed for the learning. But even if teams cannot be used all the time, they can be used *some* of the time. Team-design efforts are equally useful. Involvement by both line and staff people enhances the quality of the program—and can contribute to the education of all who participate.

Other collaborative efforts can be designed. The nature of the operation, the philosophy about line/staff prerogatives, the position in the marketplace, the marketing strategy—all these influence decisions about what tasks are assigned to staff and what tasks to line elements. But in any arrangement, a maximum number of collaborative interfaces between T & D staff, client-management, and line instructors is highly desirable. Central arrangements may prevent inventing the wheel all over again—but they also create some square wheels unless such collaboration exists!

PLACEMENT AS A PURELY STAFF FUNCTION

If you look at the organizations around you, you'll find most T & D officers occupy a staff position. As we've noted, that may bring an automatic "curse" unless collaborative activities are devised to overcome the staff stigma.

All apart from the stigma, there may be communication channel problems when T & D activities are centered in a staff location.

But the fact is, it often *is* there, and one question remains: when T & D is a staff function, to whom does the T & D officer report?

A traditional answer (probably by far the most common answer) is to put the T & D officer in the Personnel department. No matter what you call them (Vice President of Human Resources, Human Resources Development Director, Training Director, or Director of Employee Development) they report in as peers of Industrial Relations, Employee Relations, and Employee Communications.

With the kind of thinking which envisions the employee roster as a major organizational resource, and with the insight that that roster consists of *individuals* who offer unique contributions, there is a diminished rationale for placing T & D within the Personnel department.

Indeed, in some significant ways, the Personnel function and the T & D function are counterthrusts: Personnel tries to get the right people into the right cubbyholes; T & D, on the other hand, not only wants to insure that their capability matches the cubbyhole, but that it grows so they can fill other cubbyholes! T & D is even concerned with cubbyholes that haven't yet been designed or dreamed of! Perhaps this disparity of philosophy and purpose explains the recent departure of the T & D function from the Personnel department in so many organizations.

When T & D leaves Personnel, where does it relocate?

Well, if it stays on the "staff side" it tends to answer to The Vice President of Administrative Services, the Director of Support Services, or whatever title applies to the highest ranking staff officer in the organization. It is significant that the T & D position reports to the top of the staff hierarchy. The position power resulting from this placement cannot be ignored. After all, When T & D is a staff function, its representatives visit the "line territory" much as missionaries visit the frontier. This missionary status is especially noticeable when T & D specialists are consulting, designing, or instructing. As missionaries performing those tasks, it's important that they represent deities who rank high in their own heavens!

PLACEMENT AS A LINE FUNCTION

If the T & D function can report to the chief staff officer of an organization, it can just as logically answer to the chief operating officer—and with rather greater impact. Many T & D officers prefer this arrangement. Among its advantages:

- They are more clearly identified as solvers of operating performance problems.

- They are close to the operation and can give quicker response to operational performance problems.

- Their proximity to operating officers permits quick access to key data needed for analysis of performance problems.

- The entire T & D function is more clearly identified with "where the organization is"—a kind of organizational halo effect.

- The actual instruction is done by people affiliated with and responsible to operating authority, yet under the direct control of the T & D officer.

- Budgets for line operations are attractive: they are more flexible so they can respond to sudden developments; they are apt to be more realistic; they are often more generous!

Of course one disadvantage of this placement is that there is no natural mechanism by which the T & D officer can access performance problems on the staff side of the organization—and therefore no mechanism by which staff managers can access the T & D officer to get help. Obviously such mechanisms can be devised, installed, and made to work just as they have in the reverse placement.

Equally obvious is the fact that some organizations can afford—and do require—a T & D officer in both the line and staff sides at the executive level. About the only problem arising from this dual arrangement is the occasional skirmish over territorial imperatives. For example: Which one is responsible for management training and development? Who handles the training which introduces a new technology that cuts across the line/staff barrier?

An answer to these questions is the final placement we might consider in answer to our question, "Where is the Training department located?"

PLACEMENT WITH THE CHIEF EXECUTIVE OFFICER

How do you give proper authority to the T & D officer? How do you avoid wrangles about line/staff prerogatives? One answer is to have the T & D officer answer to the "big boss" . . . to the chief executive officer.

This arrangement is scarcely customary, but it is happening more and more frequently. There are some obvious advantages.

First, the position power is unquestioned. When it's necessary to arbitrate between departments battling for T & D assistance, there can be little doubt about the T & D officer's authority to make a decision. There can also be little doubt that from this position at the top of the pyramid, the T & D officer is more likely to get the funds and support for resources which would permit working on *all* the significant problems.

If it's hard to get at the facts, a person who answers to the top executive has rather a more forceful calling card than one whose boss is called Administrative Assistant or Staff Support Coordinator.

The view from the top provides a perspective permitting a pro-active approach to T & D: participation in strategic planning and crisis response permits far more effective decision making for T & D policy, priorities, and programs.

Perhaps the most important aspect of the perspective is that the news about new directions and imminent crises comes *immediately.* The T & D department is far more able to prevent fires if it has direct access to the top officer of the organization. T & D officers who are peers to the key decision-makers are key decision makers themselves! The same thing is proportionately true when the T & D officer answers to the top officer of either the line or staff organization.

It is interesting to note (though not vastly significant) that the very first page of *1984 Who's Who In Training and Development,* ASTD's official membership directory, shows six vice presidents or administrative presidents. (The four presidents listed there seem to head up their own consulting organizations, a vast industry now flourishing in this era of human resource development!)

Finally, the quality of the T & D decisions and programs tends to improve if the accountable person, the T & D officer, is in direct and constant scrutiny of the person who must make "the-buck-stops-here" decisions for the entire organization. Accountability rises in direct proportion to the position.

SUMMARY

As T & D officers gain respect by solving performance problems, their analytical skills deepen and widen along with their knowledge of what the organization is about and how it works. They become acutely conscious of who is doing what work . . . and in what direction they wish to grow. Thus it is no surprise that the T & D officer is asked to solve problems of increasing depth and breadth, problems ranging from simple knowledge deficiencies to organizational development needs involving the top officers.

Of the four inputs into an organization (people, technology, time, and material) the human resource is probably the only one capable of almost limitless appreciation in value. Directing the appreciation process is a big responsibility.

Robert R. Blake, of Managerial Grid fame, has been heard to say that the T & D officer and the chief executive officer should be one and the same person.

That makes great sense. However the facts of life are that chief executive officers do indeed delegate responsibility for a great many tasks—and human resource development is one they normally delegate. They can delegate the responsibility; but they cannot delegate active interest!

It is sheer delight to see chief executives enlist themselves in personal growth experiences, to hear them ask, "How are your new assertiveness skills working out on the job?" or to welcome them as active students rather than as quick visitors who say, "I wish I had time to stay longer, but I've important things to do!"

Chief executive officers make the most positive statement and the greatest contribution when they actively develop themselves, actively require the continuing development of their immediate subordinates, and visibly reinforce training at all levels of the organization. But they do have other things to do, too. So they characteristically delegate the T & D responsibility.

Where should they position the person to whom they make this delegation?

The training and development function should be positioned where it can give the best possible service to the largest possible number of organizational clients. The traditional dichotomy between "line" and "staff" is helpful only to the degree that it clarifies "who will do what" in solving performance problems. Since teamwork is imperative, and since the T & D specialists must access reliable data throughout the organizations, more and more T & D officers report directly to the chief executive officer.

It's a goal worth seeking—and an encouraging development.

CHAPTER

HOW DO YOU FIND TRAINING NEEDS?

DISTINGUISHING TRAINING NEEDS FROM OTHER PERFORMANCE PROBLEMS

The T & D officer is the ultimate determiner of what training will be done within an organization. To make that decision, T & D officers must know a training need when they see one—and they must be able to discriminate between performance problems which are training needs as opposed to those which are not training needs.

We have already noted that the chief test for a training need is just this: Does the employee know how to meet the performance standards for an accountable task?

If the answer is "Yes, the employee knows how," then there is no training need. There is a performance problem; but it isn't a training need, since more training will not solve the problem. The employee already knows how. There must be other obstacles to satisfactory performance.

We can look at those other obstacles later on. For the moment let's just make sure we know what a training need is. *A training need exists when an employee lacks the knowledge or skill to perform an assigned task satisfactorily.*

This implies that there are standards of performance. That may or may not be true: Not every organization has established standards for every task—and lots of standards have been informally established, but never documented. If there are no standards against which employee performance can be measured, it's very hard to conclude that the employee is not performing properly. Nevertheless, the T & D specialist, in the role of consultant, often gets into precisely that situation. Managers are dissatisfied with employee performance, but haven't identified precisely what level of performance would satisfy them. That happens a lot when new jobs are established, when the technology is altered, or when procedures are amended. It can also happen when old tasks begin to get sluffed off, or performed indifferently—or in ways which just "generally make managers unhappy."

What can the T & D officer do in the face of such vague specifications? Well, this is one time when questioning skills are very, very useful. The reputation of the T & D department doesn't gain much luster if T & D specialists just say, "Well, when you make up your mind what you want, get in touch!" This is the perfect chance to use some direct questions to get at facts; to use open questions to get at feelings; then to reflect the frustration the manager feels due to the performance problem back on the job and the hard thinking you're asking for in this consultation.

Far better that the T & D specialist and the perplexed client-manager mutually explore the issue to determine what level of performance *would* satisfy the manager whose people present a problem. Thus T & D specialists, acting in their consultant role, can be heard asking things like, "When you envision workers doing this job properly, what do you see them doing?" "What specific things would you like to see them doing—but don't?" "When you walk up to workers to tell them they're doing well, what specific things do you praise?" "When you correct them for doing things wrong, what specific things do you ask them to avoid?" "What do you ask them to be certain to do in the future?"

Even though the answers to such questions are not yet sanctioned (or is the proper word "sanctified"?) by publication in procedures manuals, the T & D specialist has begun the standards-setting process. The next decision is whether the new "specification" is a reasonable expectation of workers.

At this stage astute T & D officers try: (1) to involve *several* managers, (2) to reach agreement without pain or "lose/lose" relationships, (3) to clarify goals and start the evaluation process by discussing what "things will look like when we have succeeded," and (4) to plant the idea of some positive reinforcers for those workers who meet standard after the change effort. The truly wise ones also (5) reality test all this by involving workers themselves.

Worker comments will do many things:

●   Explain whether or not prescribed/recommended standards are reasonable;

●   Uncover interesting and productive information about hidden task interferences and conflicting consequences;

●   Help identify useful feedback data which might let them know how they're doing while they're performing; and

●   Tell the T & D specialist whether or not the job aids (present training, written procedures, and job descriptions) are accurate; all too often they are not.

In getting helpful inputs from managers and workers while defining performance standards, T & D representatives will be implanting that important concept that organizations get their work done because people fill their positions properly. They "put out the proper outputs." Positions, in turn, are made up of responsibilities, which in turn are discharged by proper completion of a number of tasks. To set standards, we define those tasks, specifying the actions to be taken and the criteria of successful completion.

In many standards-setting conversations, it's necessary to point out that "criteria" is just a big word to describe what makes the work "okay" and what makes it "not okay." This includes data about what's right and wrong; it also includes data about how many in what period of time.

Once the actions and criteria are pinned down, standard setters want to consider the conditions of performance. This includes what the worker is given to work with and what happens when there are variations in working conditions. For example: an agent who deals with the public may be encouraged to ask a pleasant question of customers. That's a "standard of performance"—unless there are more than three people waiting in line! Under those conditions, the pleasant question may be sacrificed in order to give speedy service to all three customers.

When determining standards, it's useful to think in certain terms. In *Management by Objectives and Results,* George Morrisey suggests such concepts as:

Numbers—such as hours, units, requests, completions

Dollars—sales, unit costs, resources consumed, hours-of-effort multiplied by salary-per-hour

Percent—as of overtime, turnover, rejects, or utilization

Timelapse—such as flowtime, set-up, inventory turnover

Completions—like shipments, acceptance, milestones

Skill in writing performance standards, or at least in describing human behavior, is a "must" for all T & D officers and specialists. Some organizations have begun to train managers from all departments how to define performance standards. One such firm (Kemper Insurance Companies) has conducted workshops so line managers become trainers for workshops at which still other line managers learn how to develop standards for their subordinates. Kemper stresses the importance of developing the actual standards as a joint effort between the manager and the subordinate—not as a product of staff trainers.

Once the standards are agreed upon by key people in the client department, the T & D specialist is ready to ask that all-important question: "Do the people who must meet these standards have the knowledge and skill to do so right now?" If the answer is "Yes," then no training is indicated.

For newcomers, that seldom happens. They rarely know how to do their new jobs perfectly. In those cases, we have discovered a training need. It does not follow, however, that newcomers need training in all facets of their position. Even newcomers have some ability and some knowledge, and we call this their "inventory." If we match the inventory against the standard we have set, we have a possible training need.

What the employee must do to meet the standard can be represented by the letter M for minimum mastery or "must do." From this M we subtract the inventory to discover what the newcomer needs to learn in order to perform properly.

The test is somewhat different for people who are already incumbent in their positions. We can again let M represent what the worker must do; from that we still subtract the I, or inventory. But this time the inventory is what the worker is actually doing now. The difference between the M and I is a potential training need. We now have a formula for potential training needs:

$$M - I = A \text{ potential training need.}$$

The word "potential" is accurate. Why? Because with incumbents we are not yet certain that the reason for difference is lack of knowledge or skill. We don't yet know that *they do not know how*. Only if the reason for the difference is their not knowing how do we have a training need.

It's helpful to regard the distance between the "must do" and the "is doing" as a deficiency. We can put this into our formula by assigning it the letter D. Now our formula looks like this:

$$M - I = D.$$

At this stage we are now ready to consider several different types of deficiency. When employees don't know how, we call this D_K for "deficiency of knowledge." All D_K's are regarded as training needs. If the difference between the "must do" and the "is doing" stems from other causes, we consider it a "deficiency of execution" and call it a D_E. What "other causes" might there be? To name a few: lack of feedback, badly engineered jobs, or punishing consequences. D_E's are not solvable by training.

Sometimes people know how to do the job, but have so little practice that they cannot maintain a satisfactory level of performance. This might be called a D_P, or "deficiency of practice." Training in the form of drill may solve D_P problems. (But one just has to ask why the manager of these inventories let them go to waste!)

A much fuller explanation of this approach, particularly about deficiencies of execution, appears in Tom Gilbert's "Praxeonomy: A Systematic Approach to Identifying Training Needs," from *The Management of Personnel Quarterly,* for Fall 1967. This publication comes from the Graduate School of Business Administration at the University of Michigan in Ann Arbor.

MICRO NEEDS AND MACRO NEEDS

Many T & D officers find it helpful to think of two classes of training needs: "micro" and "macro." The difference is very simple, but it has heavy impact on the response made by the T & D department. A micro training need exists for just one person, or for a very small population. Macro training needs exist in a large group of employees—frequently in the entire population with the same job classification. That happens, for example, when all clerks must be trained in a new procedure, or all managers in new policy. A manager in a specialized department, however, may develop a micro training need when some new technology is introduced into that field . . . or when performance as a manager reveals noncomprehension of one facet of good managerial practice!

When new employees enter the organization, there are assumed macro training needs: they will know nothing of policies and procedures, nothing about organizational goals or structures. These deficiencies of knowledge are assumed to apply to all new people.

However, there may also be micro training needs about the special tasks the newcomer will perform: it is a good idea to "take inventory" to see whether or not the individual meets standard on some of the skills necessary to satisfactory performance of a position.

Because there may be serious lapses in such areas, some organizations use "certification testing." These might be written exams, performance demonstrations, or both. What might they include? Typing skills, shorthand, English correctness for secretaries or salespersons; problems to solve with micrometers, tasks to perform on lathes or with typical tools for shop personnel.

One T & D officer describes the certification-testing process this way: "They are used as predictors of job performance to assure the company that each employee is ready to safely and accurately perform job responsibilities following the completion of their training." In other words, there is micro testing before there is macro training.

SOURCES OF POTENTIAL MICRO TRAINING NEEDS

How does a conscientious T & D officer discover actual symptoms of these micro and macro training needs?

Let's look first at the micro needs. What better place to start than by keeping an eye on the existing personnel systems? The actions taken to maintain personnel systems lead to the discovery of many training needs:

•   *New hires.*   Their micro need is the peculiar information required before they can feel comfortably and acceptably "at speed" in the new position. This might be local lore such as starting times, lunch and break schedules, the location of the necessary rooms, whom to turn to for help. If pre-hiring interviews or certification testing reveal any deficiencies bad enough to correct (but not serious enough to deny employment) those are also micro training needs.

(Just a note about training needs for hires: not all their needs should be met immediately. They should be trained only for tasks they will perform *soon;* they will forget—and be overwhelmed by—training in tasks they won't perform until later in their tour of duty.)

•   *Promotions.*   When one person moves into a position of greater responsibility, we may presume that there will be a gap between the person's inventory and the knowledge and skill required to perform properly in the new position.

•   *Transfers.*   Even if no promotion is involved, switching to new responsibilities is a signal that there may be a temporary mismatch between what the employee can already do and what must be done to perform satisfactorily in the new placement.

•   *Appraisals.*   This system exists in many organizations for both management and nonmanagement positions. The "suggestions for improvement" invariably are triggers for individual education and development—and thus symptoms of training needs. Suppose a superior tells a subordinate to acquire a new skill, or to master the conceptual framework for some phase of the present job that isn't being done as well as it might be. The T & D officer now has data that a perceived micro training need exits. Helping the appraised and the appraiser develop a plan for acquiring new or perfected skills is an important part of the human resource development activity. It matters not at all whether the growth recommended is to improve performance on the present position, education to prepare for the next assignment, or development to help the organization grow to fit new environments. Any suggestion calls for some response—an offer to help—from the T & D department.

● *Career planning programs.* Since these tell where people want to go, they also can reveal lacks (deficiencies) in the current inventories of those people.

● *Management-by-objectives goals.* These statements of plans for the next period can arouse trainers to action in the same way appraisals should do.

● *An accident.* An accident may signal that a single employee is unaware of certain safety regulations. If the accident report indicates the probable cause to be ignorance, the T & D department has a trigger to see that the D_K is quickly overcome.

● *Quality control records.* If the record shows the profile of individual workers (and it should if it's a dynamic management instrument!), then that profile reveals consistent errors. If the worker is making the same mistake again and again, it's time to find out why. Does the worker know better? If not, then training is needed.

● *Grievances.* When a grievance is filed against a foreman, supervisor or manager, alert T & D specialists ask if these people know what they are entitled to do and what they are constrained against doing under policy or contract statements. When they act out of ignorance, a D_K has been uncovered and some micro training is indicated.

● *New positions.* These get created occasionally as the way to handle incomplete or lagging workloads—and as a way to introduce new technology into the organization. When this occurs, the people who fill the new positions will almost assuredly have a need to acquire new knowledge and skill. If the position is filled with people from outside the organization, the newcomers will have a D_K about the policies and procedures of their new employers.

● *Special assignments.* These are vehicles for educating and developing incumbent employees. People so assigned will inevitably have some D_K's about the terms of their assignment as well as about the technology required in the special tasks.

● *Job descriptions.* Micro training needs are especially important if the job descriptions are under attack for being useless.

● *Research and development projects.*

● *Tuition refund programs.*

● *Homestudy applications.*

● *Job rotation programs.*

- *Cross-qualification decisions.* All these are possible sources of micro training needs. When people assume duties under any of these programs, even as students in homestudy programs, they inherit some lack of knowledge about the terms of the activity. T & D officers who manage the *entire* T & D function establish communication mechanisms to keep themselves informed about routine activities in all such programs. They can therefore respond effectively with good counsel about how to overcome the D_K's that inevitably are created in such programs. In many cases they get actively involved in designing the learning experiences.

That represents a wide range of potential training needs for the individual employee. Isn't it nice that most of them result because a person or an organization has grown? . . . and that they will enjoy still more growthful training?

SOURCES OF POTENTIAL MACRO TRAINING NEEDS

Certain organization events trigger the pro-active T & D officer to look for training needs involving large numbers of people. The first source of information is so obvious that many overlook it!

- *Regular management reports* tell about production, warehousing or inventory problems . . . about trends in turnover or grievances . . . about a whole array of things which cause T & D officers to ask if human performance could be a cause. There is lots of wonderful news to be discovered by reading the reports the big bosses say they need to manage the organization.

- *Special reports and requests* reveal future plans, shifting priorities, problem areas, successes, failures—many of which result from or will involve human performance. They reveal new strategies and programs which may require people to do things they never did before. That means potential inadequate human inventories, and inadequate human inventories are symptoms of potential training needs.

- *New plants* usually mean new hiring, sometimes new positions. They often signal

- *New products,* which can result only if a new technology (or significant amendments to old technologies) are acquired by significant numbers of employees.

- *New equipment or machinery* can arrive when there are new plants or new products—or simply because somebody found a better way to handle old tasks. Examples: The Accounting department gets a new computer, or the Print shop buys a new press. If many people get involved with these machines, there is a macro training need.

- *Changes in standards,* as we have noted so many times, inevitably mean that large numbers of people must be informed—and sometimes trained.

Frequently incumbents need a chance to ventilate their feelings about the change, to understand the reasons for the new standard so they can accept it more easily—or at least respond effectively by "going along with it."

• *Trends* in any operating or management index are signals for training needs for populations of employees—especially if the trend is in the wrong direction! Thus sales reports, productivity indices, cost figures, waste reports, back orders, reject rates, turnover, grievance trends, and frequent recommendations in appraisals or management-by-objectives documents—all these are good data for the T & D officer who is deciding what training needs might exist in the organization.

• *New policies* frequently result from the changing position of the organization in the marketplace. If times are tough, the employment, lay-off, benefits, and salary "package" may be changed. When that happens, the expectations of employees often change too. How will they know the new policies, and where express the new expectations, except in training-type sessions? The alert T & D officer sees that such sessions are considered.

It's quite apparent, then, that T & D officers get signals about potential needs by constant monitoring of the ongoing operation!

Is that the only way to find training needs? No . . . but it is assuredly the most reliable and the most consistent way to remain relevant and responsive. Personnel moves and operating events and indices tell management where the organization is succeeding and where it is falling short and where it is going. Paperwork which supports these activities can provide data which trigger the T & D officer to further investigation and analysis.

Furthermore, if T & D officers make intelligent use of these symptoms, they can avoid the "firefighter" trap. That is to say, instead of being purely reactive they can become pro-active . . . taking steps to solve potential performance problems before they become actual problems. By careful scrutiny of personnel moves, operating activity, and planning documents, the best T & D officers generate good training programs before any damaging deficiencies actually occur.

SURVEYS OR INTERVIEWS?

In addition to the monitoring and anticipation, T & D officers often use surveys and interviews to poll managers for their perception of the training needs in the organization.

Unfortunate results sometimes grow out of such surveys and interviews . . . if T & D officers fail to consider carefully what questions they ask and how they interpret the data.

A typical ploy is to ask managers, "What are your training needs going to be in the next year?" Line managers don't know their training needs! So they either ignore the survey, or send it in with misleading and superficial data. Hotheads with deep personal agendas send very strong signals, giving intense but distorted pictures of the "macro" situation. Conscientious managers who have nothing much to say but who think they ought to say something send back lots of data based on minimum thought or perceptivity.

There's another problem growing out of asking managers to tell the T & D specialists their training needs: they come to believe that they *do* know how to determine training needs. Over a period of time they begin to demand training for performance problems which training won't solve. At that point the T & D officer is in a weak, defensive position . . . trying to dissuade clients from doing training. It's an awkward position, even when training won't do any good!

Inherent in any survey is the problem that once line managers have made their responses, they feel they have totally discharged their responsibility for training. They need only wait until a schedule is published, nominate a few subordinates to fill up their established "quota" of enrollments—and that's it!

The trouble with all this is that in relevant training systems, that isn't "it" at all!

In relevant T & D systems, line managers in all departments and at all levels of the organization see the direct relationship between their own operation and T & D programs. If they merely respond to surveys or interviews, line managers are in a purely passive position . . . with no pro-active responsibility and no pro-active potential benefit. This passivity, which may result from a needs determination based on nothing but surveys and interviews, is unacceptable to dynamic T & D officers.

On the other hand, if the T & D department never takes its inquiry to the actual line-manager clients, it risks bad generalizations about the macro training needs of the organization. Thus the most astute T & D officers use surveys and interviews as a validation process for their own analysis of the data gathered in monitoring the ongoing operation.

Perhaps an effective summary of the relationship between surveys and interviews on the one hand, and monitoring the operation on the other would go like this:

1.   Basic signals about training needs come from monitoring the ongoing operation.

2.   Signals about micro training needs are pursued, with the T & D department using further inquiry and analysis with the manager of the potential trainees and, of course, with the trainees themselves.

3.   Signals about the macro training needs of the organization are validated by further inquiry in the form of surveys and interviews.

4. New signals which come from the surveys and interviews are validated by reference to the "hard data" from the operational monitoring.

By such a dual focus in determining training needs, the T & D officer can better validate the accuracy and completeness of the department's response to the training, education, and development needs of the organization.

There are also a number of things the T & D officer can do to make certain that the surveys and interviews actually used prove to be of maximum help.

First, one faces the question: Shall we use a survey or interviews? The answer depends on several criteria. The T & D officer must consider the size of the population, the sensitivity of the issues, and the time available.

Clearly, interviews are time-consuming and unfeasible when there is a vast population to reach. An alternative is to interview a few and send surveys to larger numbers. If the population is incredibly vast, then the T & D officer may have to sample even on the survey.

If the issue of training is especially sensitive, or if strong feelings exist about certain programs, then perhaps no survey can measure the depth of the feelings; only interviews can permit that two-way, affective exchange. On the other hand, if people are taking training too much for granted, perhaps the "hot" interview medium will rekindle the interest the T & D officer would like to generate.

The issue of time involves at least two facets. There is the time available before the data must be collected and analyzed. There is also the time the data source is willing to invest in supplying the information. No matter which one uses, interviews or surveys, the decision should reflect genuine concern for the responder. Short is best—so long as it can provide good data on which to base training decisions. Surveys should be as brief as possible, with the time for completion measured in minutes rather than in hours. Interviews should be just as long as the interviewer told the interviewee they would last—no longer!

Perhaps the decision table shown in Fig. 5.1 will provide some help in deciding whether to use surveys or interviews in the next data-gathering quest.

Regardless of the medium (surveys or interviews), the same questions are useful. True, people like to codify data from surveys (many are computerized nowadays!) and so short answers are encouraged. The issue really shouldn't be the potential for codification, but the usefulness of the data. This raises the question: "What questions should the T & D specialist be asking when searching for training needs?

The two most useful questions probably are:

If the population is	And time is	And sensitivity is	Then
Big	Tight	Low	Use survey
Big	Tight	High	Interview a sample of the population
Big	Ample	High	Interview
Big	Ample	Low	Survey with limited interviews to validate
Small	Tight/Ample	High	Interview
Small	Tight	High	Interview (This is often the initial data-gathering activity in an organization development program.)

Fig. 5.1.

Deciding whether to use surveys or interviews.

1.   What are your people doing that they shouldn't be doing?

2.   What aren't your people doing that they should be doing?

These have the value of orienting the responder toward behaviors. They focus on visible behaviors—which are the only kind we can ultimately verify. Thus these two questions put the entire inquiry into the proper realm: human performance. In addition they tend to be relatively open, yet relatively specific. Despite the passion for codification, most effective surveys and interviews contain a balance between open and directive questions.

We have already noted the futility of asking managers to tell us what their training needs are. They don't know. Besides, it's our job to determine training needs. It's their job to identify performance problems, ours to help them solve those problems. Training may be the solution—or it may not.

Another direct question, "What are your problems?" tends to be less than productive for the T & D specialist. The question itself may be too threatening: managers probably can't afford to have problems—at least not publicly. Even if they will share their problems, the question doesn't focus on human performance. It's likely to uncover facts like the inadequate plumbing, the deterioration of the community in which the office is located, or the tight labor market.

Client descriptions of performance problems are often a bit cloudy; it's easy for managers to contract a disease called "They don't make people the way they used to !"

However, when asked to do so, managers can usually describe what they would like their subordinates *not* to be doing. From that the T & D specialist can move to the next question: "What would you like to see them doing that they aren't doing now?" or "Just describe what you see your staff doing when you view the office the day after the new system has been installed." Then when that visioning step is complete, ask "Now what do you see a week after the installation?"

ACTION (What you should see them doing)	OBJECT (What they do it to)	HOW WELL? HOW OFTEN? HOW MUCH?
Type	letters and reports	with *all* errors corrected with Taperase.
Add 5%	sales tax	to *all* purchases, without error, by referring to chart on cash register.
Restock	all shelves	when no customers are in the department.
Serve	customers	whenever there are customers present.
Refrain	from chatting	with other salespersons if customers are anywhere in the department.

Fig. 5.2.

Matrix for identifying expectations.

For the client not skilled in visioning, a format or matrix like the one in Fig. 5.2 often helps.

Such formatting brings focus. It will not cure fuzziness in managers who haven't yet set their own goals or standards, but it will improve their skill in sending specific signals. T & D specialists can help managers learn to request things like "improve typing speed by 15 percent" instead of "be better typists." The format will help them ask for "will give less advice when counselling" instead of asking for a training program to make them "quit rubbing people the wrong way."

Of course there are other ways to help client managers specify what they want, for example, prioritizing exercises, like the one in Fig. 5.3. Such lists of skills "prime the pump" and keep them visioning specific behavior rather than making general complaints about the human condition.

A little of that "pump priming" can be a good thing; too much can be harmful. It limits the client manager's responses in several significant ways:

- A long list deters them from thinking of their own performance problems;
- A long list limits their creativity; and
- A long list implies that the thinking has already been done by the T & D department.

Although Fig. 5.4 brings focus by forcing the manager to rank items as in Fig. 5.3, it just lists topics; there is little implication of behavior and no mention whatsoever of standards or criteria. It would be more useful if, instead of topical lists, it listed skills such as "provides for two-way feedback when making assignments" or "voluntarily prepares zero-based budget forecasts for semi-annual, annual, and five-year cycles." Nevertheless, as it stands the

---

WHAT TRAINING DO YOUR PEOPLE NEED?

Here are the goals of some typical training programs for new managers. Assume that your subordinates could learn only one of these at the next management workshop. Put the number "1" by that goal. Then continue to select these goals, one at a time, until you have ranked all of them. You may add goals not shown here, and give them the proper priority by jotting them down in the spaces provided.

A.   Use nondirective counselling techniques.

B.   Establish performance standards for the tasks in our department.

C.   Listen for feelings as well as facts.

D.   Prepare a zero-based budget for next year.

Use these spaces to add your own and assign the correct priority number.

AA.

BB.

CC.

Fig. 5.3.

Establishing learning goals.

WHAT TRAINING DO YOU AND YOUR PEOPLE NEED?			
If you could divide 100 percent of the training effort among the following topics, how would you do so? Divide exactly 100 percent, but assign no effort at all to topics in which you don't want training.	For yourself	For your own direct reports	For those who report to your direct reports
Cashflow, budgeting, and economic planning			
Interpersonal relationships			
Time management			
Other (specify)			
Other (specify)			
TOTAL	100%	100%	100%

Fig. 5.4.

Getting training priorities from line managers.

format can help get data from client managers who are not accustomed to dealing with a training function which uses behavioral statements.

By completing such a question, line managers help the T & D director put proper priorities on training objectives and training needs—even as they give helpful data about performance problems.

It's important to include, in any structured question, a place for the responder to include fresh ideas—as the suggestions they may add to the bottom of the list in the "What Training Do You and Your People Need?" forms just examined. This is just as true of interviews as it is of surveys.

Respondents need a chance to inject their own ideas. On questionnaires, blank lines where they can add items reveal many interesting data. Open questions are excellent ways to involve respondents. For example, the T & D specialist might ask (on a questionnaire as well as face-to-face) "What in your opinion are:

- The chief duties of the T & D department?
- Your own responsibilities for training and development?
- The most significant changes this organization might make to improve its training and development activity?
- The most significant skills you could acquire with the help of the T & D department?, and
- The most significant skills your subordinates could acquire with the help of the T & D department?"

One big advantage of the interview is its flexibility. When preplanned questions fail to hit pay dirt, or when unexpected "agendas" of interviewees begin to appear, the interviewer can always move into an "open and reflective question" mode to accommodate and encourage the unanticipated data. When the responder gives extraneous answers, obviously not understanding the question, interviewers can always rephrase and redirect. In other words, a planned interview assumes that interviewer and interviewee alike can follow the structure—yet shift, add, adapt, or delete as the dynamics of the interview require. When the T & D specialists who conduct interviews cannot do so, there is a training need right in the T & D department, isn't there?

This does not mean that interviews are loosely structured. There should certainly be some forced questions to test the depth of the conviction and to ensure some common basis for comparing data from all interviewees. Any forced choice would serve this need. A parallel to the list of desired learning objectives would be something like this: "Of the seven training programs listed here, assume you could have just one. Which would it be? Which one would you least likely utilize?" This process can then be repeated, with the same list of programs, by asking the manager to do the same selection—but as if the choices were for subordinates rather than for the manager.

PRIORITIZING TRAINING NEEDS

It must be quite apparent that the T & D officer has many sources of data about potential training needs. Whether they seek micro or macro training needs, alert T & D officers keep their eyes on the operation, on key communications, on personnel moves even as they poll their client population.

If there are lots of signals from lots of sources, the training needs (or the need for some performance problem solution) may exceed the resources available to meet those needs. On what basis does the T & D officer decide which needs to fill?

At such moments a written policy statement comes in mighty handy! But on what basis does that policy rest? In most organizations, at least four criteria must be considered: cost-effectiveness, legal requirements, executive pressure, and population to be served. Let's examine each criterion individually.

The cost of a performance problem can usually be determined. It's relatively easy if one immediately knows the cost of a defective unit. For example, if typists are having to retype letters, you can get the number of letters they retype and multiply that by the cost per letter. To establish the cost per letter, one divides the total cost of the secretarial pool by the number of letters produced for an equal time period. Therefore if a letter costs $1.05 to type, and 40 percent of the 1,000 letters per week must be retyped, the deficiency costs $450 per week and $21,840 per year. If this research is too cumbersome, industry averages are available (as the $1.05 per typing used here) from many sources. Usually they're available within the organization in some of the many management control reports generated by the computer for the Controller!

Price tags for other behaviors, like managerial skills, are more elusive—but not impossible. Consider a problem in which management complains that supervisors are "soft." Further probing reveals that this "softness" reveals itself in a refusal to give decisions in grievances. Supervisors just pass them to the next level of review. The T & D officer can use the salary costs for each level to establish the cost of a single grievance. Since there is no decision, that cost is waste. By multiplying this unit cost by the number of unanswered grievances, one can establish the cost of the deficiency.

For either deficiency, the typed letters, or the undecided grievances, it's then necessary to compute the cost of the solution: development costs, salary costs, special expenses. Do they add up to less than the cost of the problem? If not, these problems don't meet the cost-effectiveness criterion. If they do meet that criterion, they may need to go into a "waiting list" because they offer fewer cost-benefits than other problems.

A second criterion is the legal requirement. Nowadays numerous government statutes dictate some of the decisions about what training to offer. Equal Employment legislation, Upward Mobility programs, Occupational Safety and Health acts—all these impact upon the T & D director's priority system. It may be necessary to implement programs for which no immediate tangible cost saving can be computed—it's the law!

Executive pressure is a third criterion. It usually comes from within the organization—and it's a criterion which smart T & D officers do not ignore. Executive desire for certain training is a reality of the marketplace for T & D officers—and it is also a pleasing symptom of management support! When T & D officers complain that they don't get support from the top, they should ask themselves how many suggestions from chief executive officers, vice-presidents, or directors they turned down recently . . . or even in recent years.

Certainly this does not mean that T & D officers should roll over and be obedient puppies just because a major execituve says, "I have a training problem," or "Why don't we have a program in Assertiveness?" Executive T & D officers use the same performance analysis they would use with similar requests from any other place in the organization—they just do it more patiently and more gently! And indeed, there may be occasions when the decision is to go ahead with the program even if it doesn't pass all the tests. The long-range support such a concession may buy could be worth this single once-only faulty decision.

Finally there is the criterion of population. Sometimes this means simply that training goes to the most extensive problem. Macro needs may take priority over micro needs. Fortunately, it doesn't always need to work that way. The factor of influence and impact must also enter the decision table. Possibly the people with defective performance occupy positions where their work impacts upon the entire operations—as senior officers. Perhaps they have product hand-offs to workers in "downline" jobs. Perhaps the value of their product gives some priority to their need.

Performance problems which affect many workers, which are costly, which are related to the law, or which interest executives—all these deserve attention. Actual or potential knowledge deficiencies (D_K) deserve training. Problems stemming from lack of practice (D_P) should produce drill, or enforced on-the-job application. Problems stemming from other causes are probably deficiencies of execution (D_E) and non-training solutions are in order.

SUMMARY

How about another chart (Fig. 5.5) to give the "big picture" of the process by which you determine training needs?

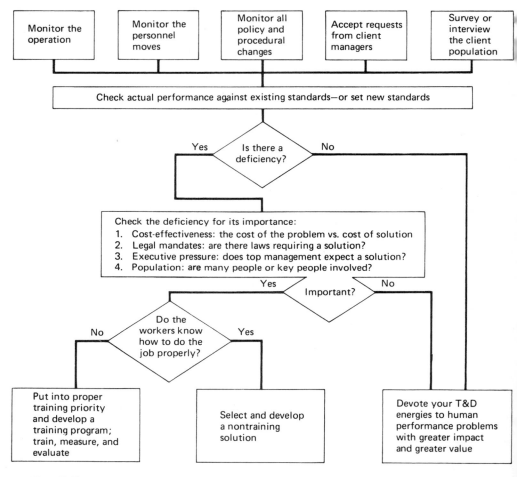

Fig. 5.5.

How to determine training needs.

CHAPTER **6**

HOW DO YOU RESPOND TO INDIVIDUAL TRAINING NEEDS?

THE IMPORTANCE OF MICRO TRAINING NEEDS

Once the T & D specialists have determined that a performance problem can be solved through training, the next step is to design or locate an appropriate program. The central issue? "How can we ensure that trainees acquire the necessary behaviors—and that they apply them on their jobs?" The two parts of that inquiry are equally important; acquisition without application is an inadequate response to individual training needs!

If we were dealing with macro training needs, involving numbers of people, we would want to make sure that the investment produced differences in the on-the-job performance of the graduates. Is it any less important when we solve an individual training need? When we meet micro training needs we "put teeth" into career-planning and assessment-center programs. We also take major steps in the total human resource management of our organizations.

The word "micro" shouldn't deceive us. Dictionaries may define it as "one millionth of a specified part," but it's hard to envision a training need for just one person in a million-person organization! Our response to an individual training need is important: it meets a genuine *human* resource need.

Performance appraisals, assessment centers, selection certification, career planning—all provide data about individual training needs. And they are all hollow exercises unless there is a relevant and *implemented* development program as a result of the data gathering.

T & D specialists respond to individual training needs much as they would respond to any other request for help: they make certain that:

1. There are some reasonably definite objectives;

2. The requesting manager is prepared to assign the "trainee" to work that will permit use of new insights, skills, or attitudes;

3. The requesting manager is prepared to reinforce application of the new behavior;

4. The training, developmental, or educational activity can be cost-effective; and

5. The "trainee" understands why this program is happening.

The first three steps do more than validate the need; they ensure management support of what may be an awkward fourth step: analyzing the cost benefits of an individualized program.

The cost of "micro training" cannot be spread across large populations, so it is an expensive process no matter what source of help you use: (1) Developing a highly individualized program with existing resources may easily cost more than the new knowledge or skills could possibly contribute back to the organization. (2) Searching for a "precisely correct" outside program means reading many brochures and university catalogs, many phone calls and risks on untested programs; it can seem like searching for a needle in a haystack. (All this presumes that no combination of existing in-house programs will meet the peculiar needs of the individual . . . that this is indeed a "micro" training need.)

The range of micro training needs is fantastic. Top executives have micro needs all the time: they need crest-of-the-wave knowledge for their unique technology, they need unusual help in solving unusual managerial problems, very often they need perceptive skills so they will anticipate future problems which haven't yet become reality! Where does the T & D staff locate that highly individualized program for them?

Nor are executives alone in this position. The high tech age in which we live means that research specialists must study overtime to lag just a bit behind their competition! Besides, the "new tech" spreads throughout the organization so many positions require knowledge and skill in a technology applied by very few employees. These are very serious, very expensive, and very *real* micro training needs.

Because they are very real, gentleness is the proper mode for the needs analysis. A battery of empathic questions may be more appropriate than hard-nosed insistence on proof of an economic payoff. Besides, client managers are asking the T & D department for training; that's no time to be hard-nosed! The gentle questioning is really designed not only to improve the quality of the decision, but also to show that T & D types understand.

For high tech or new tech requests one might ask, "How soon might the competition be able to market a product?" "How soon after your employee has this knowledge can you assign a project using this new technology?" "How soon will your unit be making a decision about a system (or product) using this new information?"

For improvement in personal skills (as failure to delegate, failure to commend, temper control, managing stress) the first questions are more apt to be reflective: "And this is upsetting you?" *Then* comes probing: "And upsetting others too?" Or another reflection that simultaneously probes: "I sense that it has been (or can be) clearly communicated to this employee that acceptable performance depends upon correcting this problem?" Or, "Are there existing assignments which, with proper coaching, could help this employee grow in the desired directions?"

No question should appear to block the request . . . only to communicate the need for orderly data gathering and analysis in meeting the micro need. More than a few managers have been known to request attendance at outside workshops scheduled in the same city the week of their daughter's marriage—or just because the locale was so attractive. (Brochures can be so beguiling! They may make learning look irresistible, though close scrutiny may reveal that there is less there than meets the eye.)

On the other hand, most organizations usually don't have internal sources of hard data about new legislation, or creative thinking about imminent economic developments and current sociological trends. These require outside resources. The same is true of highly specialized technology in scientific inquiry, or of new methods for applying management sciences and practices.

So . . . a major decision in the search for programs to meet individual training needs is the answer to the question: "Do we have, within our organization, the resources for meeting this need?"

Before we examine those "inside resources," let's review the process: We have discovered a potential training need—a performance problem. What do we do first?

Well, first of course we validate the request to make certain that it is indeed for a *training* need. If the manager is distressed about skills which workers *once did* or *can do* but aren't doing now, then we naturally work toward a non-training solution.

But if we are dealing with a genuine training need, we estimate the size of the trainee population. If there are many people involved (and it's a good idea to check that when the manager first becomes a "requester") then that's a macro training need to be dealt with by establishing objectives for a class or workshop. If there are only a few trainees, or just one trainee, we start joint discussions.

At those discussions three people are necessary; ourselves as the T & D consultant, the potential trainee(s), and the immediate superior. At this discussion the objectives are established and the search begins. It's at this point that we ask whether we use inside or outside resources. The logic of that joint analysis is essentially the process charted in Fig. 6.1.

INSIDE ANSWERS TO MICRO TRAINING NEEDS

When the T & D department agrees that reasonable objectives have been clarified for a validated micro training need, it should first look within the organization to find solutions.

Take a typical case. A manager comes to you and says, "I have this training problem—and this seminar is just what we need." Now that manager may be wrong on both points. Maybe there isn't a training need at all. Even if there were, the solution may be totally inappropriate. The manager may be mistaken—totally! But that manager is supporting training—and should be reinforced for such support! Gentle questions about the nature of the deficiency, the appropriateness of the proposed solution, and how the learning will be applied on the job are all in order.

Existing programs are the first place to check. Do the behavioral or learning goals for the need match or parallel those published for programs already in the curriculum of the organization? If there is a match, the obvious thing to do is to enroll the trainees in the next session of the existing program.

Perhaps that program has other, unrelated objectives. Well, it may be possible to attend only certain modules of that program. An individual or small group "special session" might be arranged to solve the micro training need. If the established objectives vary only slightly, minor adaptations and tutoring by the regular instructors might be an inexpensive, quick, and effective way to respond.

Self-study programs are especially adaptable to individual needs. They are thus excellent answers to micro training needs. By omitting certain segments,

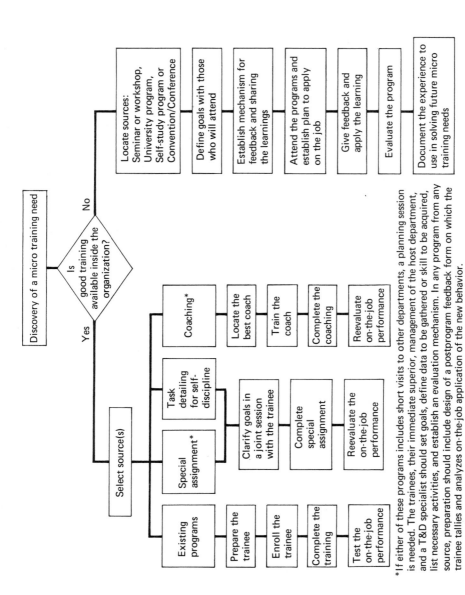

*If either of these programs includes short visits to other departments, a planning session is needed. The trainees, their immediate superior, management of the host department, and a T&D specialist should set goals, define data to be gathered or skill to be acquired, list necessary activities, and establish an evaluation mechanism. In any program from any source, preparation should include design of a postprogram feedback form on which the trainee tallies and analyzes on-the-job application of the new behavior.

Fig. 6.1. Discovering an individual training need.

or by combining several programs, T & D specialists can often "tailor-make" highly specialized programs with minimum effort. Many commercial self-study programs need trimming and adaptation to fit the peculiar needs of an organization anyway. Therefore it's wise to check the files and storerooms: one often finds adaptable and appropriate self-study programs forgotten on T & D stockroom shelves, some of them developed only a couple of years ago by the very staff that now overlooks them.

A mere "visit" or *field trip* may be adequate as the solution for simple micro training needs. Such visits can be productive—but they require careful planning. Generic visits ("just to look things over") are seldom very useful—and quite often annoying to the hosts. They easily result in superficial or misleading learnings. A pre-visit planning session is a "must." The trainee, the trainee's requesting manager, a T & D specialist, plus a "host" manager should establish a general objective, and compile a list of questions which must be answered at each position visited. It helps to regard the visit as an "Easter-egg hunt" which will answer questions, complete flowcharts, fill in organization charts, or annotate manuals. After the visit, some follow-up mechanism should evaluate: "How much is the new information or skill being used?" "Did the visit pay off?" "Should others make the same visit?"

Special assignments within the organization may be the ideal way for individuals to acquire desired learnings. This is particularly true when specialists need knowledge of practices in other departments in order to manage "hand-offs" smoothly or when middle/staff managers need insight into how other departments operate. Examples:

- To develop empathy with departments they audit, auditors might work as regular employees for several months in other staff offices, local offices, or line plants.
- Procedures writers might work in operations to know how previous work fares in the reality of the workplace, and to improve future procedures.
- Instructors might work several months in departments they will relate to and for whom they may develop future programs.
- "Ready-to-promote" employees might rotate through a number of sections in order to gain experience, perspective, and new networks.

Task-detailing for self discipline sounds a bit punitive and pedantic, but it is really an effective way to overcome micro performance problems in employees who are deficient in just one characteristic of their work. Typical of these deficiencies of execution (they usually are D_E's) is carelessness, lack of attention to detail, flying off the handle, missing parts of assignments, tardiness, lack of follow-through, or unilateral decision-making. Such personal problems can best be overcome if the trainee is acutely conscious of the problem—and aware that the temporary assignment will give maximum experience . . . plenty of chances to apply a good level of performance. Thus the phrase "task detailing;" thus the phrase "self-discipline." In such detailing, feedback mechanisms are vital. The trainee must have some sort of log which will show when there was a chance to apply a satisfactory level of performance in the deficient behavior—and how many times the opportunity was seized! Without this quantitative feedback mechanism, the assignment tends to get cloudy and discouraging. Trainees in such regimens should keep their own tallies, discussing them with their immediate supervisors at predetermined intervals. When these special detailings grow out of appraisals, they can be tied in directly with promotion, salary increases, and the next appraisal. Such integration with other processes shows that the problem is worth attention—and that there are happy consequences for overcoming the deficiency.

Coaching offers a very important internal answer to many micro training needs. It can be conveniently coupled with the task-dealing approach. Coaching has many advantages.

- It can be totally individualized.

- It can ensure total validity if the coach is the trainee's immediate superior. (That is the usual and ideal situation.) Since the "boss" is coaching, there can be no doubt about management's valuing the behaviors which are to grow out of the coaching.

- The close, one-on-one communication permits a dynamic feedback mechanism.

- The close-one-on-one communication permits a dynamic reappraisal of the learning objectives.

- Training responsibility is delegated to that point in the organization where it has the most immediate and direct payoff: the relationship between superior and subordinate.

- Manager/coaches tend to learn a great deal about the inventories of the individuals whom they coach—as well as about the whole process of motivation, directing, and communicating with subordinates.

There is, in addition, a subtler benefit from widespread use of coaching in an organization: Many managers get dynamically involved in the training process. Furthermore, managers who have served as coaches represent an empathic population for all T & D activities. As decision-makers or requesters of T & D services, they know more "of the ropes" about learning—why it is important and how it works. They are certainly useful resources in meeting future micro training needs.

None of these programs from within the organization is complete without an ongoing planning and evaluating mechanism. That is another reason for the active involvement of T & D specialists when any such solution is implemented for a micro training need. In every case, the trainee, immediate superiors, "hosts" (if job rotation, special assignments, or visits are used) and a T & D specialist should:

- Set goals,
- Define the activity,
- Describe the way in which the learnings will be applied back on-the-job, and
- Establish criteria and a mechanism for evaluating the experience.

This implies creating a post-program feedback form on which trainees tally and analyze their on-the-job applications of the new skill. Such feedback forms not only give data for evaluation; they help maintain the new behavior as well!

OUTSIDE ANSWERS TO MICRO TRAINING NEEDS

When searching for programs to satisfy micro training needs, T & D officers use such activities as seminars and workshops, university and college offerings, programs from local trade and night schools, self-study, or conventions, and conferences. Each of these options has some special value—and each requires some special consideration.

Membership in professional societies provide T & D officers and T & D staffs a rich opportunity to find out what is new in the profession, to meet people who do similar things (often in innovative, useful ways) in other organizations, to get recognition for their own accomplishments—or just to find support groups, socialize, or hold an office if they need such fulfillment. The largest groups feature local chapters, regional and/or national conferences, publications, and seminars or institutes.

The American Society for Training and Development, The National Society for Performance and Instruction and the OD Network are among the largest. The National Society of Sales Training Executives, ICEDS for training directors in the insurance field, CHART for hotel and restaurant trainers, or CUNA for credit union training managers are just a few of the active groups which serve a particular discipline or specialty within the T & D population. The Office of Personnel Management sponsors programs to upgrade trainers in the public sector.

Seminars and workshops offer one of the more frequent answers to the T & D officer's quest. Their sponsors range from independent consultants through professional societies to colleges and universities. Their length ranges from a single day (even a few hours) to several weeks. Unfortunately, their quality ranges through an even wider spectrum!

How do T & D officers locate such events? Usually they need only open their mail! Membership in any professional society (ASTD or NSPI or ASPA) will get your name on mailing lists which are then going to be sold to sponsoring agencies. Furthermore, attendance at any event by a single sponsor will guarantee future mailings—frequently multiple, because their computer lists get cross-fertilized! If these methods haven't already produced more mail than there is time to read, phoning the associations or writing nearby universities (or the American Management Association) will ensure lots of brochures in the future.

How do alert T & D officers separate the wheat from the chaff? How do they select the really "right" answer to the particular micro training need they face at the moment?

For openers, one might ask these "primary" questions about the workshop or seminar:

	Yes	No
1. Does the brochure publish learning objectives or "expected outcomes?"	——	——
2. Are those outcomes stated in behavioral terms?	——	——
3. Are the behaviors observable, measurable, reasonable?	——	——
4. Is a topical outline included in the announcement?	——	——
5. Does the brochure specify what types of employees should register? (Nature of position? Level of position? Experience assumed?)	——	——
6. Does the outline provide some time for participants to raise issues and ask questions?	——	——
7. Does the time schedule look flexible? (Could it possibly be completed? Can it adapt to the unique needs of individual participants?)	——	——
8. Is there provision for "process feedback" so participants can let leaders know to what degree their needs are/aren't being met?	——	——
9. Does the brochure mention the learning methods which will be employed?	——	——
10. Do those methods involve "action training" . . . chances for your trainees to get involved in something other than just listening and watching?	——	——
11. Is there workshop time so your trainees can contemplate ways to apply the learnings back on the job?	——	——

	Yes	No

12.   Does there seem to be an opportunity for your trainees to access the leaders in small group or one-on-one conversations?

13.   Are the leaders well known to you or to the managers in the department in which the micro need exists?

14.   Have the leaders published on this subject?

15.   Have the leaders worked for or consulted with corporate or bureaucratic organizations, or is their background entirely academic?

A really reliable seminar or workshop should score "Yes" on at least ten of those questions. It certainly should score "Yes" on five of the first six questions if it is to meet the unique learning needs of your trainee.

If the seminar looks marginal, there may be value in inquiring about the sponsor or the announced leaders. Has the sponsoring organization been in existence for at least two years? (New sponsors may be perfectly great. It's just that with established sponsors you can uncover data about their past programs.) Has it offered programs in these particular subjects for at least a year? Are the conference leaders offering similar programs throughout the area—or throughout the country? How long have the leaders worked for this particular sponsor? Remember, these questions become useful only if the more urgent questions in that "primary" list haven't given you the data you need.

If the program has been offered previously, T & D staff members can ask for rosters, and check with other organizations who sent people—T & D department as well as attendees. The whole point is to establish a mechanism for exchanging information on the usefulness and quality of public programs . . . to get data that's more user-oriented than any data you can hope to get from the sponsors or the leaders. They're marketing people while they're answering your questions! And be sure to ask the users how they're *using* the program—not how they liked it. Answers to the latter question will be contaminated with data about the food, the meeting site, the trip to and from the program, other participants. A useful list of questions to ask previous participants at seminars and workshops would include some of these:

●   Did you or your participants institute any new policies as a result of attending?

●   Did you or your participants amend or cancel any old policies as a result?

●   Did you or your participants revise any procedures as a result of the participation?

●   Did participants come home with any product they could immediately put to use?

●   What specific problem was solved as a result of attending this seminar?

- Have you calculated a dollar payoff from participation?
- If the need still existed, would you send people to this program today?
- Did others who attended really reflect the audience appealed to in the advertising—or did they admit just anyone who paid the money?
- Should our participants make any special preparation?
- In what ways did your participants get special individualized time and attention from the leaders?

Some of those questions are quite important, others far less valuable. What one probably does is select about two-thirds of the relevant ones, and then hope to get concrete answers to about two-thirds of those. When previous participants are unable to identify unique assistance or specific applications, the program may be questionable. (Of course there's a fallacy in that: users can be incompetent too—so check with more than one and with the T & D department.)

In *Professional Guide to Successful Meetings,* Davis and McCollon see modern adults as "people who are bewildered by their options. Effective workshops assist them in selection." (p. 22) Well, just as the workshop should help your employees select the options they will apply on the job, you may need to go beyond the brochure or printed description to select from an array of optional programs, workshops, or seminars.

Even for one-person training needs, some organizations like to send teams of two to seminars and workshops. This is often a good idea. Dual participation can increase pressure on leaders to respond to the uniqueness of your organization. It can cause each trainee to stimulate the other toward active participation and active contemplation of on-the-job applications. Dual participation can make "honest people" out of your trainees; they tend to acquire the needed behaviors more consistently—especially if the "partner" is their boss. Not only do behaviors tend to be acquired at workshops—they tend to be *applied*. Then on-the-job behaviors tend to be reinforced more readily if the boss has the same learnings. This merely says that team attendance (especially superior-trainee teams) results in more dynamic change than attendance by just one person. For this, as well as for marketing reasons, some seminars offer discounted rates for the second person. Team members should be warned against isolation . . . instructed to mix with the group.

University programs take a variety of forms. They may be short seminars. They may be "one-night-a-week" programs offered through regular channels or through extension services. They may also be fulltime investment of the trainees' time and energy during a period of release from normal work responsibilities. Such "release" programs sometimes lead to degrees—as a "year at Harvard" or an M.B.A. from the state university.

Regardless of the money invested, regardless of the time and energy spent, regardless of the organizational level from which trainees come, university programs should be investigated and evaluated. Like any training investment, it should pay its way—if not in documented dollars and cents, then in ideas which are brought into the organization.

How can T & D officers assure investments in university programs?

To begin with, they can check the programs for relevance and quality in the same way they check seminars and workshops. Colleges and universities will invariably have been in existence for more than a year; their reputations as sponsors are already established. (Sometimes for good, sometimes for bad sponsorship!) But it's dangerous to be beguiled by good reputations. Colleges with good reputations in general may be very poverty stricken in the department from which you need help. Institutions with shabby reputations in one department may excel in others. And besides—it isn't the institutional reputation that matters so much as it is the competence of the professors who will teach your trainees!

But beware. A glittering array of renowned authorities on the faculty does not guarantee that those luminaries will actually teach your people! Astute T & D officers check, and get a commitment about:

- The precise name of the instructor.
- The amount of time the learners will be exposed to each faculty member.
- The nature of that exposure. (Will they listen to lectures? . . . get to ask questions? . . . get small-group or one-on-one time to discuss unique problems?)
- The size of the class.
- The nature of the testing. (Will your trainee be held accountable for the learnings?)

When no guarantees can be made about the faculty's willingness to deal with the special needs of your employees, a longer search may be a good investment of time and energy. Often the truly motivated trainee or manager will do the searching—a healthy action which gives them some "ownership" of the final decision.

To insure commitment to make learners accountable, a "contract" may be in order. T & D people, in concert with the manager and trainee, identify specific ways in which the learnings will be applied on the job. For example:

- Delivering four oral reports within three months of completing a university course in public speaking;
- X percent drop in rejects after a welding course; or

- *X* percent increase in the number of decisions at meetings chaired by a manager who attends a conference leading course.

Although such "contracts" can and should be simple documents, they indicate that both student and manager accept accountability for the expediture of money and energy and support by the organization. They also show both the businesslike and the supportive nature of the T & D function. What these contracts say is that the payment of the tuition (and sometimes compensation for time in class) is a business transaction, with evaluation criteria and accountabilities established at the start.

Such commitment to learning and on-the-job application can erase some of the stigma of academia, some of the "ivory-tower" reputation that tarnishes college programs. It also is a basic mechanism for meaningful evaluation, encouraging immediate feedback when students find the program a doubtful route to the targeted application objectives. For general tuition aid programs, these contracts are recommended parts of the policy guidelines.

"Renewal" programs like the Dartmouth or Aspen Institutes defy such precise contractual clauses. These programs, lasting from a month to a year, open new horizons and rebuild old foundations. Wives often attend with their husbands: a Texaco wife called it a "refresher course in being a human being;" said a bank official, "It filled a gap created when we stopped doing our homework to do our job."*(Business Week,* August 14, 1978)

Topics like existentialism and Shakespeare show that these are for reorientation and renewal, and though evaluation is necessarily perceptual, debriefings are vital—not as schoolteachers patrolling the playground, but as T & D people who care how it went, and who want a candid database to help evaluate the program for future requests.

That debriefing should be documented, as should evaluative data of any outside program. This isn't for record keeping about the number of trainees, or training hours or expenses: it's for that database to use when selecting, recommending or avoiding these programs as solutions to future micro training needs.

Rehabilitation programs for various addictions or psychological disorders are now relatively frequent, and often are covered by health insurance. Any reputable program of this genre has its own inherent evaluative indicators. For such personal development, the T & D department needs to adhere to two vital policies: supportiveness and confidentiality.

Self-study is another medium for meeting micro training needs. Sometimes these self-study programs already exist within the organization; they've been bought for previous similar needs. Sometimes they are available through local educational institutions. More often they are available as books or packages, sold through publishers or commercial vendors. Again, membership in professional societies gets the T & D director onto mailing lists describing such programs. Subscription to training magazines will also uncover many sources of such "software," as well as the names and addresses of suppliers. In addition, attending conferences (or local merchandising sessions by publishers) lets T & D specialists know what is on the market, which sources to respect, and whom to turn to when a really unique micro training need arises.

The self-study solution may come in the form of a book, as programmed instruction, or as a "package" involving audio-visual presentations. Such packages usually involve some equipment: audiotapes, filmstrip projectors, or teaching machines. The sophistication of the presentation is relevant to the decision only if it involves unavailable equipment or unreasonable costs. More important is the appropriateness of the presentation to the learning goals.

If the goals involve acquiring knowledge, then reading a book may be the best solution. Other training needs may involve a retention and application which is possible only through programmed instruction, or lessons mailed to and reviewed by an instructor on the vendor's staff. Other needs involve psychomotor skills which can come only if the program provides visual displays—and perhaps equipment with which to perform the tasks.

In evaluating self-study programs, the usual questions arise:

● Are the behavioral (learning) outcomes clearly defined? (This may not apply to books, but it should be a minimum test for accepting any programmed text!)

● Is the scope of the content clearly specified?

● Are there indications of the "normal" time required for completion? (Beware of averages; look for upper and lower limits.)

● What do previous users say about their use of learnings from this program?

● What do other users say about the learning processes stimulated in this program?

Professional conferences and conventions provide another source of learning to meet micro training needs. They are seldom structured as behaviorally oriented learning systems. Thus they often become "head trips," intellectual bazaars at which people discover new trends in their fields. As such, they can be an effective way to bring state-of-the-art and wave-of-the-future knowledge into an organization. At other times they clarify state-of-the-art concepts which had previously been only fuzzy phantoms that worried management—but not in sufficiently concrete form to do the organization any good. Hopefully, people who attend conferences and conventions will bring back ideas which they will try out, or at very least share with their peers.

Many conferences develop questionable reputations. "They are too large. Nothing new ever comes from them! They are just big drinking parties." The first two are serious charges; the third is a personal matter: If there are social temptations, individuals must solve that in their own way. On the other hand, T & D directors who support convention attendance should take some measures to see that participants handle their social schedule without jeopardizing the acquisition of all "that good stuff" that gets shared at the scheduled sessions.

This involves some preparation so delegates can: (1) distinguish between "rubbing elbows" and "bending elbows"; (2) make intelligent decisions about which sessions to attend; and (3) realize their obligation to apply or share the acquisitions when they return to the organization.

To meet these requirements, the T & D officer can take certain steps. First, there can be an obligatory chat between delegates and their superiors. (If managers are properly trained, the T & D staff doesn't need to be present!) At this chat the boss and the delegates can make initial decisions about which sessions look most promising in terms of applications within the organization. They can even discuss the relative qualification of presenters, treating each event as if it were itself a workshop or seminar. The analysis is far less profound, but the same primary issues apply. Second, the T & D department can see that not all the delegates attend the same conference. Within any discipline there are usually several societies, each offering its own convention. Gentle prodding by the T & D officer can see that members of that discipline divide their attention among the conferences. Finally, the investment can be protected by establishing a policy that short follow-up reports or briefing sessions must follow attendance at all conventions. This should not be arduous or punishing. It may be a staff meeting, or merely a copy of the report required by their own management.

Outreach programs, or placement on a university faculty is a new, but growing and sophisticated solution for micro development needs. The typical placement in such programs is for at least one full academic year. IBM calls this its Faculty Loan Program, and since 1971 has put over 430 executives and employees on faculties as diverse as tiny Haskell College in Kansas . . . or Rutgers and Columbia. At one point in 1984 there were 53 employees from offices and laboratories in IBM's Faculty Loan Program.

In such arrangements the university naturally has some control and criteria: they may insist upon full academic qualifications or service in other than professional duties, such as meeting informally with students.

A magazine article on this (*Sky,* March 1984, pp. 101–104) asked what these full-time temporary faculty members gained. It then replied, "A chance to let down their hair, to test out some of their own theories." A college official called it an opportunity to "develop the essential blend of the conceptual and the pragmatic, so often missing in the public arena," and "said that it also can serve to add an understanding that it is human beings, not abstractions or cartoon figures, wrestling with difficult issues on a day-to-day basis." (Let's hope this was not his behavioral objective for any outreach program!)

All of these policies or activities, introduced into the organization by the T & D officer, send the important signal that attendance at conferences and conventions is an investment—not mere fun and games. They also imply that such attendance isn't a mere, thoughtless ritual; it happens because it's a response to a real or potential micro training need.

And that introduces the idea of systematic control over the programs used to solve the micro training needs of an organization.

A CONTROL SYSTEM FOR SOLVING MICRO TRAINING NEEDS

Micro training needs come from all parts and all levels of the organization. The solutions to micro training needs are elusive. Even the search for solutions can be expensive. Cost per trainee is apt to be high because the population to be trained is so small.

All these facts conspire to a requirement for steady but gentle control over the processes by which organizations meet micro training needs.

In actual practice, many micro training needs come to the attention of the T & D officer because managers arrive saying "I have this problem," or "Can you help me with the funds to send some of my people to . . .?" Intelligent T & D officers reinforce such initiative. They also subject it to gentle analysis. That analysis tests the validity of both the request and the suggested program. It asks, "Will the people learn something *new*? Will the program supply what they need to learn? Will the learnings actually be put to use on the job? If not, will the experience permit intelligent rejection of the technology in the program?

Even if the T & D officer is not informed or involved in all the decisions, the control system is needed—and it is the responsibility of the T & D officer to see that managers at all levels comprehend and apply the system whenever they solve a micro training need.

It's not a question of control for the sake of control. It's not a policy designed merely to keep the T & D officer informed of what's going on—although that is not an insignificant item. The reasons for a centralized, systematic decision process are many. They go like this: A control system for meeting micro training needs:

1. Eliminates duplicate searches.

2. Increases-the probability of selecting an effective, appropriate solution to the micro training need.

3. Increases the probability of selecting an appropriately priced training program.

4. Increases the probability that the learnings will actually be applied on the job. A feedback device can be designed for each program.

5. Provides a data bank for meeting future micro training needs.

6. Establishes a data bank about the quality of vendor's products and services.

7. Keeps the immediate superiors of all trainees actively involved in setting goals and following up each training investment.

8. Makes a statement to the entire organization that training is an investment which must be justified and evaluated.

9. Provides data to monitor the actual dollars being spent on training, education, and development.

10. Keeps the T & D officer informed about the genuine training needs. From this data, trends may emerge; and the organization learns when micro training needs have become macro training needs.

In other words, astute T & D officers put special stress on steps 3, 8, and 9 of the control process in Fig. 6.2. Step 3 deserves special attention. Especially important is the presence of three parties in the joint planning. The T & D department is obviously involved—but just as important is the active involvement of both the trainee and the immediate superior of the trainee! Without their inputs there is no real assurance that the learnings will be useful to the organization, that they will be properly reinforced after they have been acquired—or even that the trainee understands the purpose of the training!

However, the basic message of the process chart is the need for central control. When micro training needs are solved from any source (inside or outside the organization) the process should not be hit-or-miss. Such decentralization produces chaos . . . chaos in the form of poor decisions, wasted money, duplicated search, and lack of follow-up to ensure that the organization gets its money's worth and puts the learnings to work.

The theme of those advantages is application and accountability. A word of caution applies here. The reservation which needs to accompany the policy is an admonition, "Be gentle." In other words, the T & D staff must use tact during performance or cost-benefit analysis of a micro training need—or

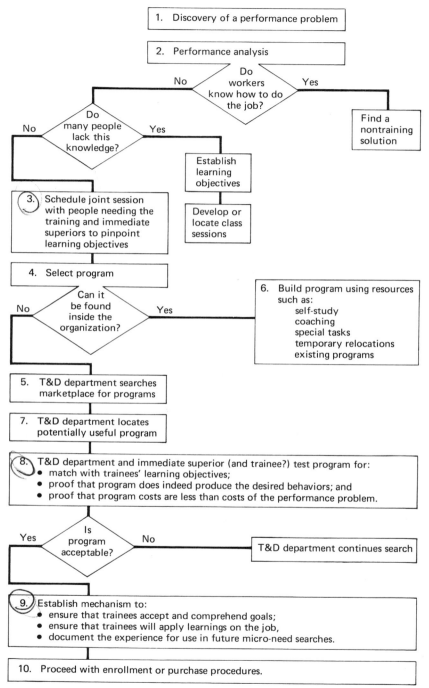

Fig. 6.2. Control process for solving micro training needs.

when denying funds for one! With diplomacy, the logic of the system (Fig. 6.2) appeals to most managers.

In fact, if there has never been a control system to govern the way individual training needs are met, the T & D officer might very wisely institute the control system one step at a time. Perhaps it should start with only the most expensive investments. Then it can gradually be applied to additional cases until it becomes the norm. It's probably just good psychology, good politics, and good management to reinforce with liberal decisions those managers whose requests are most valid and most cost-effective. (If we were discussing reinforcement theory, we'd call it "successive approximations"!) Furthermore, if the control system is valid it will gradually earn its own good reputation.

The alternatives to such gentleness are frightening. T & D officers who are too rigorous, too hard-headed, will soon observe some unhappy consequences. First, they will get fewer requests for their consultative services. Second, they will grow increasingly ignorant about the many employees who attend special training. That is to say: client-managers who want training will find a way to get it—whether they get the proper training through the proper channels or go the "bootleg route."

These are the days of assessment centers, appraisals, career development, and career planning . . . of outreach programs and tuition assistance. At their best, all of these are part of a long-range individual training and development system. The T & D officer wants to be a major factor in the design of those programs for individuals . . . and in the follow-up and evaluation that refines the programs and gives them their real impact to both the individual and the organization.

SUMMARY

A training need which exists for a single person is just as real as a training need which exists for vast numbers of people. For this reason, the micro training needs cannot be evaluated on the same priority system used for macro training needs. In other words, the total impact on the organization may be smaller—but the need must be evaluated on its own merit. It cannot be thrown into the same general hopper as the macro training needs.

Whether it be a response to a performance appraisal, a career plan, or an assessment decision, the micro training need is part of the T & D officer's job.

Controls are necessary. Over a period of time a firm control system can be established by a gentle, intelligent analysis of each micro training need. When that system is fully operating, an organization is ready to process all its human resource growth needs—the little ones as well as the big ones.

WHAT DO YOU DO WHEN YOU DON'T GIVE TRAINING?

WHY TRAINING ISN'T ALWAYS USEFUL

As we have often noted, there is no sense in training people to do what they already can do. Training is an appropriate solution to job-related problems for people who have deficiencies of knowledge or performance . . . who have what we call a D_K or a D_P.

But what about all those other occasions when workers *can* do their work properly—but just don't?

In this chapter we will look at a way to analayze these situations, examining the non-training solutions used by T & D professionals to solve the performance problems in the organizations they serve. The chapter explores the expanding role of T & D officers: no longer to they merely see that "programs get run!" They are in reality, the solvers of the human performance problems for their organizations.

As we look at this expanded role, we will consider:

1. The questions T & D officers ask when they consult with client departments, and

2. The solutions they evaluate and select to overcome the problems which concern the client.

Graphically, the process looks like Fig. 7.1. Our focus is the left side (deficiencies of execution) . . . the problems which training will not solve. As solutions for the D_E we will consider feedback systems, contingency management, job engineering, and organization development.

FEEDBACK SYSTEMS

When T & D specialists discover cases where workers *can* do the job properly but are failing to do so, it's intelligent to ask, "Do they know, while they do their work, how well they are doing?"

That question is really geared to discover if the workers are getting feedback. Why is feedback so important?

Feedback systems are attractive alternatives to training because they motivate workers, are inexpensive, and can be part of the regular management reporting system.

First, let's see why feedback is in itself something of a motivator. When workers see their own acomplishments, they have more reason to be interested in their work, more reason to be satisfied with their assignment, a greater sense that they are needed, a keener awareness of their contribution.

Unless graduates of training get on-the-job feedback about the skills they acquired in that training, they tend to lose the new behaviors. Feedback, on the other hand, can "control" their performance. In short, feedback gives workers more reason to care . . . more *motivation* to perform well.

Secondly, psychologists who specialize in adult behaviors stress the fact that mature humans regard self-evaluation as having primary importance; evaluation by others is secondary. It just naturally follows that when workers have a simple method for continuing their accomplishments they find the very process of counting both reinforcing and motivating.

Thus T & D "consultants" ask questions like:

• How do workers find out how many times they have completed the task successfully?

• How do they discover whether their units of work are satisfactory or unsatisfactory?

• Do they ever judge their own work to determine whether it is or is not satisfactory?

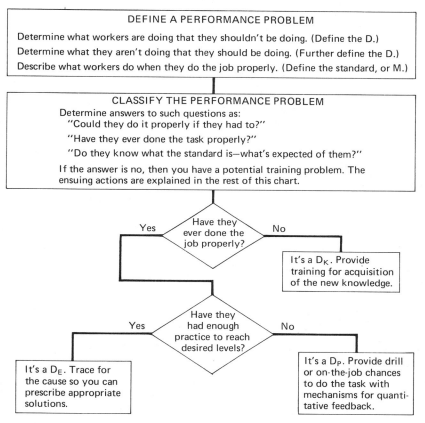

Fig. 7.1.

The expanded function of training and development.

- What tally do they see showing the number of successful units, or the ratio of satisfactory to unsatisfactory units?
- Who keeps that tally? Themselves? Their immediate superior? A quality-assurance specialist?
- At what intervals do they see the data about the quantity and quality of their work?
- What positive reinforcement is made as a result of high achievement?
- What follow-up (consequence) is made for low achievement?
- Do the workers themselves have control over the action which corrects their poor performance?

When such questioning reveals that there if no feedback, the T & D specialist may have found both the cause of the performance problem and a possible solution.

There are many success stories about the results of simple feedback systems. The trouble is, they're so unbelievable . . . they produced such dramatic results in such short time. Yet they happened. In one firm clerks retrieved millions of dollars in lost business per month simply by recording the dollar value of shipments resulting from matching backorders with unnoticed inventory in the warehouses. Performance went from the low teens to mid-eighties in one week. An airfreight forwarder reported overnight strides in a big problem: failure of agents to consolidate small shipments. Workers merely kept tallies of how often they might have consolidated—and how often they actually did. In both cases, the new high performance levels were maintained for long periods just through feedback.

The sports worlds abounds with success stories about feedback. Athletes know the attempted passes, number of completions, conversions on third down, percentage of free-throws made.

Several principles are important to successful feedback systems:

1.   The feedback mechanism must be simple. If it's cumbersome or time-consuming, requiring lots of work or lengthy reports, it will be an unpleasant task—and thus demotivating. Obviously, simplicity also contributes to the economy of the performance maintenance system.

2.   The workers should check their own work and enter the data onto the feedback form. Why? Because adults perceive self-evaluation as more valid and more important than evaluation from anybody else.

3.   The data in the feedback form should be quantitative. Many experts feel that if it can't be expressed in numbers, it shouldn't be done. Thus workers can count units completed, opportunities captured, dollars of revenue. They can also make distinctions between "okay" and "not okay" units. By tallying the ratio between these two, they give themselves feedback on both the quantity and quality of their work. Other units of measurement can be time-taken-to-do-a-task, or numbers of successive performances without an error.

4.   If at all possible, the form on which workers give themselves feedback should be a part of the regular reporting system already installed to tell management what it needs to know about the operation.

5.   The feedback should enable the workers to modify both their performance and the system itself. By checking themselves they can modify their performance without feeling "snoopervised." If they repeat the same error for an external reason, their reporting the interference to management can lead to modifying the system itself.

Skeptics ask if workers won't "cheat" when given such control over the feedback. The answer seems to be, "Oh, now and then—but not as much as one might expect." And anyway, the form can be designed so there is no payoff for cheating. For example, with the freight forwarder: There would be no sense to showing opportunities not taken, and the consolidations they actually did make are a matter of local record. In other words, there is no point to manufacturing data about units completed if the total system output won't support your data. But the main point is this: There is little evidence that people cheat very much on self-controlled feedback systems.

There is, however, strong evidence that when people have the mechanism for controlling their own output, they perform in the desired fashion—and do so more frequently. Such improvement in quality and quantity of performance is, after all, what both T & D officers and client managers want!

CONTINGENCY MANAGEMENT

"Contingency" is merely a technical word for "consequence" or "result" or "effect." Contingency management is based upon the belief that every human action causes some consequence. If workers find joy in the consequences (contingencies) of doing a good job, they will tend to repeat their good performance. Thus a main thrust of contingency management is providing positive consequences for performing at the desired standards.

Management sometimes (. . . often?) argues that workers get positive reinforcement for proper performance when they collect their paycheck. The trouble with that logic is that so many workers collect their paycheck whether they perform properly or not! One reason they ceased long ago to see a direct connection between proper performance and salary is that the checks come anyway.

Another reason is the considerable delay between the behavior and the consequences. Merit raises are granted months after the good work was completed.

Anyway, the increments are usually very small; people who were truly outstanding get just a *little* bit more than those who were "above average."

Finally, merit raises stir up lots of questions about why the other fellow "got more than I did!" Such jealousy is often based on pure rumor, since management works so diligently to keep confidential the amount of merit increase granted each individual.

For all these reasons the merit raise is not seen as a positive consequence at all. Overtime, on the other hand, shows up directly and soon in the paycheck. (It also makes a statement that what the organization will pay for is "time at work," not the quality of performance.)

Most T & D officers have encountered situations in which management had its contingencies all mixed up. Bosses think they are reinforcing positively, but are perceived by the worker as punishing. Need an example? The new stenographer stays late to get some important work out on "voluntary overtime." Guess who gets rewarded with the invitation to give some more voluntary overtime the next day we're in a pinch? Another frequent example occurs when one level of management says, "Do it this way,"—and a different level screams, "But that's all wrong!" Workers caught in these inconsistent responses can only wonder, "What in thunder do they expect around here?" From the workers' viewpoint the standards are dim—all because of the conflicting verbal signals given in the reinforcements.

Swingshift foremen may stress quality; dayshift foremen scream for more units of work. Whom is one to believe?

And then there is always the supervisor who thinks a great bit of praise has just been handed out with the words, "Not bad!" But the worker remembers only the word "bad" and wonders why they never give you any praise around here. "Not bad" seems like damning with faint praise . . . just another glum bit of judgmental feedback from management.

Again, B. F. Skinner states this phenomenon well.

> Organized institutions exert a powerful and often troublesome control in ways which effectively reinforce those who exert it . . . Those who are controlled then take action. They escape from the controller, moving out of range if he is an individiual, or defecting from a government, resigning, or playing truant. Or they may attack . . . as in a revolution, strike, reformation, or student protest. In other words, they oppose control with countercontrol. (*About Behaviorism*, p. 190).

The suspension of the infracting employee offers an interesting insight into people—and into reinforcement theory. Many contemporary managers are astounded that employees today don't mind being suspended. In other words, workers may value the free time even more than they value the salary. With many younger workers, suspension is not punishment at all: suspension permits them to hunt, fish, or loaf—all far more attractive than going to work!

T & D departments which go to work rearranging consequences may have a tough job on their hands. It isn't just that new schedules of rewards upset tradition: It's very hard work to discover what the *real* rewards and punishers are. Consultative skills come into full play. Expecially important is the ability to get the individual value systems identified—and to get honest recognition of what the true contingencies are. Furthermore, in getting them out into the open, it's necessary to see how workers perceive them.

Thus, to make contingency management effective, the real operative consequences must be identified, verified, and changed. That involves perceptual data from the organization and from the worker—they may not see the contingencies in the same light at all! Beyond that, the contingencies to the learner-worker need to be identified for both short-range and long-range timespans.

Thus successful contingency management requires an analysis which includes *all* the thinking illustrated in Fig. 7.2. This means completing a matrix that honestly shows the positive consequences for being bad and the negative consequences for being good!

The analysis in the Fig. 7.2 matrix deals with a universal safety problem: exceeding posted speed limits.

Until all the areas have been filled in, the matrix is incomplete—and so is the analysis. Once it is apparent that there are no positive consequences for doing the job properly, the next step is to add some. In the example, rewards for accident-free periods of driving (as a full month) might be added as a positive consequence. Once it is apparent that the system may actually be rewarding noncompliance, those positive reinforcers should be eliminated. In the example, the organization might well afford to quit paying the fines for drivers who are caught speeding! Once it is apparent that there are aversive consequences for doing the job properly, the organization should try to remove them. In the example, supervisors would need to desist from "chewing" drivers who abided by the speed limits—even though that meant some late deliveries now and then.

This often happens in contingencies affecting safety practices. Management says it wants care and attention to details of the regulations, but actually "chews out" all the people who slow things down by complying. It happens again when management says it wants careful workmanship, but reinforces only volume of production.

The corrective process, once the real reinforcers have been determined, includes such steps as:

- Removing negative consequences for proper performance.
- Removing positive consequences for improper performance.
- Adding positive consequences for proper performance.

Changing the contingencies imposed by long-established systems is arduous work—but there can be big payoffs. T & D departments have helped avoid more than one costly and fruitless sales training program by helping management see that they were actually punishing good performers by raising their quotas. Sizable reductions in safety training costs are available to organizations which find effective positive reinforcers for compliance. Management

		THE DESIRED BEHAVIOR IS: Driving within speed limits.		THE CURRENT UNDESIRABLE BEHAVIOR IS: Exceeding speed limits while driving.	
		Consequences		*Consequences*	
		Positive	*Negative*	*Positive*	*Negative*
To the *worker*	Now	None	Customers often chew you out for late delivery; supervisors may chew you for "goofing off."	More deliveries mean more wages; might get time off with pay during accident investigation and hearing.	*Might* get hurt if an accident happens; *might* get chewed by supervisor; *might* get a speeding ticket *if* caught.
To the *worker*	Later	None	Lower total deliveries mean smaller paycheck.	Get variety by going to court if you get a ticket; get paid for court time.	May waste time in court without incentive pay if you get a ticket.
To the *organization*	Now	Less supervisory time spent in checking; fewer accidents; fewer speeding fines to pay.	May get behind schedule in deliveries.	More deliveries.	Downtime if drivers are arrested and have to go to court; cost of accidents; cost of fines if convicted of speeding.
To the *organization*	Later	Lower costs for fines, accidents, and insurance; less downtime costs while drivers are in court	Fewer total deliveries; less total revenue.	More deliveries with greater total revenue.	Same as short-range, except cumulative totals impact on efficiency of the operation and adherence to budget.

Fig. 7.2.

Matrix for analyzing consequences.

development becomes a reality under managers whose salary and promotions are directly related to their discovery and development of other managers. The T & D department attracts talented personnel when effective performance as a T & D specialist leads to responsible positions in other departments rather than to permanent "detachment in the T & D function."

JOB ENGINEERING

Not all performance problems lie in people. Sometimes they lie in the position itself.

The problem can arise just because some workers are misplaced. People with low verbal skills probably shouldn't be asked to write manuals—or even many reports. But if the position demands writing, then those people are in the wrong job—and all the training in the world will help but little. Workers who like to tinker with machines may be ill-suited to managerial assignments. Creative systems analysts may make terrible supervisors.

Positions which require crisis management (law officers, aircraft pilots, or hotline counsellors) may require special mind-sets or value systems; people who must satisfy customers may need to demonstrate their extrovertism—not to mention their patience; problem solvers probably need to demonstrate both logical and creative capabilities; secretaries may be expected to enter an organization with pre-determined speed and accuracy competencies in both typing and shorthand.

However placement/employment specialists in Personnel or other branches of Human Resources departments usually have the responsibility to fit the person to the position. They sometimes use "Selection Certification," some test for personal adjustment, or some inventory of an applicant's values as ways to get the right people into the right job.

But when T & D officers think of job engineering as an alternative to training, they have a different technology in mind. Job engineering is generally concerned with positions which are either too demanding or too simple. Let's look at each situation.

Overloaded jobs are apparent when there is just too much work to be done, when there is too great a variety in the nature of the tasks, or when the worker must make discriminations that are too taxing. For example, it's easy to separate green units from yellow units, but discriminating between nile green and pea green units may be just a bit too much. The answer to difficult positions is simplification and specialization. Such work is normally the task of industrial engineers. Frequently the T & D specialist merely calls such engineers into the problem-solving team when the performance problem stems from over-difficult positions.

In recent years, however, there is strong evidence that the industrial engineering movement toward specialization may have gone too far. Simplification and specialization have produced many "impoverished" jobs. As a result, some jobs are not done properly because they are so narrow, monotonous, and tiresome that workers just can't maintain satisfactory levels of performance. It is easy—but dangerous—to think of this as applying only to assembly line jobs. In most organizations there is a discouraging array of management level positions in which no decision-making is assigned, where problem-solving consists only of carrying out solutions someone else has adopted! Whenever this happens at any level, job enrichment is indicated.

Sometimes job enrichment clashes with the value system of the industrial engineers. Sometimes job enrichment is little more than an attractive fad for an organization which likes to keep up with the times. On other occasions job enrichment has begun with the T & D officer's own position—and to good effect for the T & D function and the entire organization! At its best, job enrichment is an attractive and important new tool for the T & D officer's kit.

Whether T & D staff members actually manage job-enrichment projects or merely recommend them (handing them off to specialists for implementation) is a moot point. The central question is the ability of the T & D specialist to know when it is appropriate and how to launch a job-enrichment project.

To do so, today's T & D specialists need to know what constitutes an enriched job. Specialists like Herzberg and Ford mention several factors.

A complete piece of work emerges from an enriched job. An auto might be a complete piece of work. Indeed, one manufacturer once boasted that its workers made automobiles—not transmissions. A right front wheel placed on the car does *not* qualify. A letter written for another's signature, a complaint recorded but not processed, a sketch for a visual aid which someone else will develop—none of these seems to represent a complete piece of work.

Enriched jobs *do not damage, humiliate, consistently bore, or degrade* the worker. That says a lot! It pleads for variety, for safety, for dignity and for challenge.

Frequent feedback about performance is another dimension of enriched jobs. This chapter has already said enough on that subject.

Utilization of the worker's valued existing skills is a mark of an enriched job. In his study of andragogy (adult learning theory), Malcolm Knowles points out that during their time as learners, adults want to apply their past skill and experience in acquiring new learnings. Job-enrichment technologists apply this same human need to the way workers relate to their jobs. People with good skill in communication enjoy investing that skill in activities where they've never before been responsible for communicating; people who have solved other problems like to be part of the problem-solving team in issues which impact upon their work.

An opportunity to acquire other skills characterizes enriched jobs. Instructorships should qualify very well on this. Instructors need to develop—and then develop some *more*—skills in communicating . . . both as senders and receivers! They can grow in comprehension of learning theory, methodology, feedback, and evaluation techniques. But teaching the same old course again and again and again with the same materials is a de-enriching trend in what is basically a rather enriched position.

Enriched jobs *enhance (or at least do not impair) the worker's ability to perform other life roles.* Strangely enough, many managerial positions rate rather low on this. How many times have you heard managers complain, "My time isn't my own any more! The job takes 24 hours a day!" Or the exasperated, "Just what does this outfit expect out of me?" Enriched jobs leave something over; they permit incumbents to be parents, deacons, citizens . . . to coach the little leaguers or to lead the scout troop.

Now that we know the elements of an enriched job, let's look at steps in job-enrichment projects. Professional "job-enrichers" know that there is much more to it than the seven steps we'll examine here. They also know that in any single project, not all these steps will apply. But generally job enrichment takes place when one or several of these things can be done:

1. Remove controls—but raise the accountability.

2. Add accountabilities. This often means providing training; there will be knowledge deficiencies about how to discharge the new accountabilities.

3. Add new authorities for decisions.

4. Find natural units which can result from the way tasks are assigned to individual workers.

5. Add feedback decisions for the worker to make about accomplishments. For example: "Does the product meet all standards?" or "Shall I speed up or slow down in order to avoid bottlenecks in the total system?"

6. Assign specialized tasks to the total job requirements. This is often an effective way of letting the worker utilize existing skills, and of becoming an "expert" in one part of the operation. Note that this is an *added* specialization. It doesn't substitute the specialized skill for the total task; rather, it gives a new dimension to the job.

7. Introduce more difficult tasks. The degree of difficulty is important. Just adding more of the same type doesn't enrich a job; it merely adds what some experts call "horizontal loading." For example, a gardener who pulls up ragweed scarcely occupies an enriched job when the scope of the job is extended to pulling up dandelions too!

It must be apparent by now that positions as well as people can cause performance problems. When turnover is high, or when absenteeism and tardiness afflict a work station or an office, one possible cause is that the jobs are improverished. Astute T & D officers who find these symptoms consider the possibility that job enrichment is an appropriate solution for the D_E they face.

ORGANIZATIONAL DEVELOPMENT

When is organizational development a useful solution to performance problems? Why would the T & D officer, or a staff member serving as consultant to a performance problem, suggest OD?

Most organizations (corporations, bureaucracies, or associations) have a mission. As they grow they add subsections to the structure with which they carry out that mission. These subsections develop missions of their own. On occasion the missions of the subsections come into conflict with one another. They may even become counterproductive to the mission of the parent organization. Sometimes individuals within an organization are more motivated toward their personal goals than toward organizational goals. They then begin to invest their energy and influence in activities which are destructive to the goals of the larger organization.

When such conditions exist, it's quite possible that changing the behavior of individuals will not overcome the problems. And "problems" is the right word! There are apt to be so many of them that one can truly say that it is the organization that needs fixing—not the individual behaviors or the jobs themselves. Shakespeare had Prince Hamlet reflect the need for OD in an entire nation when the Prince said, "Something is rotten in the state of Denmark."

Organization development may be required in cases where trust levels are low or nonexistent. It can be needed where gossip is prevalent—or worse, where gossip is used as the basis for decisions. Other symptoms may be decisions which are slow to come or missing altogether . . . personal frictions that are high and pervasive and persistent . . . progress reports that are misleading, ambiguous, or downright falsified. All these are symptoms of organizational illness. In short, when the environment of the organization prohibits or seriously deters the proper performance of individual tasks, then OD may be the solution.

Let's examine one of the standard definitions: Organization development is a change effort within an organization, managed from the top, using a third-party consultant to reallocate resources in order to improve processes and attain organization goals with maximum effectiveness, satisfaction, and efficiency.

That last part ("attaining organization goals with maximum effectiveness, efficiency, and satisfaction") may sound a little like a testimonial to mother-hood and Pollyanna—but it is, after all, a description of what most organiza-tions would like to be. The other elements of the definition merit individual analysis.

"A change effort." This is essential. There is no point to development efforts which merely maintain the status quo. By definition, "development" implies change in mission, structures, policies, or relationships. Unless management of a distressed organization is open to change, there is no reason for the T & D staff to invest energy. Consultants in OD efforts are often heard to say, "We're testing to see if there is energy here to . . . " They say that at all phases, but especially in early activities.

The phrase is often completed with words like, "if there is energy to change communications channels, or reporting relationships,"—even, "the way we relate to one another," or more often, "to change our mission statement."

"Within an organization." The organization need not be the total organiza-tion. It might be the Accounting department, one plant within the Manufactur-ing department, or even one office within that plant. But it must be a unit, and the person at the top of that unit must be involved. Thus the next item.

"Managed from the top." If the person at the "top" of whatever unit is being developed is absent from the activity, there will be no sanction for change from the power structure. Active involvement and assent for the change effort is vital. It is equally vital as each change is analyzed and adopted. Consensus with the consultant about what will and what will not be permitted during the developmental activity is essential too.

A written "contract" usually specifies constraints. For example, if no partici-pant can lose a job due to disclosures made during the OD process, that's specified. If there may be no changes in reporting relationships or salary reductions, that too is specified—though if such constraints are applied, one must wonder if the change manager at the top has any real energy for changing anything!

The contract may also detail whether or not changes may be made in span of control, distribution of responsibilities, or communications channels. These things must be specified at the very beginning, since the active involvement of all managers (perhaps of all employees) is required if the organization is truly to re-*develop* itself. If peoples' position and power and accountabilities may be altered, they are entitled to know the rules of the game.

"Using a third party consultant." The objectivity of this consultant is vitally important. As catalyst to—and observer of—the development processes, the consultant needs to be immune to the contingencies of the organization. That is to say, the consultant should be totally free to share observations, to focus

discussion, to provide instruments and activities which facilitate the process. Consultants who may be rewarded or punished by the group are not effective in those activities. Thus the third party from "outside the organization" is not an empty description of a nice situation; it is a realistic and necessary criterion.

"To reallocate resources." This is an apt way of explaining what goes on in typical OD interventions. The human resources in particular may be fulfilled in a lot of different ways; and OD process considers reallocation in ways which individuals find fulfilling and which are more effective, pleasant, and efficient in reaching the organization's mission.

One objective of an OD effort is for the organization to identify and solve existing problems. An equally important objective is to develop a mechanism for identifying future problems and for solving them before they once more paralyze the organization. Thus the third-party consultant seeks to eliminate the need for similar services just as soon as that mechanism is designed and ready to function. The sooner the consultant can depart the OD intervention, the more effective the consultancy!

Definitions don't always say much about the process. The definition we have just analyzed *does* reveal quite a bit about what happens during an organizational development effort. For an activity so shaking to the organization, no one formula can be developed. Even if OD practitioners (a term they like to use when referring to themselves!) have a standard approach, they will need to vary it so it fits their initial contract with the "change manager."

"Change manager" is an excellent name for the person at the top of the organization. It is this person who is truly responsible . . . this person who indeed does manage the developmental change process. The initial plan, made with the active involvement of both the consultant and the change manager, may need to be amended on the basis of data emerging from early activities. It may even be dropped in favor of a new plan with a new contract. Thus flexibility if a key attribute in both the consultant and the program.

Nevertheless, some similar and inevitable phases tend to occur in all organization development interventions.

First comes the problem identification phase. The principal members of the organization get together to try to identify the problem and its causes—or their *perception* of the *problems* and what is *causing* them. This may be more difficult than one would think, so most consultants use structured devices to stimulate and maintain honest communication.

Small teams may postulate their ideas about problems and causes, then compare these in reports to the total group. There may be "More and Less" exercises when subunits or individuals make a list of "I wish you'd do more" and "I wish you'd do less" for every other unit or every other person. These relate closely to "Role Identification" exercises in which members define their own role and then hear how other people think it should be!

Sometimes the data gathering gets rough, with consultants using potent devices to stimulate and maintain openness of honest communication. Fordyce and Weil in their *Managing with People* discuss many of these activities. Their chapter on "Methods for Finding Out What Is Going On" is especially helpful. You'll read of relatively "cool" instruments like interviews in which consultants ask traditional low-key questions like: "How are things going around here?" or "Who is most influential in your organization?"

There are also "polling" activities in which members fill out a blank form indicating with which people they most enjoy working—and whom they least enjoy as work partners. Such data are later shared as part of the problem definition and in action plans for personal change.

Polling can take the form of "Physical Representations" in which group members position themselves along a wall to express personal concepts of how they behave or impact. For example, on an "Influence" axis, those who see themselves as most powerful stand at one end; those who fell ineffectual at the opposite. Not until everyone is placed so people on both their left and right accept the position is the exercise complete. To attain the final representation, each person must do a bit of influencing, even if that means doing a bit of influencing to prove one's lack of influence!

Another type of physical representation tells members to stand very near those with whom they enjoy comfortable working relations—but far away from those whom they find difficult. The participants keep moving until all are happy with their position in relation to everybody else. This may require some deep conversations. And those deep conversations have been known to result in changed relationships—at least in changed perceptions. It's easy to envision the potential emotion generated by such "hot" data-gathering techniques. Quite clearly, OD assumes that feelings are facts in organizational behavior . . . that they must be identified, examined, and managed if human resources are to work together toward effective organizational processes.

Second-step activities involve generating optional solutions to the identified problems. This is feasible once participants have agreed upon the nature and the cause of the problems. It should be noted, however, that when the entire group is dynamically doing this analysis, the analytic and communicative process itself solves some of the problems.

The consultant will probably urge the group to a literal translation of the word "options." If they have choices about solutions, they will have greater satisfaction in their involvement in the action planning and implementation. These action plans are, of course, another facet of this second phase. In addition, this is the point at which many consultants start to work with the group in developing some mechanism to identify and solve future problems before they become serious. Perhaps "mechanism" is an unfortunate word; the way to avoid future crises may merely be patterns of responsibility, communications, and accountability which permit individuals to spend their energies constructively. The open communication of the facts of feeling if inherent in nearly all the activites—and assuredly implied as a part of the "mechanisms" of the future.

When an action plan and a mechanism for evaluating the organizational health are adopted, the consultant is ready to exit. Note that the second phase is not regarded as complete until the evaluation criteria and mechanism have been agreed to by all participating parties.

Evaluation constitutes the final phase—but of course this was started near the very beginning when the group agreed upon a vision of "how it will look and how it will feel around here when we are working together to achieve our departmental and personal goals." Such group visions offer a very rich exercise in participative goal-setting; revisiting it from time to time is a potent way to measure progress toward becoming a nice organization to work in and live in.

The final evaluation requires not only data gathering to measure results and satisfaction levels . . . not only agreement that old problems have been eliminated or alleviated, and that new problems are being processed as they arise; it also requires agreement that the developmental process has given the group a skill (or an enduring mechanism) which it can use in dealing with future problems before they again paralyze the organization so badly that it needs OD.

When that agreement happens, the organization may be presumed to be sound and has indeed been "developed."

The organization regards itself to be sound, to offer an environment where behaviors acquired in training can persevere on the job. Above all, the energy of the "human resources" is being expended in ways which contribute to organizational goals and which pleasantly reinforce the contributors.

Quite clearly, organizational development is a comprehensive program. It is appropriate to profound and widespread distress within an organization. Astute T & D officers will know when it is necessary through the accurate analysis of performance problems within the organization. Proficiency in OD interventions involves a vast technology—a great many skills not in the inventory of all T & D officers. Yet large numbers of T & D specialists know that many performance problems cannot be solved with anything less than OD. They are therefore busy acquiring the necessary skills—or actively recruiting staff members or consultants who can help solve the problem when an entire organization is sick.

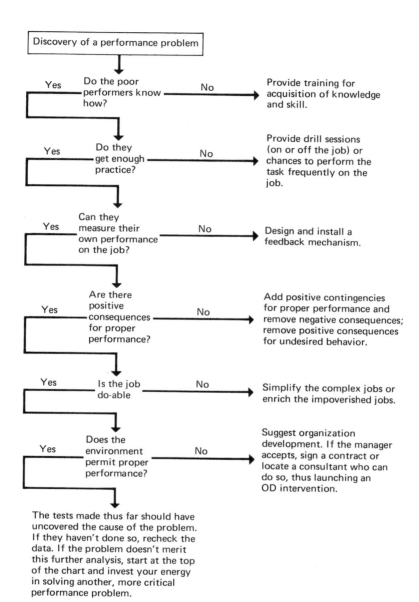

Discovery of a performance problem	

Yes / Do the poor performers know how? / No → Provide training for acquisition of knowledge and skill.

Yes / Do they get enough practice? / No → Provide drill sessions (on or off the job) or chances to perform the task frequently on the job.

Yes / Can they measure their own performance on the job? / No → Design and install a feedback mechanism.

Yes / Are there positive consequences for proper performance? / No → Add positive contingencies for proper performance and remove negative consequences; remove positive consequences for undesired behavior.

Yes / Is the job do-able / No → Simplify the complex jobs or enrich the impoverished jobs.

Yes / Does the environment permit proper performance? / No → Suggest organization development. If the manager accepts, sign a contract or locate a consultant who can do so, thus launching an OD intervention.

The tests made thus far should have uncovered the cause of the problem. If they haven't done so, recheck the data. If the problem doesn't merit this further analysis, start at the top of the chart and invest your energy in solving another, more critical performance problem.

Fig. 7.3.

Decision tree for locating appropriate solution.

SUMMARY

Today's T & D officer is expected to solve performance problems—not just to run training programs. The logic used in locating the appropriate solution is graphically expressed in the ''Decision Tree'' in Fig. 7.3.

CHAPTER

LEARNING OBJECTIVES: WHO NEEDS THEM?

JUST A BIT OF BACKGROUND

A gentleman named Robert F. Mager made a major contribution to the T & D profession by publishing a book in 1962. The book was called *Preparing Objectives for Programmed Instruction,* and its thesis was simple: "If you're not sure where you're going, you're liable to end up someplace else—and not even know it."

The book was a big hit. Later retitled *Preparing Instructional Objectives,* it sold about a million copies. Few other books about training and development can make that statement! In some parts of the world, pirated copies were sold under the counter to escape copyright constraints. In 1975 a second edition appeared, retaining the fundamental principles of the first, but suggesting that "performance objectives" might be a better word for the goals of training.

Despite the success and impact of the book, a few resisted its thesis and technology. For such readers, Mager ended his 1962 and 1976 Preface with the words, "If you are not interested in demonstrating achievement of your objective, you have just finished reading this book."

Some T & D officers took Mager at his word; they still ignore objectives. But if there is current contention about learning objectives, the issue is not "Do they have value?" Rather people ask "Must *every* objective be totally observable and precisely measurable?" Or "How can we avoid the limiting effect of such total precision?"

Today most T & D officers expect themselves and their staff to be able to write objectives. Why? Their consultation includes establishing learning goals; their course designs are guided by these expected outcomes; their learning experiences include an early examination of the objectives; their evaluations ask, "Did the learners achieve these learning goals?"

THE CASE FOR WRITING LEARNING OBJECTIVES

As we've noted, a great many T & D specialists took Mager at his word—but read beyond his Preface. As they put the technology of specifying performance objectives to work, they discovered some significant reasons for attempting to define what the learner would learn to do as a result of the training. Among these reasons they mentioned that:

1. Trainees who know precisely what is expected of them are much more inclined to invest energy in pursuit of the goal—and thus to get there more quickly.

2. Instructors can better control the stimuli they use on students, and can better re-respond to the learners' reactions, when they have a clear statement of the desired behavior to be produced by all this stimulus-response-restimulate-re-respond activity.

3. Management knows what it is getting for its investment when it has statements of the outcome.

4. The bosses of the trainees have a tool for motivating the learning, for communicating expectations. They can establish accountabilities for the learning and for applying it on the job after. the training.

5. The T & D department can more honestly evaluate its own achievements when the T & D officer and instructors have a clear statement of what they are supposed to produce.

6. Clear statement of learning accomplishments can serve as validation of performance standards, or as a way to get standards set where none have existed in the past. If none have existed, the learning objective should be approximately equal to the expected performance standards.

7. The distribution of printed objectives makes a documented statement to all the organization that "training means business" and that learning is work.

The "work" to be done in training is achieving the objectives—just as work on the job is typing letters, assembling or repairing machines, providing a product or a service.

But writing performance (or "behavioral" or "learning") objectives is hard work. Thus there is predictable resistance. It's probably helpful to look at the arguments against learning objectives—and at the same time to examine questions to raise for each objection. We can learn something from this process. In the left-hand column you'll find typical objections; the center column poses counter-questions; the right-hand column draws some conclusions about the legitimate role of learning objectives in an effective T & D system.

Pro/Con Analysis of Learning Objectives

Arguments against	Counter-arguments	Conclusions for the T & D staff
You just can't define some jobs!	Then how does this job survive during a crisis? Who would miss it if it were eliminated?	One way to determine the learning (behavioral) objective for an ambiguous task is to identify the product (or "accomplishment") resulting from successful completion of that task. Example: Managers are decision-makers; therefore the product of that process is a decision. What are the qualities of effective decisions in their organization? The objective of the training program would be to produce decisions which meet those criteria.
They take too much time!	Did you cancel your vacation just because it took a long time to decide where you wanted to go?	To get at behavioral objectives, ask such questions as: • Describe them (or yourself) doing the job perfectly. What do you see? • When you see them doing the job the wrong way, what do you see that you don't like?
There are no standards to work from!	Then how do you now know when the work is okay? . . . when it should be rejected? . . . when to insist that the work pace be accelerated? . . . whom to promote?	When standards do exist, that's where learning objectives start! Thus learning objectives may be a way to validate existing standards—and to generate them when they're missing.
	Are you certain? Better check again for manuals or documents which specify standards.	Sometimes standards "vanish" because nobody ever enforces them, because there is no steady feedback about their achievement—or because they are not realistic and people conveniently "rise above them"!
We've been getting along just fine without them!	Are any of your people getting by with less than good on-the-job performance? Well, maybe that's what we've been doing by not trying to define the output of our training.	Resistance to change is one of the perpetual realities with which T & D specialists learn to cope . . . in themselves as well as in others.

Pro/Con Analysis of Learning Objectives (*Continued*)

Arguments against	Counter-arguments	Conclusions for the T & D staff
	Do you agree that we might find a better way to do training?	The technology with which training is accomplished is the peculiar domain of the T & D staff. If that staff says it wants learning objectives specified, then it has final authority to try to do so.
They're hard work!	Of course they are. Aren't lots of your jobs hard work? These learning objectives are about as difficult as anything we do in T & D—but we keep working to get them. Can you help us? . . . so we can do a better job for you and your employees who come to us to be trained?	As Maslow says: "Instincts toward growth are weak, easily stifled by bad habits, education, or environment; by lower needs like security and safety, and by the tendency to doubt or fear our own ability." The T & D specialist may need to take the first steps: first drafts to show the client manager, asking, "Would you say their job was being well done if your people did it this way?"
The ones I've seen sound so phoney. They don't relate to the reality of the workplace.	Then would you help us correct them—so they are realistic and relevant and useful?	Don't settle for trivial, or self-fulfilling objectives! Martin Broadwell contends that when client managers resist learning objectives, T & D staff people set standards and teach what they want to. Example: participative management in organizations which actually reinforce autocratic practices. This misappropriation is, Broadwell says, "near criminal." (*Training*, May 1975, p. 50).

HOW TO WRITE LEARNING OBJECTIVES

To be useful, learning goals need to contain:

- An action (Mager says it must be an *observable* action) and
- At least one criterion (*measurable,* says Mager) and
- Conditions of performance (*usually,* per Mager.)

The recipe sounds simple, but it requires rigorous thinking. Observable actions are hard to find; we tend to think of covert actions that we assume to be "hidden inside people somewhere." These are *affective* goals, and we need to find an outer observable action. We're also reluctant to pin down precise criteria—even more reluctant to insist that they be measurable.

Observability and measurability are important if we wish to evaluate: without actions both learners and we can see, or criteria that we can measure, how will we know we have succeeded?

For people who *want* them, observable actions and measurable criteria can be established.

It's always helpful to start with the clause, "After training, the worker will be able to . . . " Within those words is the magic phrase: "*will be able to.*"

Next, let's think of verbs (they express action) and objects. For example, "compute the tax" or "relieve tension." With these verbs and objects we have our observable action.

Now for "measurable criteria," which answer such questions as "How often?" "How well?" "How many?" "How much?" "How fast?" or "How high?"

"Conditions" can best be expressed with prepositional phrases as "without reference to the manual" or "unless the customer points a gun at you."

Through such grammatical/mental exercises, we can translate ambiguous objectives like "counsel effectively" or "understand adequately" into concrete performance standards which are also learning goals or, in Mager's words, behavioral objectives. These are behaviors learners can see and give themselves feedback for achieving as they progress in class; these are behaviors managers can see and reinforce when graduates do them on the job.

Let's look at a range of tasks from the very concrete to the rather abstract. Fig. 8.1 shows four examples: salesclerks are learning beginners' skills in the example across the top; the middle example deals with drivers; the third is from customer relations training; managerial skills appear in the example at the bottom. The vertical columns identify the action, criteria, and conditions of performance for each of these four cases.

Success in establishing useful learning goals depends largely upon the willingness to do the necessary thinking . . . willingness to make the effort to envision successful performers.

There is no magic formula for writing good learning objectives, no list of "right and wrong" words. However, for novice writers, the words listed in Fig. 8.2 are often "doorways." If accompanied with some honest analysis, these words can lead to the actions and criteria desired in some of those ambiguous tasks.

Three domains: cognitive, affective, and psychomotor

Another tool for specifying learning behaviors is the Bloom *Taxonomy of Educational Objectives*. Compiled by a committee of college and university examiners, and published by David McKay of New York City, this list arranges objectives into three general categories. They call these categories "domains." The three domains parallel what industrial T & D departments

	THE OBSERVABLE ACTION MAY BE EXPRESSED AS: Verb (or action)	Object	MEASURABLE CRITERIA ANSWER QUESTIONS AS: How often? How well? How many? How much? How will we know it is okay?	CONDITIONS OF PERFORMANCE What's given? What are the variables?
After training, the clerk will be able to	add	6% sales tax	exactly 6% on all sales	by checking a chart on the cash register.
	identify	corporate officers	18 of the top 20	by looking at a photo or by hearing the title.
After training, drivers will	activate	the turn signal	for all turns	by using the automatic signal in the car.
	1. raise	left arm	upward at elbow for straight left for	right turn / left turn — if no automatic signal.
	2. extend	right arm	$1/8$ mile before turning	when driving in country.
	3. give	proper signal	or $1/4$ block before turning	when driving in the city.
After training, the worker will be able to	smile		at all customers	even when exhausted or ill / unless customer is irate.
	express	concern at the fact that the customer is unhappy	with all irate people by brief (fewer than ten words) apology only after customer has stopped talking	no matter how upset, or abusive, or profane the customer becomes!
After training the manager will be able to	ask	open questions	which cannot be answered yes or no or with facts	whenever probing for feelings.
	relieve	tension in subordinates	by asking open questions	when employee seems angry, frustrated, confused, or tense.

Fig. 8.1. Standards for learning (behavioral) objectives.

Observable action words		Measurable criteria
Choose	Collect	At least ____*(#)*____ correct.
Categorize	Trace	At least ____*(%)*____ correct.
Copy	Count	With no more than ____*(#)*____ errors
Chart	Classify	With at least ____*(#)*____
Define	Describe	Accurate to ____*(?)*____ decimal points
Diagram	Designate	In _____ (amount of time)
Detect	Distinguish	At ____*(#)*____ per hour
Differentiate	Discriminate (between)	
Document	Repeat	
Locate	Identify	
Find	Label	
Isolate	Match	
Mark	Note	
Name	Place	
Rank	Order	
Provide	Select	
Quote	Underline	

Fig. 8.2.

Useful words for learning objectives.

have always said *they* did: produce new knowledge, different attitudes, and new skills. The three domains (coming from the campus as they do!) use bigger words: *cognitive,* for mental skills; *affective,* for growth in feelings or emotional areas; *psychomotor,* for manual, physical skills. The Bloom group produced in intricate analysis for each of the first two domains, but none for the psychomotor domain. Their explanation: They have little if any experience in teaching manual skills at college levels.

In the cognitive domain, the toxonomy cites six distinct types of behavior:

Behavior	*Definition*	*Examples*
Knowledge	Recall of data	Name of the officers of an organization. Recite the pledge of allegiance. Quote a policy.
Comprehension	Translation; Interpolation or Interpretation	Explain the principles of performance objectives. State a problem in one's own words.
Application	Unprompted use of an abstraction; Using a concept in a new context.	Use an organization manual to calculate your own sick leave. Apply laws of trigonometry in practical situations. Solve a discipline problem by relating it to the union contract.
Analysis	Breaking down systems or communications into components	Troubleshoot a machine that isn't working properly. Distinguish facts from hypotheses. Outline an essay.

Behavior	Definition	Examples
Synthesis	Building a structure or pattern from elements found in diverse sources	Write an essay. Design a simple machine tool to perform a specific operation.
Evaluation	Making judgments about the value of ideas, works, solutions, materials	Select the most efficient solution from an array of options. Select the most qualified candidate for a specified position.

The affective domain covers learning objectives which change interests, values, or attitudes. This would include the development of appreciations, adjusting to new systems or policies. The domain specifically identifies:

Behavior	Definition	Examples
Receiving	Attending; Awareness; Willingness to hear; Controlled or selected attention	Develops tolerance for a variety of types of music. Listens to others with respect. Listens for and remembers the names of people to whom one is introduced.
Responding	Willingness to react; Acquiescence or satisficing in responding	Keeps still when the situation calls for silence. Forces oneself to participate with others. Willingly serves the group of which one is a member.
Valuing	Sensing worth; Commitment; Conceptualizing a value	Feels self to be a member of a group. Speaks up at a discussion in class or at meetings. Writes management on matters about which one feels deeply.
Organization	Organizing values into a system; Determining the interrelationship of values; Establishing dominant or pervasive values	Forms judgments about an organization's responsibility to practice ethically. Develops techniques for controlling aggression in socially acceptable fashion.
Characterization	Reliable performance of value systems; An individual's unique characteristics	Revises judgments and changes behavior in the light of evidence. Develops a plan for regulated rest in accordance with job demands.

The Bloom group felt that at about the level of Organization, the schools reached their ultimate accomplishment . . . that they were powerless to build an organization of value systems, or character. They point out that the schools are less influential than other developmental forces like the family and peer groups.

The two volumes of the "Bloom Taxonomy" further subdivide each objective into even more specific levels of behavior. They do regard these as "levels," each successive behavior being more difficult than the previous. It's easier to teach Knowledge than Comprehension. Either of those is definitely easier than Valuing, they contend. This is partly because each behavior involves earlier learnings. For example: people cannot make evaluations without having analyzed, cannot analyze without knowledge. Yet one wonders about all those people who constantly make judgments with no facts at all! The point is that educated minds *do* insist upon facts first.

In *Planning, Conducting and Evaluating Workshops,* Davis and McCollon say values are hardest to change. (p. 23) They also suggest that for affective objectives, words like "convincingly, comfortable, unflinchingly and unhesitatingly" are okay, and further identify "judges" in the criterion element of all objectives. Thus for affective objectives they can accept phrases like "To your own satisfaction," "In the opinion of the boss," or "In any way that seems natural." (p. 88) More rigid formulators of learning or performance standards would probably see these as "copouts"; they wouldn't "be comfortable" with such words and phrases in learning objectives they themselves created.

From the Bloom list, T & D specialists are particularly impacted by the conclusion that affective behavior is more difficult to develop than cognitive—and that psychomotor is the most difficult of all! One rationale for this conclusion is that useful manipulative, physical behavior does indeed rest upon highly trained minds and emotions. Then as the books themselves say, "We find so little done about it [psychomotor skill] in secondary schools and colleges." (Vol. 1, pp. 6–7)

Other educators have developed a set of sub-objectives within the psychomotor domain, but this domain has never been the problem in organizational training. The manipulative skills very easily reveal observable actions and measurable criteria. It's easy to define learning objectives in the psychomotor domain.

There is a lesson here—particularly for T & D specialists who find their organization reluctant to define learning objectives, or for T & D officers who find that some of their very own T & D specialists resist all the hard work that goes with "pinning down" the learning objectives or performance standards. Why not begin in the psychomotor domain? Why not get good observable and measurable statements for programs with manipulative skills? The "smell of success" there can often encourage reluctant T & D specialists to apply the technology to more ambiguous tasks. It can gradually create the norm that, "We like crisp learning objectives in this organization." It's a place to start in getting good objectives for future programs: later on managers come to expect and demand that there will be good objectives for all learning programs.

WHO WRITES LEARNING OBJECTIVES?

By now it must be apparent that useful and valid learning objectives result from collaborative effort between the client management and the T & D department. But writing these objectives is hard work, and only the T & D specialists are masters of the technology. Does it follow then that they should be held accountable for the initiative and for the final product?

Precisely!

But it also follows that T & D specialists should never do the work alone. The statement may be for a totally observable action with a thoroughly measurable criterion and well-defined performance conditions. It is worthless if it isn't also a realistic statement of what the client organization needs and of what it will reinforce on the job.

Thus a team approach seems critically important in the process of creating professional but practical learning objectives.

Who should be on that team? Several elements need to be represented. First there is top management in the client department; they must give approval to the final objectives. These top managers may not be actively involved in selecting the words—but their final "sign-off" is critical, and they must be involved in a two-way conversation reviewing those statements. Only such scrutiny by top client management can ensure the legitimacy of the program.

Actually, three elements are necessary representatives of the client (line) organization: (1) top management, at least for review and approval; (2) typical, or representative, superiors of the workers who will attend the training; and (3) representative workers. Without those superiors and actual performers, there is little chance of total realism and reasonableness in the final version of the learning objectives.

And of course the T & D department should be represented. Probably two types of T & D expertise are needed: the consultant who helps analyze the performance problem and defines behavior, and the designer who must create learning systems to develop those behaviors. These functions may very well be combined in or performed by just one person, but the process requires both skills: pinning down the behavior and making certain that some learning method can be devised to achieve it. Without the consultant's active involvement there is a possibility that the real problem will go unsolved; without the designer's participation there is a possibility that unrealistic learnings or inappropriate methods will be attempted.

The team which produces the learning objectives should probably be organized as shown in Fig. 8.3.

SUMMARY

Should every training program have a behavioral objective?

Should every development effort have a pre-determined behavioral outcome?

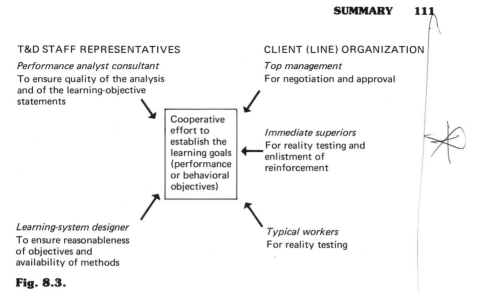

T&D STAFF REPRESENTATIVES

Performance analyst consultant
To ensure quality of the analysis
and of the learning-objective
statements

CLIENT (LINE) ORGANIZATION

Top management
For negotiation and approval

Cooperative
effort to
establish the
learning goals
(performance
or behavioral
objectives)

Immediate superiors
For reality testing and
enlistment of
reinforcement

Learning-system designer
To ensure reasonableness
of objectives and
availability of methods

Typical workers
For reality testing

Fig. 8.3.

Team for establishing learning objectives.

Should learning objectives be precisely defined?

What about tasks that aren't so easy to define?

To be certain that the T & D department is giving the organization what it wants, learning objectives are highly desirable. They document the behaviors and imply a pledge that client managers will reinforce those behaviors when the T & D department produces them. They give managers from all departments a clear picture of "what things will look like around here after we've solved this performance problem."

There is great value in the joint effort by T & D people and client personnel like the SME, smart new jargon for "subject matter experts" or top performers. The SME helps define the task, criteria, and conditions. Client managers *may* help define, but they *certainly* approve the final version of the behavioral objectives. Their involvement obviously has great long-range value for the T & D function!

It seems apparent that even if T & D specialists cannot establish precise goals for all learning, there is value in doing it for those tasks for which they are able to establish observable, measurable behaviors.

Perhaps the most sensible conclusion goes like this: To the degree that the learning can be specified, instructors have a better basis for making good decisions while teaching . . . learners have a better sense of why and how well they are learning—and the organization has a better idea of what it is getting back from its training investment.

CHAPTER

HOW DO PEOPLE LEARN?

WHY IT MATTERS

How do people learn? Nobody knows for certain, but in recent years there has been a flurry of interest in answering that question.

B. F. Skinner says we learn to behave in a certain way because the consequences of that behavior are reinforcing. Carl Rogers says we make significant learnings when external threats are at a minimum. Herbert Kohl, in *The Open Classroom,* says that the starting point of change is discontent.

Since experts can't agree, why worry?

Well, T & D designers need some learning theory upon which to base the activities they specify in the learning systems they create. Professional instructors need some theoretical basis from which to operate. Consultants and administrators serve as change agents for the client organization—and to produce change, they need a theory about learning. After all, change begins with learning that there may be a better way!

But there are many learning theories; which one should you use? If you must have just *one* theory, use the one that caused you yourself to learn—if you know what it was! If that seems fuzzy, or that route a narrow base, use the theory permeating the department where you work.

But as you gain experience helping others acquire new behavior, *keep your eyes and ears and mind open!* Chances are you will use many theories doing what must be done to help people change. By observing your successes and failures, *you will develop an eclectic but consistent learning theory of your own!*

Perhaps this chapter can help you launch your growth toward that objective. Newcomers can think of opportunities to try out these ideas; old-timers can guard against the temptation to dismiss them because they're unfamiliar, or because they tried them once and they didn't work the first time!

So our learning objective reads: "After reading this chapter, the reader will comprehend the similarities and differences among four learning theories: Sensory Stimulation, Reinforcement Theory, Facilitation, and Andragogy." An application objective (as advocated by master trainers like Patricia A. McLagan) would be: "will develop a personally satisfying and realistic theory about helping others learn."

SENSORY STIMULATION THEORY

This approach to learning says simply that for people to change, they must invest their senses in the process. The people who manage that process (instructors and trainers, parents, or bosses, or friends) thus try first to stimulate and then to control what students see, hear, touch, and do during a learning session. More attention is paid to sensory experience than to mental processes or emotional involvement.

Special stress goes to the sense of sight. Advocates of the sensory-stimulus approach maintain that 75 percent of what adults know was acquired through the eyes. They credit hearing with about 13 percent, and say that the remaining 12 percent of what people know was acquired through touch, smell, or taste.

This stress on visual senses as the source of learning results in a heavy attack upon the lecture method—unless, of course, it is accompanied with a lot of visual stimulation. Sense stimulators point to studies showing that people retain only about one-tenth of what they have heard 72 hours after hearing it. They add that these same students retain about 30 percent of what they have seen. When the stimulation appeals to both ears and eyes, the retention goes up to about 70 percent. Advocates of this approach point out that the more senses involved, the more lasting the response. Thus to "motivate greater

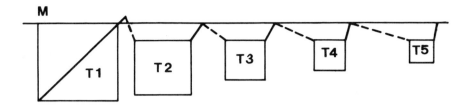

Fig. 9.1.

The learning-forgetting process.

learning," designers and instructors use stronger statements, louder sounds, more colors and more intense colors, bigger pictures, multimedia presentations.

The focus is quite clearly upon the acquisition and retention of knowledge. Learning theorists who reject this approach do so on several bases:

1. They argue that the research is faulty, based on just a few subjects and ignoring other variables which might have affected the outcome. For example, there are no data to indicate that the learners knew in advance that they were accountable for acquiring and retaining the information. Today many people believe that virtually no learning at all occurs unless students know their accountabilities.

2. There is also no evidence about sequence. In what pattern was the material presented? Would retention have been different had another pattern prevailed? The question here is: "Does retention depend upon some patterned sequence as alphabetic, geographic, or chronological?" The results in the studies may or may not have benefited from such continuity, sequence, or pattern.

3. The tests deal only with acquisition and retention over a short timespan. Most T & D specialists feel that the ultimate behavior expected of adult learners is to *apply* knowledge over a long range of time, not just to acquire and retain it for a few days! They therefore deplore any system that stresses memorization and question the value of retaining even 70 percent of unapplied information!

The sensory stimulation theory recognizes the problem of forgetting. It thus stresses retraining as an integral part of the learning process. Schematically, that process looks something like Fig. 9.1.

The acquisition shows up in the five solid diagonal lines, while the forgetting is reflected in the four dotted lines. The heavy horizontal line near the top represents M or satisfactory level of performance. The rectangles at the bottom represent training sessions, and are labeled T for that reason. You'll note that they get smaller, and occur at longer intervals as the learning overpowers the forgetting.

Although many industrial training systems rely upon such scheduling, even those who practice the method agree that there are some puzzling problems associated with it. For one thing, it isn't easy to get trainees back into the classroom for the retraining. Far from it! In low-impact T & D departments it's difficult enough to get them to the training in the first place!

Overteaching makes a lot more sense when building habits, but the extra energy comes in the form of repeated drill by the learners—not as semi-relevant extra information dragged in just to "stimulate" them!

In other contexts, though, overteaching can be devastating. There is often unbearable repetitiousness and wasteful redundancy. In those situations instructors end up working harder and harder and learners end up working less and less. Overteaching also often involves adding related background—presumably to make the stimulus "stronger." The relevance of that background is often highly questionable.

Probably the major argument against making sensory stimulation the basis of an entire T & D system can be summarized this way:

1.   Students take a purely responsive role. It's possible that they will become so passive that even gigantic stimuli elicit little response. Eventually even the strongest stimulus proves to be not stimulating at all.

2.   The burden of the activity rests on the instructor's shoulders. This leads instructors to become more and more showmen—less and less managers of the learning process.

3.   When the trainee response isn't what the instructor intended or desired, the teacher-student relationship deteriorates to one of mere control, or dominance and attention. As Tiger and Fox have pointed out in *The Imperial Animal,* those are "political rather than instructional considerations," and T & D systems run into trouble when they confuse the two. (p. 167)

REINFORCEMENT THEORY

When B. F. Skinner's behaviorist psychology arrived, it brought a major variation to traditional ideas about stimulus-response learning. The essence of Skinnerian psychology appears in the study of contingency management in Chapter 7.

However, one element called reinforcement theory applies especially to learning theory. It guides the dynamics of the instructor-learner relationship.

Skinner himself objects to theories, saying that they lead to wasteful testing effort. However, the findings of his own research are widely published under the general name of Behavior Modification or Reinforcement Theory.

Just for review: Behaviorism teaches that a behavior is controlled by its consequences. Humans will repeat a behavior which seems to produce pleasant consequences, and will avoid behaviors which seem to lead to unpleasant consequences. If one applies this to learning theory, the conclusion is simply that people learn because of what happens to them. To translate that to the instructor-learner relationship is a simple (but dangerous) step: teachers can cause students to behave in desired ways by "rewarding" . . . giving positive, pleasant consequences to students who "got it right."

This *is* a dangerous conclusion because it is terribly incomplete and partly incorrect. Why incomplete? Because it ignores the fact that reinforcement between humans is a two-way transaction. Learners are constantly shaping the behavior of instructors just as instructors are attempting to shape the behavior of the learners. How incorrect? Because behavior isn't that simple.

First, the reinforcers should be *positive*. Why? Because happy consequences teach behaviors and unhappy consequences teach the avoidance of behaviors. Slot machines never tell their "one arm" to attack the player in the chest or stomach! They carry no taped recording to chide, "You jerk! I just paid off two spins ago!" When slot machines reinforce, they reinforce with happy consequences . . . with good news . . . with *positive* contingencies. Gamblers continue to insert coins because they never know when or how much that positive payoff will be.

Psychologists urge positive rather than aversive (negative) reinforcement because positive reinforcement can instill the desired behaviors, while negative reinforcement can only get rid of undesirable behaviors. Thus spankings follow naughtiness; jail follows lawbreaking; suspensions follow infractions. But many respected psychologists dislike negative reinforcement: they say that even if it does eliminate an undesired behavior, it often produces other less desirable behaviors. For example: a spanked child will beat up on baby sister or bite the neighbor; a suspended employee will "bad talk" the company amongst steady customers.

Since most T & D departments seek new behaviors, there seems to be little need for aversive reinforcement. In *The Technology of Teaching*, B. F. Skinner explains it this way: "Only when the good will and affection of the teacher has failed need we turn to the use of aversive stimulation."

Wade Burck, tiger master for Ringling Brothers, and Barnum and Bailey's Circus, trains his pupils via the reward method: a piece of meat for a job well done. "But if an animal is good for two months, then all of a sudden doesn't do a trick, I don't beat the animal." Most organizational trainers have no desire to experiment to prove Burck wrong!

Burck offers still another insight: "Animals are basically like people, and each one has to be dealt with as an individual." (*Sky*, August 1984, p. 46)

The *principle of individuality* is expressed in the old cliche, "One man's meat is another man's poison." Transactional Analysis has given us another version: "Different strokes for different folks." Thus it is that time off without pay is a negative reinforcer for those who value doing their own thing.

This individuality of reinforcers sometimes makes contingency management systems very hard to administer. Varying the reinforcers can conceivably clash with organizational policy, union contracts, laws, or standard management practices. Many managers can tell you that they've driven themselves desperate trying to treat each person as an individual and yet treat everybody alike! Perhaps this very problem offers insight into its solution. If people are individuals, and if managers are hoping to reinforce them with their peculiarly individual "stroke," then the manager must know a great deal about *every* worker on the staff!

The *principle of immediacy* is also important. A consequence will control a behavior if it follows the behavior at once—or at least soon enough that the performer subtly perceives the consequences. Behaviors really have two consequences: one immediate and one delayed. The immediate consequence will control future behavior more than the secondary contingency.

In *About Behaviorism* (p. 178), B. F. Skinner explains this. Drinking alcohol has an immediate, positive, and pleasant consequence: feeling "high." Unfortunately, there is also a delayed negative consequence. It's called a hangover! During this delayed, aversive consequence, drinkers may resolve never to touch the stuff again! But they do. Why? Because the immediate consequence is so pleasant. That's what controls their consequences. In the same vein, spanking a child next Sunday for today's impertinence won't do much toward making a polite child. Suspending an employee next month for yesterday's infraction will not produce desired behaviors. A good performance appraisal next year for last winter's extra effort will not be very reinforcing.

The *principle of strength* means merely that the consequence needs to be noticeable. Weak reinforcers don't control behavior; witness the gentle taps some parents call a spanking, or the small variations in salary increases spread across an employee population. Unless the reinforcement is perceived to be significant, it doesn't encourage a repetition of the desired behavior. Slot machines know that; if they give you back anything at all, they usually give you back at least twice the amount you inserted. Which takes us to the next principle.

The *principle of variability* ties in closely with strength. The strength must not only be noticeable; it must vary. Slot machines are programmed perfectly for this principle. Sometimes they return twice as many coins as the player inserts; sometimes they pay off at a rate of five-to-one, ten-to-one—or even with jackpots! The players just never know when they're going to get paid—or how much. Some sociologists feel that our criminal justice systems are actually encouraging criminal behavior by the erratic penalties applied for conviction of identical crimes. The logic of the criminal goes: "Even if you get caught, you might get off easy. You can always get a soft judge, you know." Slot machines are also programmed to apply another important principle of contingency management.

Mutuality is another principle which governs the transaction of reinforcers in interpersonal relationships. We don't always stop to think about it, but we are constantly cross-reinforcing one another for our behaviors. Consciously or subconsciously we give either positive or negative reinforcement to the people with whom we interact—*and they are continuously doing the same thing to us!* People who don't believe this need only observe how quickly little tots teach their parents to shout! Instructors who introspect can agree that cooperative students control the instructor's behavior at least as much as the teacher controls the student.

It takes real discipline to pay less attention to those who are constantly smiling than to those who seem not to be responding at all. Also, it often is easy to over-respond to troublemakers at the expense of learners who are investing constructive energies in acquiring the new behaviors!

Successive approximations represent another significant principle of reinforcement theory. Those big words simply describe the small steps people take toward the ultimate objective: those small steps are "successively approximate" to the desired behavior.

Students rarely "get it all right" the first time. They certainly don't get the complex objectives of most adult learning programs totally correct with their first tryout of the new skill, the new idea, the new value. They do, however, do *some* of it properly in their early efforts.

Learners approach mastery one step at a time: rarely do they sit down at a sophisticated computer and write a successful program on their first effort; hardly ever to they embrace a quantitative feedback element in a new appraisal system the moment it is first explained to them.

Successive approximations work for all of us from infancy to senility. Instructors of adults really need to understand this phenomenon.

Why? Because adults so often need to reacquire the skill of open inquiry. Too many adults have closed their minds to new ideas, methods, or options. A learner's experience is a double-edged sword. It can be "a rich resource or an impenetrable defense" against new learnings.

Just recall classroom situations in which you've participated. You will surely

remember plenty of times when instructors missed the opportunity to reinforce learners who, though a long way from mastery, were moving in desired
directions. You can probably also recall cases where trainers actually punished learners for successive approximations. Teachers who exclaim, "But
you forgot to cross the 't' in the second word!" are ignoring all the other
words which the student completed properly. Phrases like, "Not bad!" may
seem to be praise to the instructor, but rejection to the learners who aren't at
all sure of their progress. They may, indeed, not be at all sure they want to
acquire the new learnings, and such ambiguous reinforcement may help
them make up their minds—in the wrong way!

Instructors easily "put down" adult learners who challenge the instructor's
ideas. What does that put down really say to the entire class? It says, "Hey,
fella! We don't want inquiry in this session." Instructors need to nourish
questions which challenge the system or policy rather than argue with the
questioner. After all, such questions show interest, some slight willingness to
receive, and are thus successive approximations of the valuing which will
ultimately bring compliance.

What the Skinnerian reinforcement adds to the traditional sensory stimulus
theory is not merely the encouragement of positive reinforcement. It is the
implication that the learner is doing something more than listening to or
watching an instructor who is trying to stimulate. The active involvement of
the learner is inherent in successful, reinforcing learning experiences. In one
of his books Skinner points out: "To acquire behavior, the student must
engage in behavior."

Even from this quick analysis it should be apparent that the traditional sensory
stimulus and reinforcement theory are quite compatible. It's just that reinforcement theory goes further in describing an inter-reaction of the instructor,
the learner, and the course content. Above all, it assumes that such an interaction exists—and that the learner is actively engaged in that interaction
whenever learning is really happening.

Having discovered this compatability, let's examine what may appear to be a
sharply different approach to learning.

FACILITATION

In *Freedom To Learn,* psychiatrist Dr. Carl Rogers outlines a different theory
of learning. He places far greater emphasis on the learner's involvement in
the process. He examines far more deeply the relationship between the
learner and the instructor, identifying this relationship as the primary ingredient in the process.

The Rogers approach is called "Facilitation." Why? Because Rogers sees the role of the instructor as a facilitator of, rather than a stimulator or controller of the learning process.

Rogers believes above all that humans have a natural capacity to learn—even an eagerness to do so. Yet he describes this eagerness as "ambivalent" because significant learning involves two kinds of pain: one with the learning itself and the other with giving up previous learnings. That is why he believes that external threats must be kept at a minimum. The instructor is there to facilitate the resolution of this ambivalence . . . to assist (never to force) the student in doing so.

When learning involves changing one's concept of oneself (Organization), says Rogers, it is all the more difficult. Indeed, it is threatening—one of those "significant learnings" which truly interest Rogers. Thus Rogers and Skinner would agree about the instructor's use of aversive stimulation: they both deplore it. So do Davis and McCollon, who say in *Planning, Conducting and Evaluating Workshops,* "The ability to change is directly proportional to the degree of comfort adults feel." (p. 23) Tiger and Fox comment, in *The Imperial Animal,* that the "Optimal conditions for learning when we are young are astonishingly different from those when we are young adults. The one phase demands security, the other risk." (p. 176) One presumes they are not talking about external threats—only about the risk provided by the significant learnings themselves.

But Rogers goes even farther. He points out that facilitative instructors are:

- Less protective of their own constructs and beliefs than other teachers,
- More able to listen to students—especially to their feelings,
- Able to accept the "troublesome, innovative, creative ideas which emerge in students,"
- Inclined to pay as much attention to their relationship with students as to the content of the course,
- Able to accept feedback, both positive and negative, and to use it as constructive insight into themselves and their behavior.

Thus Rogers's concept of facilitation involves permitting students to make responsible choices about the direction of their learning, and to live responsibly with those choices. This means living with mistaken choices as well as correct ones—and to do so as part of the learning process.

The learners themselves are rich resources for the learning in facilitative systems. Their participation is both process and materials for their own and everyone else's learnings.

How does this relate to the course content in a typical T & D department training program? There may be a sharp conflict. Facilitative objective-setting and the established performance standards may not turn out to be one and the same thing. The learning objectives have presumably been established and validated by management, and revalidated with reality testing through typical workers. These objectives will hopefully be reinforced by the managers of all successful graduates.

The potential conflict is quite obvious: organizations are unwilling to alter standards just to permit craftspeople to fulfill themselves! Only in organizations where Quality Circle philosophies permeate do workers even have a lot of say about what standards will apply to all who perform the same task.

However, in programs for supervisors, managers, executives, and staff professionals, many apply Rogers's advice: they stress individual development programs growing out of appraisal and goal-setting sessions with the immediate managers. In a few workshops, participants may select individualized learning goals relevant to their current position or to those they may reasonably be expected to occupy soon—but the most frequent example of "Learner Controlled Instruction" in most organizations is employee participation in selecting which programs or conferences they will attend.

Learners increasingly select the sequence with which they will acquire new skills, or the materials they will use. Sometimes learner and trainer work together to describe adequate tests of their learning accomplishments.

This last activity reflects the principle of self-evaluation—a critical facet of Carl Roger's philosophy. He insists that self-evaluation is basic, that evaluation by others is secondary.

One principle of facilitative learning is totally compatible with organizational T & D efforts: the belief that learning should be oriented toward the solution of significant problems—not to the history of the task or the profession. As a result, both seek students who become self-disciplined professionals attempting to cope with significant issues. What organization wouldn't like to have that sort of employee working at every level?

Another comment from Rogers identifies "maturity" as the ultimate objective of a facilitative learning system. "The most useful learning is learning the process of learning . . . a continuing openness to experience, incorporating into oneself the process of change." (*Freedom To Learn*, p. 163)

Many public schools and a few universities are moving in the direction of facilitative programs. If schools continue this trend, corporate and bureaucratic organizations can expect to hire increasing numbers of workers who are unwilling to accept education and training in which all the decisions about goals and methods are made by the T & D "establishment." Skill as facilitators of learning will then become increasingly important to organizational designers and instructors.

As an advocate of facilitative instruction, Carl Rogers is perceived as a humanistic psychologist. Indeed, he is one of the founders of the Association of Humanistic Psychology. Recent developments within that movement include the concept of "holistic" education.

As the name implies, holistic education maintains that the individual personality contains many elements. It contends that education and development are effective only to the degree that they activate *all* six elements: the intellect, emotions, body, impulse (or desire), intuition, and imagination.

Most holistic educators envision these six elements as linked together by the will. To visualize this, imagine a pie sliced into six pieces. Then envision an apple ring at the center, linking all six slices. That ring at the center is the will. Now imagine a pole sticking up out of the center of that ring, straight up from the pie. This is a line to a "higher self," the individual's linkage with deity or divinity. Some ask if this "higher self" is the same as Maslow's supraconsciousness.

Until the will is activated, through exercise of the six elements, there will be neither growth nor learning. When the will is activated, that is called "intentionality," and once the growth begins there is a linkage with the higher self.

In a very real sense current creativity workshops based on the right brain/left brain dominance theory are holistic in their orientation. Recent research identifying seven distinct types of intelligence (including musical, spatial, kinetic, and above all *intrapersonal*) reflects holistic thinking.

Holistic humanism may therefore involve a certain mysticism. One facet, psychosynthesis, boasts of roots in the East, West, Europe, and North America! Holistic lesson plans (a term which will surely upset any true humanist!) involve music, chanting, self-actualization, sensory heightening, expressive movement, consciousness raising, guided fantasies—all this in addition to the normal verbal exchanges between instructor and learner.

But the instructor–learner relationship is notably different in holistic settings. For example, the "centering," a vital activity in any design: traditional trainers center on one topic by discussion of the learning objectives and (maybe) students' personal goals for the program. In holistic sessions, however, the centering will probably be experiential since holistic educators believe that an "energy field" must be created so the six human elements can energize the will.

There is thus a dual emphasis: expanding awareness and exploring the unconscious. This may sound exotic and esoteric, but humanists make a strong point about the necessary activation of the will and *taking responsibility for the direction of one's own growth and life.*

In all humanistic holistic education, the self-image of the participant is vital.

Jack Canfield and Harold Wells have developed a book about this: *100 Ways to Enhance Self-Concept in the Classroom.* The "100 Ways" are exercises, developed with young learners in mind. However, with imagination and caution, they can be adapted for experiental training involving adults. This self-image is basic in holistic, humanistic, and facilitative learning experiences, since all stress that significant learning occurs when learners feel secure in the learning environment.

Because of its mysticism or because of a few "touchy-feely" learning activities, holistic education is avoided by some organizations.

There is also growing sentiment against "Me Generation" and self-actualization psychology. "Many of us are unable to break the habit of self-absorption, unable even to live with someone else because it interferes with our own space." (*Time,* April 9, 1984, p. 78) Hans Selye, guru of stress management, advocates an "altruistic egoism" in which individuals fulfill themselves through serving causes beyond their own needs. (*Psychology Today,* March 1978)

Some proponents of facilitative learning designs and relationships feel that there is an impenetrable barrier between the beliefs of behaviorists like B. F. Skinner and the tenets of Carl Rogers. Others contend that good positive reinforcement is merely facilitation between two humans with mutual respect for one another's values. They argue that one must care enough about other people to discover what they find reinforcing. It's facilitative, they say, to see that others get positively reinforced for behaving in mutually desirable fashion. That, they say, is facilitation at its most practical level.

Can this be applied to the instructor-learner relationship? Perhaps a facilitative interchange of mutual reinforcements can avoid that "controlling" pattern deplored by Tiger and Fox. When instructors and management have clearly identified to learners which behaviors will produce approval, the instructor can function not as a showman who goes to great limits to attract and maintain attention, not as a policeman who hands out tickets to transgressing students—but as a facilitator who leads adults to pleasant acquisition of useful new skills.

ANDRAGOGY

To become an elementary teacher, a person may study "pedagogy." T & D specialists in the past few years have become interested in "andragogy." The difference is quite simple. "Ped" is a Latin root meaning *child;* "andra" derives from the Greek "aner," meaning man, not boy. Thus andragogy studies how adults learn. It asks if they learn in ways which are significantly different from the ways in which children acquire new behaviors.

Leading this inquiry is Malcolm Knowles. He points to several differences in the inventory adults bring to the learning. While children are dependent, adults see themselves as self-directing. Children expect to have questions which must be answered by outside sources; adults expect to be able to answer part of their questions from their own experience. What may be more important, children expect to be told what they need to do; adults have a very different viewpoint on that issue!

In part, this stems from their view of their own experience. Children are well aware that they haven't been around a great deal. Thus they put a rather low value on their experience. But adults weren't "born yesterday," and they *do* value their experience. They value it so much that they want to invest it in the learning experience . . . want to test new concepts and behavior against what they have previously learned. And to test what they now think against new research.

You can recall from your own schooldays the times when the teacher said, "Now someday this will come in handy." Children may buy that; adults ask, "How soon?" Children accept a delayed application, but adults tend to de- mand immediate application of the learnings. This harmonizes with Rogers' viewpoint that learners want to be problem-solvers. Knowles simply adds the word "soon."

Thus andragogic learning designs involve a number of features which recog- nize the essential maturity of the learner:

- They are problem-centered rather than content-centered.
- They permit and encourage the active participation of the learner.
- They encourage the learner to introduce past experiences into the pro- cesses in order to reexamine that experience in the light of new data . . . new problems.
- The climate of the learning must be collaborative (instructor-to-learner and learner-to-learner) as opposed to authority-oriented.
- Planning is a mutual activity between learner and instructor.
- Evaluation is a mutual activity between learner and instructor.
- Evaluation leads to reappraisal of needs and interests—and therefore to redesign and brand-new learning activities.
- Activities are experiential, not "transmittal and absorption" as in stan- dard pedagogy.

These andragogic concepts have tremendous implications for the T & D specialist. Early activities need to allow maximum participation by learners, so they can invest their experience and values in the learning process—and so instructors can note this inventory. Andragogic instructors use more questions, realizing that learners *do* know a great deal . . . that tapping that inventory permits the learners to invest more energy in new learnings.

For example: if learners know how digits are positioned in a decimal system they can be expected to interpret displays in binary or octal numerical systems. This is sometimes called "letting the learners go from the known to the unknown." But note those andragogic words "*letting learners go*" rather than the pedagogic "*taking* learners from the known to the unknown."

A major aspect of andragogic systems is the learner's active involvement in establishing the learning objectives. And so we have the same potential conflict between the needs of the organization and the needs of the individual. As we noted earlier, in management development learners may be able to select their own learning objectives; in skills training that doesn't happen very often.

Not all organizational T & D programs can permit full delegation of the learning goals to the learners themselves—but none of them prevents an activity which allows learners to analyze learning goals, and why they are important to the organization—and to the individual learner.

Understanding the reasons for (or "owning") the objectives is sometimes called "motivation." One popular theory insists that until the learner has this ownership, little useful learning will result.

But even when learning objectives are predetermined, the processes of andragogic sessions vary sharply from those in pedagogic classes. In fact, andragogy raises interesting questions about the proper role of the instructor. Are the best instructors those who can speak well? Those who can maintain a benevolent but consistent control? The andragogic learner-instructor relationship escapes the dominant-teacher and dependent-learner image altogether. It features reciprocity in the teaching-learning transaction.

The primary function of the instructor is to manage, or guide, andragogic processes—not to "manage the content," as in traditional pedagogy. To achieve this, learning designs involve establishing the norm for a great deal of two-way communication. This may very well include learner inputs, querying, or establishing the objectives and the methods.

It follows that the andragogic climate stresses physical comfort, variety, and mobility. (Learners need to get to their chosen resources for the learning; class or conference rooms may not be the ideal environment for this.)

The process, if presented graphically, looks something like Fig. 9.2.

Instructors need to focus on goals and inventories . . . to use frequent skillful questions and empathic reflection to help learners invest their energies so there is growth for both the learner and the organization. Thus in andragogic designs, trainers serve as facilitative counsellors to each learner. This requires

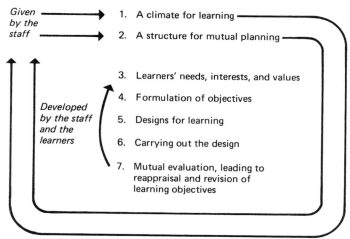

Fig. 9.2.

The process of andragogy. (Adapted from Von Bertalanffy, Ludwig, *General System Theory*, New York, Braziller, 1968. Used by permission of the publisher.)

a wide range of the competencies listed in the ASTD model: Understanding of Adult Learning, of Organization Behavior and of the organization itself, of the Training and Development Field and of Training Techniques; plus skill in Writing, Counselling, Questioning, Feedback, Group Process, Intellectual Versatility, Peformance Observation, Objectives Preparation, Negotiation, Research and Writing!

This andragogic kind of guidance is a big order—and further evidence that T & D specialists do indeed need a solid, personalized learning theory to use as a consistent basis in dealing with learners.

When T & D departments adopt andragogy as the philosophical basis of their learning designs, they are saying that they intend to make maximum use of student inventories. Remember that standard formula, $M - I = D$, or Mastery minus Inventory equals Deficiency. Learners are encouraged to invest their considerable pretraining experience in new learnings. Skilled instruction is required to make certain the investment is a wise one—particularly in organizations which are unaccustomed to andragogic designs.

SUMMARY

Is a single learning theory possible?

In 1965 Gagné pointed out in *The Conditions of Learning*, "I do not think learning is a phenomenon which can be explained by simple theories, despite the admitted intellectual appeal such theories have."

If no single theory can be derived, then why try to have one?

The exploration of sensory stimulation, reinforcement theory, facilitation, and andragogy have answered that question. Hopefully it's apparent that the designer and instructor of learning experiences need a theoretical basis in order to make concrete, consistent decisions about arranging the events of the learning experience and managing the dynamics of the learning activity. For consistent and fulfilling growth, administrators and consultants need a personal philosophy from which to serve the T & D organization.

Learning is a verb—not a noun. It is a journey—not a destination. Thus the designers of the highway and the drivers of the vehicles definitely need a consistent philosophy from which to operate.

How do these four major approaches to adult learning relate to one another?

● *Sensory stimulus:* The instructor presents the motivation. The theory is that the more effective (or sensory) the stimulus, the more intense the motivation-response.

● *Reinforcement theory:* The instructor presents the original stimulus. After that, there is a mutual exchange of adapted stimuli. Hopefully this exchange is punctuated by positive reinforcement in which the learner and the instructor share the desire to offer happy consequences for mutually beneficial behaviors.

● *Andragogy and facilitation:* In a two-way climate, the goals are determined or examined. Feelings as well as cognitive values of the learners become actual materials of the learning. Removal of external threats and identification of resources for enabling change become prime skills of the instructor.

By now it is clear that the learners' involvement results in part from the instructor's behavior—and in part from the original design of the learning system . . . in effect, from the "lesson plan." Both the execution and the plan itself invariably reflect the learning theory assumed or consciously adopted not only by the T & D department, but equally important, by the instructor.

CHAPTER **10**

**WHAT
METHODS
SHALL
WE USE?**

WHAT ARE METHODS?

Interstate I-70 is a fine highway if you want to get to Topeka—but don't take it if Birmingham is your destination. The Ohio Turnpike is great for travelers from Ohio to New Jersey, but a terrible road to take if you're going from Fresno to San Francisco. Reverse role-playing is great for learning to see the other person's point of view, but not much help for people trying to learn to read light meters.

And that's the point about instructional methods—more happily called "learning methods." They are just as good as they are contributive toward the achievement of a learning objective. In fact, it's often helpful to think of methods as highways which lead to cities (objectives) and of training materials (visual aids, case study write-ups, roleplay descriptions) as the ingredients of those highways.

Students may need to travel several highways in order to reach a given destination. Certain students may progress most rapidly if they discuss; others may learn more rapidly and more significantly via programmed instruction. For other goals, there may be several equally appealing and productive routes. When these issues arise, and at all phases of the design activity, the T & D specialist faces the question, "What methods shall we use?"

The decision is multidimensional. It involves the learning objectives, the inventory of the learners, and the norms of the organization—to say nothing of the available budget! But a fundamental criterion in selecting a learning method should be the appropriateness of that method to the learning objective. Davis and McCollon explain, for example: "Rhetoric and argument do not produce change in the emotional framework." (p. 23)

There is a strong trend toward "experienced-based" or "experiential" training in programs which seek to alter the behavior of adults. The terms are not yet terribly well defined. Fig. 10.1 merely indicates three approaches to the

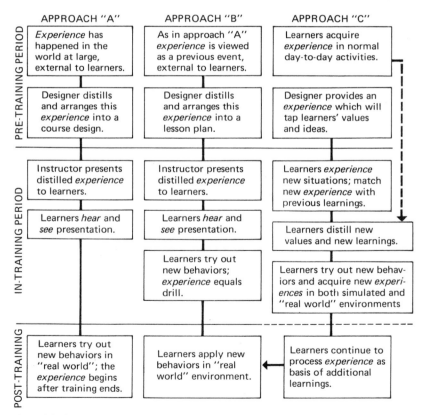

Fig. 10.1.

Three approaches to the use of experience.

use of "experience" in learning systems. Approach "A" is the rather traditional system, giving little emphasis to experience by the learner; Approach "B" increases learner activity, or experience; Approach "C" allows many variations, but involves actual experience by learners as part of the process.

When learning goals involve on-the-job use of new skills, then the drill involved in Approach "B" is essential. When the expected future behavior involves application of new values, or when it implies that people will respond in unfamiliar ways to familiar stimuli, the kind of experience in Approach "C" is useful. These kinds of training programs are often referred to as "attitude development"; they invariably involve behaviors in the affective domain of the Bloom taxonomy. Again, Davis and McCollon have a relevant comment: "Behavior change does not necessarily involve attitude change." (p. 23)

A LOOK AT SPECIFIC METHODS

All modern learning theories stress that adults must have a degree of ownership of the learning processes . . . that they want to invest their previous experience in those processes.

Such ownership and investment are achieved by designs in which the learners actively talk about what they've done in the past, or what they are thinking and feeling right now as they experiment with new behaviors during the learning process.

The document of these designs is called a "lesson plan." It describes the learner activities, with headings like:

TIME & A/V	INSTRUCTOR SAYS AND DOES:	STUDENT ACTIVITY

Fig. 10.2 shows a duo-dimensional array of methods, noting both instructor control of content and learner activity levels.

One logical sequence for examining learning methods is in order of increasing learner involvement; another is by the delegation of content. The duo-dimensional matrix does both.

Does student involvement automatically bring delegation of content? That can happen—but needn't if the participative activity is designed properly. Do participative methods take more time than pure lecture? No question! But the issue is: should instructors cover content or cause learning?

Those who opt for delegated content call it "the discovery approach," and

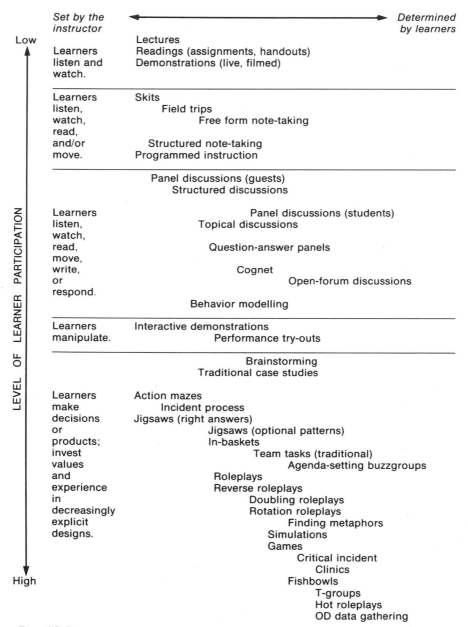

Fig. 10.2.

Duo-dimensional list of methods.

design activities which cause learners to *discover* content the instructor would otherwise have to "tell" the class.

However, delegating content control does not automatically increase learner participation: in open forums the learners control all the content except the topic, yet they aren't necessarily more involved than when manipulating hands or arms in trying out a psychomotor task.

Delegating content does not mean withdrawing control of the processes. In a critical incident, for example, learners supply all the cases and examples, but an instructor leads discussions. The real control, however, comes in the *design* of the activity, not from forceful leadership by an instructor during the session.

For example, the in-basket materials provide their own control. During the class session the instructor merely gives a few preliminary instructions, then watches the process, staying available for student questions. If the instrument has been well designed, there should be few if any questions.

The sequence of the methods on the chart makes a helpful sequence for us to use in analyzing all those methods. Let's look at each method, proceeding from that method in which learners are least participative to those where their activity levels are highest.

Lectures

The lecture is, by definition, words spoken by the instructor. It is thus a verbal-symbol medium, offering a relatively passive and unstimulating experience for learners . . . unless the speaker has unusual vocal and rhetorical talent. The lecturer needs plenty of interesting examples to illustrate theory, colorful and persuasive language to enhance a well-organized pattern of ideas, and a pleasant and stimulating voice.

Lectures were popular in the Middle Ages when the *tabula rasa* theory of education prevailed. The mind of the learner was perceived as a blank tablet upon which ideas were inscribed by a great teacher, lecturer, or professor. It still prevails in a great many universities. Though under constant attack, the lecture method has apparently proved overwhelmingly appealing to professors who enjoy the security blanket of dog-eared lecture notes and the absence of feedback.

At the very minimum, lecturers should:

- Speak loudly and clearly enough to be heard. Amplification is recommended if classes include more than 25 learners. In these cases, of course, microphone technique is a requisite skill for the lecturer.
- Organize each lecture around a single theme or "thesis."

- Develop inherent, mutually exclusive "areas of discussion" which thoroughly and relevantly develop the thesis.

- Develop each area of discussion with a variety of evidence. This includes analysis, concrete incidents, illustrations, quotations, statistics, and (if possible) physical objects to display.

Nothing prevents speakers from supplementing their words with visual aids. This adds a whole new dimension to the sensory stimulation. Nor is there any good reason why speakers cannot be interruptible. They can offer "swiss cheese" lectures . . . presentations with "holes in them." In this way learners can make inquiries or comments which accelerate their comprehension. Nor need all the questions come from the learners, though that's probably the most productive arrangement. No law prohibits the lecturer from asking questions or pausing for discussion.

Added accountability for receiving the content can result from supplying learners with a syllabus, a carefully structured notepad on which they can take notes. The careful structure ensures their copying down key words; it establishes key relationships by using charts and tables as well as incomplete sentences or the "bare bones" of the topical outline.

In itself, the lecture is a nonparticipative medium. It does offer an efficient way to *deliver* material. To qualify as an effective learning method, lectures must also contain provisions to test *receipt*.

Readings

Reading assignments don't do much to stimulate the senses; they merely require some concentrated seeing of words on pages. They can, of course, efficiently expose learners to large quantities of content. Reading assignments, like the lecture, should be accompanied with some feedback activities which measure and assist the retention of the content.

Presumably even slow readers will read more material than they could hear in the same length of time. If the reading relates to illustrations or diagrams, some added interest (sensory stimulation) may result.

To make a reading assignment more meaningful, astute instructors build in accountability. They announce discussions or tests on the content—activities in which learners apply new concepts to real-world problems, projects, or products. If the tests or discussions are oriented to application (rather than memory recall) they need not be academic and sterile.

Another approach to this accountability is to supply a syllabus, or structured notepad. Students complete this while reading, thus being guided to focus on the most important points. The reading experience thus becomes a kind of

"Easter-egg hunt": readers search out the critical data hidden in the reading assignment.

When instructors use reading as a post-class exercise, such accountability may appear less necessary. That assumption needs to be sharply challenged. Any reading which does not permit further growth is a questionable investment. Any growth deserves follow-up. Such follow-up might include discussion, participation on a panel of students, testing, or application to a simulated problem. Without such follow-up, the post-training reading assignment risks a very low return on investment.

Demonstrations

Demonstrations are merely illustrated lectures or presentations. We usually think of manipulative activities in a demonstration, though mere pictures of the process sometimes replace the "model" which the demonstrator manipulates. Such pictures are appropriate for processes which can be comprehended through schematics or drawings. Demonstrations are especially suitable for psychomotor objectives, but can of course be used (as in "modeling") to illustrate interpersonal skills, interviewing, communication, discipline, or counseling.

The key to successful demonstration is a close integration of the spoken and the visual stimulus. Hopefully they will be simultaneous. If there must be a lapse, let the verbal stimulus precede the visual—but only by a split second. This means that good demonstrations probably proceed one step at a time, with all visual materials concealed until they come into play. Careful planning and ample rehearsal help. Good demonstrators:

- Analyze the process, breaking it into small sequential steps.
- Have all their materials in place.
- Check the operation of all equipment just before they start the demonstration!
- Position, or scale, their models so all learners can see all the parts all the time.
- Explain the goals of the demonstration at the beginning, hopefully in a two-way discussion with learners.
- Present the operation one step at a time, based on the task analysis completed earlier.
- Allow the earliest possible try-out of the demonstrated skill. This probably should be at the end of the first step. Performance try-out can then be repeated at the end of each successive step in the operation. If andragogy is correct, adults want immediate application of all acquired skill and knowl-

edge. Why keep them waiting until the end of a complete operation to "demonstrate" to themselves that they are learning and growing?

• Reinforce everything learners do correctly in their try-outs. Instructors need to reinforce these successive approximations of mastery of the total task. This also becomes part of an ongoing goal-setting process; learners themselves identify the differences between their try-out and the ultimate desired performance.

Skits

A skit is a prepared enactment, with precise dialogue provided for the "actors," who are usually students reading their roles from scripts. They may sit at their regular positions, or if movement is required, stand and move about to simulate the actions of the situation they enact. Rehearsals are not usually necessary.

Skits effectively transfer to learners the task of "modelling" verbal behaviors: what to say when counseling, asserting, giving directions or reprimands. Skits may also reflect differing points of view, with several "characters" facing a common crisis which they approach with dramatic differences due to their contrasting value systems. The skit personifies and vivifies what might otherwise be a dull theoretical lecture.

Field trips

Field trips, excursions, observations, or tours may or may not be participative learning experiences. That depends pretty much on how well instructors set up expectations and objectives *before* the trip takes place—and upon the mechanism developed to make sure that learning happens.

Again, the image of the "Easter-egg hunt" seems helpful. Here's how that works. Instructors give each trainee a set of questions for which answers must be supplied. These answers can be discovered on the field trip. They can be reviewed at a feedback session in the classroom following the tour. If different learners are asked to locate different "eggs" on the tour, there can be a mutual sharing and comparison in the discussion which "debriefs" the participants after the tour.

If such accountabilities for learning seem inappropriate, then at the very minimum the instructor should preview the tour with the class. This means setting up expectations about what to look for. It means letting class members determine, in a mutual exchange, how the field trip will contribute to the announced objectives.

A major argument in favor of field trips is that they permit learners to experience sensory impressions which could never occur in classrooms or conference rooms—but which are characteristic of the environment in which the new behavior must persevere. The trip thus assists the "generalization" process, permitting behaviors acquired in an isolated or unnatural environment to persist in a less focused "real world."

Further, field trips effectively let people who work in one part of the system comprehend the impact and dependencies they have upon other departments. This desire for organizational empathy is highly commendable, and field trips are probably infinitely more successful than "guest lecturers" from alien departments. These guests often manage to be not much more than mediocre lecturers. Too many orientation programs are just "parades" of people who assume far too much about the learners' inventories and curiosities. They thus do a great deal to confuse and to dampen enthusiasm for the new employment!

But when field trips are used to develop insights and empathy into other parts of the operation, accountability for gathering answers is critically important. The best method is probably to have the learner actually work with an employee of the visited department—not to stand apart and watch the operation. Specially plannned "Easter-egg hunts" are in order. The questions need to include things like, "How many times did the clerk have to . . . ?" or "How did the agent handle . . . ?" or even some specific technical information, as "What is DFT?" or "What does ARUNK mean?" Such questions more nearly guarantee that the learners will come home with clear, definite comprehension of how they depend upon other departments—and of how other departments depend upon them. The learners can also better comprehend how these "downline" and "upline" dependencies in the total system require close adherence to established performance standards. In any case, managers of both the visited and the visiting departments need to be involved in setting precise goals, action plans, and evaluation mechanisms for the field trip program.

Note-taking

Note-taking by learners is somewhat controversial. Theorists like to argue about its value and about the proper way to control note-taking. Does note-taking enhance or impede the learning process? Chances are the answer is "Yes" . . . to both alternatives. For some people note-taking may be necessary to "imprint" the data. These people need to hear it, to see it in the visual aids, and then to see it again as they begin to "own" the idea by writing it down themselves. They may need to "hear it again in their mind's ear" several more times as they reread the notes they have taken. For others, all note-taking may be a distraction.

At any rate, when notes are taken in a free form (as in most college lecture halls) the students are in almost total control of what gets transcribed to the paper. That conceivably can be a bad thing. They may copy what they *think* they hear, or they may abbreviate in ambiguous ways which produce later misinformation. Knowledge is the probable objective of a lecture, and misinformation is destructive toward the acquisition. Some lecturers are shocked and appalled when they see the "pure fiction" that shows up in student notepads.

To prevent such distortion, many lecturers provide learners with a syllabus. The syllabus may take the form of a sheer topical outline, with room enough for learners to complete the headings and statements as instructors say things like "The third category is minerals . . ." while students write the words in alongside the "3" in the syllabus. Even more structured is the syllabus which includes most of the key statements, with blank spaces left for essential words. For example, the syllabus for a lecture on andragogy might have an entry like this:

"A child's self-image tends to be _____ ; adults see themselves as _____ ."

From the lecturer's comments, the learners are able to fill in the proper words: "dependent" and "self-directed or increasingly self-dependent."

A variation is a matrix onto which student make notations as the lecture or demonstration continues. For example, a matrix syllabus for a lesson in which the objective is to distinguish between pedagogy and andragogy might look like Fig. 10.3. As the lecture or discussion reveals the answers, students can put words like "dependent" and "self-directed" or "limited and of little value" or "extensive and worth investing in the learning process" in the proper boxes.

As that example reveals, the answers to be inscribed in a syllabus need not be supplied by the lecturer; they can just as easily come from reading or discussion among the participants. This is especially true in review sessions where

	PEDAGOGY	ANDRAGOGY
Self-image		
Experience		
Time perspective		
Orientation to learning		

Fig. 10.3.

Sample matrix syllabus.

the learners bring a big inventory to the learning situation. Used this way, the syllabus is more a training aid than a learning method—but if it contributes to the achievement of the objective, who wants to quibble about categories?

Programmed instruction

Programmed instruction gets heavy support from its advocates for two major reasons:

1. It requires active involvement of the learners. They make overt responses to a question-stimulus which follows the presentation of small bits of information.

2. It provides immediate feedback about the quality of the learner's response. Learners are told the "correct" answers right away, and can compare their response with the preferred answer.

Although effective programming requires mastery of an extensive technology, these two virtues reveal a great deal about the nature of the method. Small-step learning is perceived to be important: learners are given just a bit of data, then asked a question about that data. The "program" (whether it be printed in a book, presented in some audio-visual "teaching machine," or stored in a computer) supplies an appropriate answer. Learners access this answer as soon as they have made their own response to the question. The program then does one of two things: if the answer is correct, the program directs them to another bit of data so they can continue their study; if the answer is incorrect, the program *may* redirect them to a previous or an altered stimulus so they can change their insights, or supply a more appropriate answer.

The bits of data are called "frames" and the two methods are called "linear" or "branching." In linear programs the learners are usually given the next bit of information regardless of their answer; they control the decision about revisiting previous frames to clear up misunderstandings. (Advocates of this linear approach contend that if the program has been properly validated, it will control the stimulus so carefully that there is precious little chance of mistaken answers.) In "branching" or "intrinsic" programs learners are routed to different frames depending upon their choices at any given frame. They thus proceed through the program on branches which may be entirely different from those followed by other students studying the same program.

As noted, the total technology is complex. Sizing and sequencing and wording the frames requires patient validation. What does this validation imply? First, that there will be trial drafts of each frame. Second, that these trial drafts will be tested on typical learners. Third, that each frame will be redrafted as a result of the experience gained from analyzing student responses. Most T & D departments will publish and implement only programs which are validated at 85 percent or higher. This means that every frame of the final program has been answered correctly by at least 85 percent of the test audience before the program "goes to press." Some organizations insist upon more than 90 percent validity before they publish.

Because of this complexity, professional upgrading is necessary before T & D designers can become effective programmers. Some upgrading in the proper administration of programmed instruction is indicated for any instructor who uses programmed modules. At times they may need to supplement the published frames; they may be called upon merely to administer the program. There is a strong possibility that they will be called upon to serve as counselors to learners who are temporarily frustrated or immobilized by the initiative required the first time they experience self-administered programs.

Programmed instruction obviously represents total control of the content by the designer or instructor. Andragogic T & D departments therefore like to use PI (the short title of Programmed Instruction) in conjunction with real live instructors. Another problem with some PI is that the frames have been excessively simple. There is little thrill in the learner's soul when asked to copy a word from one frame as the answer to that frame. For example:

"The President of your company is R. J. Frieder."
Who is the president of your company?

_____ . _____ . _____

(Write your answer here.)

However, problems like the absence of a human facilitator or stupid frames can be easily overcome. Therefore PI is an important method in modern training systems. It is especially helpful in organizations which:

- Hire only a few people at a time in any given classification.

- Are widely separated geographically and must train individuals on a one-at-a-time schedule.

- Employ minimum numbers of instructors and need to delegate the teaching function to some mediated instruments.

- Have a heavy commitment to mediated programs, but need a mechanism to provide feedback to learners about their learning progress.

- Need to teach intricate procedures which aren't easily communicated in classroom visual aids or group-instructional modes.

- Have a heavy commitment to individual education and development, and thus need a wide range of programs to serve a small population.

Panel discussions

Panel discussions represent a variation on the structured discussion format. Sometimes they are called colloquies; sometimes they are called symposiums (symposia). Panel symposiums tend to be short lectures by a variety of people rather than a long lecture by a single lecturer. In effective panels each speaker concentrates on a single subtopic, delivering a unique thesis (clearly different from any other panelist) and relating that thesis to the unifying objective.

The problem with many panels is that they tend to be so structured that learner participation is very low. Thus the control of the content (to say nothing of the control of the processes!) rests too heavily with the panelists. An antidote for this is a question-answer session after the final presentation. (If the question-answer session comes too soon, later panelists may be seriously impeded in what they say, or influenced to amend a viewpoint necessary to total achievement of the objective.) Another antidote for the low vitality and one-way communication of the panel format is a post-panel structured discussion in which one leader channels comments as well as questions from the listeners—or between panelists themselves.

To increase the learner involvement in panel discussions, many instructors assign advance readings to class members; then they let learners serve as members of the panel. The reading is thus given greater meaning, and the learners take greater responsibility for developing the subject. As this happens, accountability for comprehending the subject and achieving the objective is transferred to the learner's shoulders.

Structured discussions

Structured discussions are conversations between trainees, aimed toward specific learning objectives. Such objectives distinguish them from mere social conversation, or from the discussion at staff meetings.

For structured discussions, this learning objective should be clearly announced in advance, or during the first moments of the discussion itself. It is usually helpful to post a written statement of the objective where all can see it throughout the discussion. Structure can be further imposed (and meandering correspondingly controlled) by using such devices as a syllabus or a publicly posted agenda. Such agendas may even include an estimate of the appropriate amount of time to devote to each subtopic.

Facilitative instructors like to let the class develop these agendas and timetables themselves. This permits ownership of the entire proceeding by the learners. A heavy instructor-supplied agenda may be totally inconsistent with the climate needed for adult learning. Yet even structured activities planned by the leader permit learners to share their experience and feelings. While this is going on the instructor gets data about the learners' initial inventory and their progress toward desired learning goals.

In such cases the instructor may opt to use no control devices. They feel they can always inject control when irrelevant excursions or counter-productive dynamics might prevent achievement of the posted objective. How? Simply by reminding the group of the objective, or by challenging the relevance of the current activity.

Thus a typical "preparation" for discussion leading is to predefine the objective, and to build a list of questions to give to the group. These preplanned questions are used as the initial stimulus, when each subtopic has been thoroughly developed, when discussion wanders, or when the group needs restimulating. The "lesson plan" merely lists the objectives and questions; the teaching materials sometimes include printed versions of these for display or distribution to individual participants.

Norman R. F. Maeir coined the phrase "Developmental Discussion" after discovering situations which required structure as opposed to free (or "forum") discussion. W. J. McKeachie describes it in *Teaching Tips* (p. 52) as a technique in which the instructor subdivides the topic into parts. Thus all group members are working on the same part at the same time. "One of the reasons discussion often seems ineffective and disorganized is that different members . . . are working on different aspects . . . and are thus often frustrated by what they perceive as irrelevant comments by other students."

The structured discussion is appropriate when there are predefined objectives and when the learners do not bring a negative viewpoint to those objectives. Open forums are indicated when the learners need a chance to ventilate their apathy or hostility toward the learning goals.

Panel discussions by students

The panel, though deadly if poor speakers are invited from outside the class, may prove a lively affair when a topic is broken down into subtopics and assigned to the best students in the class. Some tips and precautions apply:

- Give the panelists adequate time to prepare . . . to read some specified material, analyze it, and synthesize it into an effective presentation.

- Allow time for other students to ask questions.

- Delegate the role of moderator too. Then brief the student moderator on: (1) the relationship of the subtopics, (2) how to communicate that over-all design to the class, (3) how to keep the discussion moving, and (4) how to provide a lively atmosphere without uncomfortable confrontation.

- Select as panelists those students who have shown unusual speed in acquiring and synthesizing information; make this an "enrichment" and a positive reinforcement for good work in earlier parts of the program.

- Don't select donkeys, mules, or pairs of people who might reduce the discussion to a two-dimensional debate. What you seek is analysis of the several facets you have assigned to each panelist.

● The criterion for selection is always the ability to present and interact in the discussion, not social roles inside or outside the class.

Topical discussions

Many people call these "general discussions." If that implies a general topic and minimal prescribed substructure, great! If it implies that instructors just name a topic and immediately launch a discussion, well, not so great! Impromptu chitchats too often meander, miss the mark and bore the learner.

For useful topical discussions instructors should:

● Announce the discussion far enough in advance to permit a bit of required reading, plus time to analyze and synthesize that *new* information;

● Announce precise time limits;

● Announce one or more specific objectives; and then

● Lay low! From there on in it's up to the group to meet the objectives of their analysis of this topic. Well . . . it's probably also "cricket" to

● Tell the group that it's up to them to keep the discussion on track and to meet the objective(s).

Question-answer panels

In more controlled Q-A sessions, instructors announce a topic and a reading assignment, plus the key requirement: a list of questions to be brought to the session itself. The session may be the next meeting of the class; it may also be "after an hour of research and analysis." When the time for the Q-A session arrives, the instructor calls on the learners for their questions. The answers may come from a panel of the students in a sort of "stump the sudden experts" activity. The answers may come from the instructor—but that will only prove that the instructor is smart; it won't develop much learning in the students! The answers may come from invited guests, though that also causes minimum growth in the learners. Whenever the answers come from someone other than the instructor, the instructor need participate only when the data given as answers are inaccurate or incomplete. Of course instructors may be chairpersons . . . but that robs a learner of a participative opportunity!

In Q-A sessions there may actually be no panel at all. Since students generate the questions (individually or in small buzzgroups) they may also be the "experts." They can acquire their expertise by special reading, research, or experimentation achieved during the training program! In fact, "stump the experts" or "information please" panels of students have been known to enliven many classes that once covered less content through instructor-driven lectures.

When making the assignment to develop questions, instructors need merely point out a general objective for the session, reminding the question developers that each item should contribute toward that over-all goal. Sample goals might be:

- To make a personal decision about using zero based budgets;
- To decide which operations in my office might effectively be computerized; or
- To complete a Pro/Con analysis on the use of robots.

Cognet

Cognet is short for cognitive networks, and is (You guessed it!) appropriate for cognitive objectives. All participants do some reading and answer the same questions before they gather—but only several people read the same material. When they gather these "homogeneous" groups meet to prepare group answers which they share in reports to the other teams.

For example, biographies of Harry Truman, Howard Hughes, J. Edgar Hoover, Joan Crawford, Geraldine Ferraro, and Henry Ford might be assigned as pre-reading with questions about their planning strategy, leadership style, interpersonal relations, management of meetings, or behavior in crises.

After the initial report, there is usually another phase of Cognet when new teams are formed by people who want to probe further into those subpoints. Thus there will be new and different reports on planning strategies, people handling, or leadership style—or new issues may emerge, as positions on womens' liberation, unionism, technology, armaments, or politics.

The virtues of the method are that: (1) a lot of information can be processed at whatever depth the group (or instructor) chooses; (2) the information is analyzed from at least two dimensions; (3) each participant gets to "network" with a number of different people; and (4) each learner can integrate the reality of their own situation and perceptions into the theory contained in the literature.

Open-forum discussions

Open-forum discussions are useful when the learners can accept full responsibility for the content of the discussion, or when they need to "ventilate" their feelings and opinions. Generally, only the topic is announced—although more dynamic discussions result when that announcement involves presession readings or analysis. Learners tend to filter their experiences and biases through the reading, thus arriving better prepared to learn.

In the forum format, any member of the group may speak to any other member. A moderator is usually there to prevent everybody from speaking at the same time, or to "patrol" debates when more than one person is speaking simultaneously. Of course, simultaneous speaking isn't always a bad thing, and forums tend to encourage such interchanges. Such free-for-all catharsis can be a useful way to ease threatening learnings—especially if those learnings involve affective behaviors where feelings run high. Objectives involving responding or valuing often profit from open forum discussions.

Behavior modelling

The words of this method tell what it is: a "model" or ideal enactment of a desired behavior lets learners discover what actions and standards are expected of them. Typical behaviors to model would be managerial skills, as making assignments, delegating, counselling, asserting, or disciplining. The model is usually presented via a medium like film or videotape, but may be performed by instructors in what amounts to a skit.

Behavior modelling differs only slightly from a demonstration. But it fits intellectual-cognitive rather than psychomotor objectives, and it usually presents the total skill before learners try out any behavior themselves. This has the virtue of offering a gestalt, or "big picture" overview of what may be rather complex interpersonal behaviors.

Interactive demonstrations

Any good demonstration is interactive—but unfortunately there are a lot of bad demonstrations!

The difference is that interactive demonstrations allow learner-watchers to do something instead of merely observe. They have things in their hands and they move those things in purposeful ways; they start doing so at the earliest possible moment. They move around, they ask questions, they *interact*.

Job Instruction Training (JIT) is a perfect format for this. Once the climate is set, the instructor tells and shows the first step of the task, as learners *do* that first step right along with the instructor. This permits cumulative repetition and the practice that makes perfect. After seeing and hearing how the second step is done, learners do both the first two steps, and then the first three, and then . . . .

Performance try-outs

Performance try-out is probably a necessary element in any "tough-minded" learning experience. Performance try-outs serve as ongoing feedback activity during the learning and as "criterion" tests at the conclusion of the program. Lest this imply that the performance try-out is used only for measurement and evaluation, let's remind ourselves that it is a significant learning experience too.

Trying out the new skill offers the "immediate application" andragogists urge for adult learning. Facilitative learners like Dr. Carl Rogers point out that much significant learning is acquired through doing. Trying out the new behavior starts the practice required to form habits. If tied into the rest of the learner's jobs, this practice can make the relevance of the new skill apparent to all learners.

"Performance try-out" is an integral, inevitable step in the four-part Job Instruction Training used so successfully during World War II to train quick replacements for drafted workers (see page 166). At its best, JIT lets learners try out the first step of a new task as soon as the trainer has completed the "tell and show" for that step—and before the "tell and show" of the second step, and is therefore an interactive demonstration.

Psychologically, a performance try-out is a perfect chance for learners to give themselves positive feedback for what they have already achieved, and to do some goal-setting for what they can still improve. By making this analysis, they re-examine the ultimate criteria and buy into the necessary self-improvement to get there. They have concrete evidence about the criteria they didn't achieve on their first attempt; they can better individualize their further efforts. But above all they have evidence about what they *did* achieve. This is a practical application of the "Look Ma! I'm dancin'!" effect that makes learning and instruction so exciting.

A performance try-out implies:

1. Completing the entire task, not just successive steps;
2. Remembering and adhering to the proper sequence;
3. Coordinating all the necessary skills and knowledge;
4. Meeting criteria for each step in the task; and
5. Demonstrating mastery, proving that the skill is available for use on-the-job.

We naturally think of try-outs of psychomotor skills, yet demonstrated mastery is just as vital for cognitive and affective learnings. When managerial and interpersonal behaviors involve a step-by-step process, an intellectual formula, or an emotional discipline, then performance try-outs are necessary. It would be unthinkable, for instance, to use behavior modelling which wasn't followed with performance try-outs by all learners.

Roleplays or simulations, or any exercise in which students do the calculations or the paperwork of a process are effective vehicles for performance try-outs. Sometimes the environment in which the behavior will be performed on the job is critical; if so, some simulation (noise, interruptions, temperature, outages) should be provided.

Brainstorming

Brainstorming is a specialized form of discussion. It is commonly used in real problem-solving situations. As a training method, its most frequent use is to teach learners to suspend judgment until a maximum number of ideas have been generated. A second use is to train people to listen positively to the ideas of others, refraining from negative comments which might cause the creative process to dry up.

Brainstorming applies the synergistic theory that groups can generate more ideas, and better ideas than all the individual members could do if they worked independently. It is therefore a useful method only when there are numbers of trainees; five or six is probably the minimum for a workable brainstorm.

The learnings occur because participants must discipline their inputs to the discussion. The controls occur through the instructions and through the behavior of the leader. Those instructions usually include these points:

1. Generate, don't evaluate. There will be time for evaluation later. In brainstorming, quantity is the goal: the more ideas the better. This doesn't mean that quality is unimportant—only that when people stop to challenge quality during the creative processes, they inhibit their creativity by moving into a judgmental mode too soon.

2. Create new ideas by amending those which have already been suggested. This amendment can take such forms as increasing, decreasing, adding, deleting, consolidating, substituting elements, or reversing. The "reversing" specifically prohibits negative statements. For example, one participant might say, "Promote her." It's okay for another to say, "Demote her," but it's not okay to say, "Don't promote her." To offer an alternative (demotion) is to generate another option; to state the suggestion negatively is simply to start the analytical debate.

3. Post all suggestions on a visible list in front of the group. This serves as a reinforcer for those who contribute and as an encouragement to further participation. When participants begin to analyze or question or debate, the leader uses "neutral reinforcement." That is to say, the leader at first ignores such behavior. Because there is no visible posting to the list, and no verbal response, the tendency to debate or analyze generally "goes away." If this neutral reinforcement doesn't work, the leader may remind the group that the analysis will come later.

The total brainstorm includes three phases: generation, analysis, and action-planning. In the second step, analysis, participants ask the contributors to explain strange terms or an unfamiliar idea. Analysis also includes evaluation. At this step the participants establish criteria for selecting the best ideas, then test each idea against those criteria. As ideas "fall out" because they don't meet the criteria, the group is left with a workable list of options. From these they can select the "best" solution. They are then ready to move to the third phase, action-planning. This consists of outlining the steps needed to put the adopted solution into operation.

Case studies

Case studies have been a popular way to get involvement and to bring discussion down to a reasonable level of concreteness. Case studies are thus antidotes for the tendency to avoid real issues by talking about theory rather than about its application.

In traditional case studies, participants receive a printed description of a problem situation. The description contains sufficient detail so learners can recommend appropriate action. The printed description must therefore include sufficient detail to ennable some recommendation but not so much that learners are distracted from central issues—unless, of course, sharp analytical skills and ignoring trivia is part of the learning objective.

Control of the discussion comes through:

- The amount of detail provided;
- Time limits, frequently rather stringent;
- The way the task is postulated, often a description of the desired output, such as a recommendation, a decision, or the outline of an action plan; and sometimes
- A list of questions for the group to answer on their way to the final total product.

There are numerous commercial sources of case studies. Training reference books contain a rich supply of tested cases. Creative T & D designers can develop cases typical of the organization for which the learning is designed. Andragogic instructors permit participants to write their own cases from real-life problems. They then exchange or share these home-grown cases as the material of the learning experience.

When participants generate the cases, the control of the content is assuredly more in their hands than in the hands of the instructor—and there can be little question about the perceived relevance. To make certain that pre-prepared cases are equally relevant, good T & D specialists ensure that each case contributes toward identified insights or a specified learning objective.

To increase the total participation, instructors often divide the class into small teams or buzzgroups. Because there are fewer people in each group, individual learners are more inclined to participate at higher levels than they would or could if only one large discussion were going on.

Action mazes

An action maze is really just a case study which has been programmed. Participants usually receive a printed description of the case, with enough detail to take them to the first decision point. The description gives them options from which to select. After the group discusses these alternatives, they request the leader to supply them with the next "frame." That frame will explain the consequences of their decision; not by a theoretical background, but in terms of the case itself. Let's look at an extremely simple sample:

> Donald Lipson has been on your shift for nearly seven years. You regard him as a marginal worker at best. At times he comes close to insubordination, and he once was sent home without pay for three days for fisticuffs in the canteen. He has been tardy seven times in the last two weeks. Today he arrives for work 45 minutes late. You feel you should:
> A. Give him one more chance, so you do nothing.
> G. Discuss this with him, so you ask him to see you at the next break.
> H. Discuss his tardiness with him. You thus stop at his work post just as soon as he reports for duty.
> S. Suspend him for one day without pay.

The group would discuss this phase. When they reach a decision, they inform the instructor, who then gives them a prepared response to their choice. Let's say they opted for "S." The prepared "consequence" might very well say:

> When you tell Lipson of his suspension, he merely shrugs and gives you a sneer as he packs up his tools and walks out. You wonder how anyone can be that cool, clearly feeling superior to the situation.
>
> Three days later the shop steward hands you written notice of Lipson's formal grievance. The basis of the grievance is that as a member of management you have interfered with Lipson's personal affairs and prevented him from discharging his duties as parent of a minor, handicapped daughter.
>
> On the basis of this, you decide to . . .

Of course the case continues, with additional options appropriate to the current state of the situation. When participants have made wise choices, they should face a new set of increasingly desirable options. When they choose badly they may be offered another chance at a previously rejected option, but in general bad choices lead to limited numbers of unattractive options. It's just good reinforcement theory, however, to leave them one chance to retrace their actions and work their way successfully out of the maze.

Instructors may elect to let the group "split" according to their choices. Thus in the Lipson maze, part of the class would select "S" as indicated. However others would follow the path for other options such as "A," "G," or "H." Similar splits and regroupings can occur at later phases of the maze. This permits homogeneous groups to work together. It is sometimes an effective way to let people discover the value of dissent, debate, confrontation, and compromise.

Even greater involvement is possible by allowing groups to generate original options when they are restless with the printed alternatives. The instructor may reinforce these by "inventing" desirable consequences—or route the group directly back into the maze if their solution would bring consequences similar to the published options.

Like any other training activity, each maze (indeed, each step of the maze) should teach something specific—as in the Lipson case: "Get the facts and the feelings before taking disciplinary action."

Incident process

The incident process is a specialized form of case study. It is usually used to teach analytical skills, or techniques for special problem-solving tasks such as handling employee grievances.

The incident process differs from normal case studies by giving participants far too little data to reach any decision—even preliminary decisions as in an action maze. The data are available to the instructor, usually in easy-access printed form. However, the instructor reveals the data only when asked a specific question to which the datum is a correct and relevant answer.

Learners thus acquire skill in knowing what questions to ask, how to phrase them, how to draw inferences from the data thus uncovered.

Because it teaches skills of interrogation, analysis and synthesis, the incident process is a popular tool for courses in labor relations, grievancehandling, accident investigation, investigative techniques and problem-solving.

Jigsaws

Jigsaws are about what their name implies. We all know what a jigsaw is: Participants put pieces together to complete an integrated "picture." Applied to the learning situation, participants may be given parts of a design or of an organization; they assemble these into a "System" or an "Organization Chart." They may be given the elements of a letter or a report; they put it together into a logical outline. They may be given the key variables of a decision-making problem; their task is to select from the pieces of the jigsaw the proper action to take for every conceivable combination of variables.

When instructors are teaching a prescription, there is only one way to assemble the pieces properly, and the review makes that clear. When the objectives are more individualized or creative, the design provides for ambiguities: different people (or teams) may assemble the pieces in different ways, then discuss the reasons and relative merits of each pattern.

Jigsaws are thus useful in teaching synthesizing skills, problem-solving skills, or organizational skills.

In-baskets

In-baskets are a form of simulation which gets at the realities of a job through the paper symptoms of that job. Learners get all the materials one might expect to find in an "IN" basket on a typical work-day. They must then process that paperwork until all the items are in the "OUT" basket. Thus the title. Usually the situation is described so participants must use only their own resources. For example, the directions may read: "You are alone at the office, and will be out of town the next week. You have just 60 minutes to dispose of the items in your IN basket. Complete as much work as you possibly can. Do not delegate decisions or actions unless it is proper for you to do so when you are actually at your desk."

Quite typically the exercise contains more work than can reasonably be completed in the allotted time, thus training in managing stress as well as in the content of the basket: learners deal with not only the rational decisions of the management problems, but also with the added realism of working against the clock. To enhance this, some instructors simulate emergency interruptions which require new decisions about priorities and add to the pressure.

Needless to say there is a review of how learners handled each issue raised by the paperwork. To provide feedback in time to be useful, instructors may have to do homework on their "evening off." They can ease this burden with numbered checksheets on which oft-used comments are pre-printed. For example:

    #11   Glad you handled this first.
    #17   Right! This section should be eliminated from the report.
    #23   How about putting this idea up into the first paragraph?
    #24   Would phrasing it as a question make it less "demanding?"

Instructors can also add some individualized comments, but a copious amount of basic feedback can be communicated by merely writing numbers on student papers.

After the comments are returned, group discussion is productive. It can: (1) clear up misconceptions, (2) re-examine common problem areas, (3) reinforce class-wide achievements, and (4) allow self-evaluation and goal setting. Because of this high potential as a measurement tool, in-baskets are attractive pre/post instruments. Assessment centers also make extensive use of in-baskets in their task of determining management potential.

Team tasks, Buzzgroups and Syndicates

Team tasks for buzzgroups (small teams of participants) result in some product, decision or recommendation to be shared with similar groups in the class. For example, case studies may be assigned to small teams rather than to the entire class. Whatever the task, the small groups report their findings or present their "product" in a report to other buzzgroups.

Typical products for these buzzgroups, also called "syndicates" in many parts of the world, are reports, decisions, or a set of recommendations, a Pro/Con analysis of some issue. The assigned task can run the entire gamut of the designer or instructor's creative imagination. It is limited only by its relevance to the announced objective and by the learners' perception that it is a useful endeavor.

Here are some samples:

1.   On the enclosed chart of a typical organization, indicate where the training and development responsibilities should rest. Specify the title, responsibilities, and reporting relationship of each T & D position.

2.   By referring to your instructor-outline for a training program now filled with lectures, identify: (a) content which the learners could probably supply from the inventory they bring to the class, and (b) the specific questions or tasks you would use to get them actively sharing what they already know about the subject.

3.   List the key criteria to be considered when selecting locations for branch sales offices in a metropolitan area. Include everything you can reasonably consider for such a decision.

4.   Do a Pro/Con analysis of short-interval scheduling applied to the revenue-accounting function. Be certain to consider variations within the sub-departments of Revenue Accounting.

Buzzgroup tasks can range from the one-level activities of those samples to such sophisticated tasks as those outlined in *Structured Experiences for Human Relations Training,* by Pfeiffer and Jones.

Buzzgroups can also be used to permit the members to generate an agenda for extremely andragogic programs. In any event, buzzgroup activity early in the learning process permits an andragogic investment of the learners' inventories. It also permits the instructor to get acquainted with the goals and personal styles of the participants.

Team tasks may be time-limited (as "Spend ten minutes developing your findings.") or open-ended. In the latter case the instructor says something like, "Let's keep at this as long as it seems a profitable investment of our time. I'll be around and amongst you, so give me a signal when the task is completed or when you begin to feel restless with the value of the task." In this open-ended approach, instructors need to be "sound sensitive." The noise levels of the buzzgroups tell instructors how teams are progressing through a task. Patrick Suessmuth (*Training,* June 1976) identifies four stages of sound level:

1. The Start-Up, when the sound level quickly peaks and plateaus.

2. Thought Collecting, a relatively quiet time. Sound levels drop sharply and then rebuild slowly. Suessmuth urges instructors to trust the silence and not to interrupt.

3. The Main Working Stage, when noise levels are generally high but fluctuating. This stage lasts a lot longer than either of the first two stages.

4. Finishing, the final stage, is characterized by a sharp drop in the noise level, and any rise after that is apt to be mere chatting. With these renewed noise levels, instructors should check groups to test their task completion. Thus many experienced instructors proceed to the reports after they have heard "the second lull" in the buzz levels.

Suessmuth further defined ideal group size. Two is "not really a group." Three is the "barest minimum." Four is reasonably effective. Best results come when five or six are in the group. In groups of eight or nine, subgroups or splinter discussions occur.

Agenda-setting buzzgroups

Teams of buzzgroups for agenda setting constitute a special use of the "small-group concept." We have already noted that they present an andragogic method of gathering inventory and goals-data from participants. This implies that the members determine all or part of the course content. This can mean that they decide on the objectives and areas of discussion; it can also mean that within an assigned list of objectives or within an assigned subject, they determine the issues or skills of special concern.

Such buzzgroups offer an excellent instrument for probing the feelings of learners about their achievement in reaching course objectives. In this context the groups meet after the program is well under way to recommend courses of action for the remaining time together.

Here are two examples: In an Effective Business Writing program, participants form small teams for 20 minutes to compile a list of questions they want answered and key issues they wish to discuss. A typical list would include things like, "Getting it through the boss without heartbreaking changes," "Can you use a preposition to end a sentence with?" and, "How to get rid of gobbledygook." The second example is from a workshop for experienced instructors. They might develop two lists. One is, "Things we already know for sure about teaching." The other list is, "Questions that come up to haunt us about our teaching."

Lists so generated are usually the basis for lively discussions by the entire class. At the same time they effectively let instructors know where the trainees "are really coming from," where they truly want to go—and how they feel about getting there.

Roleplays

Roleplays permit learners to reenact situations which they face on the job, or which they will face in the future, or which they perceive to be job-like. Through such reenactment they can reexamine previous behavior, try out behaviors they have just acquired, or experiment with behaviors which strike them as potentially useful.

Since there is some pressure associated with roleplaying, adult participants (even some trainers!) may resist this learning method. This seems unfortunate, so instructors frequently:

● Use the "multiple roleplay" format with many small roleplays going on simultaneously in various parts of the room.

● Keep the cast of characters quite small when using the multiple format.

● Reinforce the experimental behaviors of the roleplayers—never their "theatrical effectiveness."

● Keep the physical facilities, or "stage setting," at an absolute minimum. Attention focuses on the content or processes of the situation being enacted, not on the theatrical aspects of the play or the players.

● Move into initial roleplays with a minimum of fanfare. For example, a trainee might comment, "I have this problem with an employee who keeps evading the issue." The instructor then asks a question which will get the trainee to "play" the employee. It might be, "What was the last thing they said while evading an issue?" Once the trainee quotes the evader, the roleplay has begun. The instructor may soon ask the class, "Who would like to carry on this conversation?'' Or the instructor may designate someone to carry on.

- Call the process something else—as "a simulation" in the example above.

Such spontaneous roleplays add involvement, variety, reality, and specificity to the learning experience. When roleplays are more structured, role descriptions are given to participants. These often include not only the characters in the situation, but also an "observer's role." When observers are used, the points to watch for are listed much like those used in any other observation sheet. These are, after all, learning aids which help "imprint" action steps and standards in the minds of the observers.

Each role description should give the character a goal to shoot for in the conversation or situation—and perhaps a motive for that goal. Specific tips about how to play the role should be avoided at all costs. For example, it's probably better to instruct the player: "You intend to keep at this supervisor until you get an apology," than to say, "You regard yourself as a hardheaded individual who takes no nonsense from anyone—and you don't intend to give this supervisor any satisfaction whatsoever while the two of you are talking." That locks the players in, and prevents any real growth as they experiment with behaviors in reaching a roleplayed understanding.

Specific time limits can be assigned. This helps the roleplayers focus on reaching their objectives and cuts down on the occasional horseplay. When time is up, the instructor can merely clap hands to refocus attention and launch the next step. It is not important that the situation be "resolved" as in fiction or in the theatre—only that critical moments be reenacted. If roleplayers fail to reach their objectives in allotted times, they may very well be learning something! Indeed, they almost certainly are learning something about which behaviors are nonproductive. This can be a very rich learning if they have another opportunity to replay the situation using different behaviors.

The processes and the learners' perceptions of those processes are apt to be the appropriate focus on roleplays. This indicates the vital importance of a feedback, or debriefing session after the roleplays themselves. Such feedback may very well deal with the feelings as much as it deals with the intellectual content of the transactions. When the instructor wishes to focus on content, a checklist like those given to observers is useful.

For example, in a roleplay teaching the use of the open, directive, and reflective questions, the situation might very well call for reenacting an oral proposal to a client manager. Checklists for observers and post-roleplay feedback might consider such questions as:

- What objections were raised to the proposal?

- Which type of question did the proposer use when this happened?
- List any examples of "loaded" questions which slipped into the conversation.
- Check each time the proposer used an open question.
- How many reflective questions did the proposer use?
- How many of each type did the manager use?
- List examples of the open questions used by the proposer.
- List examples of effective reflective questions.

If the roleplay is designed not to focus on such specific techniques as questions, but rather to focus on feelings and perceptions, then the checklist for the observer's sheet might ask things like:

- What nonverbal symptoms appeared when there were differences of opinion?
- What did the participants say to share their feelings?
- When feelings were openly shared, how did the other people react?
- In what ways did the participants handle conflict?
- How did the participants show their regard (or non-regard) for the feelings of other participants?
- How did the participants show their regard (or non-regard) for the opinions of other participants?

To make the roleplays totally relevant and realistic, instructors sometimes ask participants to write up their own roleplays. The very exercise of describing a problem situation or a problem employee often creates new insights into the troublesome situation. To enact it, with peerlearners playing familiar roles, often gives trainees an entirely new perspective on the situation. More poignant learnings can result when the creators of the situation take an active role—even to "being" their own problem personality!

Reverse roleplays

Reverse roleplays are helpful methods for gaining understanding of another person's viewpoint. It works equally well when the objective is to see how oneself is perceived by others. As the title implies, at a critical moment in the roleplay, participants switch roles. Thus the "supervisor" becomes the "supervised"—and may get brand new insights into what it feels like. Interviewers, playing an interviewee in class, can better emphathize with the penetratingly personal questions they themselves asked just a moment ago—or that they ask every day on the job.

Reverse roleplaying requires sensitive monitoring by the instructors. First they must know just when to switch the roles. Next they need to make certain that during the debriefing or feedback session, all participants have the chance to share the feelings they experienced during the enactment.

Doubling roleplays

Doubling roleplays lets observers of the roleplays get into the action when they feel moved to do so. They simply step behind the current player and become another "body and voice" for that character. If their reactions to the dynamics and interplay differ sharply, then the roleplay is indeed exposing varied perceptions to a single stimulus.

There are several reasons why observers might want to get up out of their seats and take an active part in the roleplay. Perhaps they want to help a current player out of a distressing situation. Perhaps they feel that a current player is missing an opportunity. Perhaps they think a current player is being unrealistic. Perhaps they just want to offer another solution to a problem.

When doubling is used to encourage examination of alternative ways to handle a situation, it constitutes a kind of brainstorm at the application level. If we look at the methods on a kind of continuum, we can see that doubling is an enacted brainstorm just as roleplaying is an enacted case study.

Rotation roleplays

Rotation in roleplays is just a slight variation on doubling. Instead of several people ending up as one character, one learner replaces another participant in the roleplay. Such replacement can be spontaneous, like the "tag dances" at the senior prom. In this case the learners are in greater control of the content and processes. The rotations can also be managed by the instructor, who quietly asks an observer to enter into the roleplay as a designated character.

An obvious advantage of rotation is that the participative base can be spread throughout the class. More subtly, this form of roleplaying permits added dimensions to the analysis of the situation or to the motivation of the characters.

Finding metaphors

When humans are emotional, they call things by the wrong names. Out of anger we call someone a beasts; out of love we call the same person a baby doll! This is metaphor, and the search for metaphors can be a growthful experience.

To come up with the right image, we must analyze and synthesize; above all we must imagine . . . must use that creative right brain of ours. Many searchers for metaphor occur in adult training:

- The T-shirt exercise: you inscribe a T-shirt with a saying that captures my character or behavior; I do the same for you,
- The Library Exercise does the same thing with book titles,
- The Movie Marquee does it with film titles,
- Collages are pictorial metaphors from photos in old newspapers and magazines assembled by a person or a team to capture the spirit of an idea, a movement, an event, or an organization—or whatever else instructors or students wish to symbolize in order to express their feelings or ideas.
- In Cinquain individuals or groups compose a five line poem:

    1.   The name of the object;

    2.   Two words describing it;

    3.   Three action words: what it has done, where it is going, what it will do;

    4.   Four words of feeling: what it means to you or to someone else; and

    5.   A one word synonym: how you feel about it.

As the instructions for one metaphoric search explain: "All of us seek ways to understand, interpret, and synthesize our experience. We now call this 'Putting it all together.' Ancients did so with poetry; they sought synonyms, comparisons, images, metaphors." So do adults in T & D settings seek meaning by finding metaphors for their projects and problems, their loved ones, organization, or one another . . . even for "this training program."

Simulations

Simulations are somewhat like action mazes being roleplayed. Usually they are extensive designs with carefully programmed decision points. Participants may serve as the board of directors or members of a consulting team, working with a mythical firm. They are given data about a number of external conditions, internal situations, and critical decisions.

Their roles may be "generalized" ("You are all members of . . . ") or specified. In the latter case, one person is specified as Chairman of the Board, another as Vice-President of Finance, another as T & D officer, and so on until all critical viewpoints are represented in the simulation.

In either format the participants discuss the critical situations and make their decisions. When that step takes place, they get feedback about the consequences of those decisions. The programs are sometimes simply printed for instructors to distribute, sometimes put onto a computer as a form of computer-assisted instruction.

Titles like "Planet Management," "The Redwood Controversy," or "The ABC Corporation from 1980 to 2050" reveal the scope of existing simulations.

Typically, simulations involve teams of learners working together. They are thus effective in team-building programs, or in providing a "laboratory" of group dynamics. In-baskets are actually simple, one-person simulations.

Games

Games result when simulations are made competitive, with teams vying to see who makes the more effective decisions. Some T & D specialists feel that the gamed simulations increase the energy and commitment of the participants . . . that they add motivation to the learning.

Simpler games are used in a variety of ways. Tinker-Toy®projects can be used as a medium for learning team processes. Some games can be used to make didactic points. Among these are structured games such as those published through agencies like Science Research Associates of Chicago. A typical SRA product is Erwin Rausch's "Supervisory Skills" from the Simulation Series for Business and Industry.

Even simpler didactic games can challenge individual learners. One of these is the common puzzle about connecting nine dots into four interconnected straight lines (Fig. 10.4). The instructions prohibit lifting the pencil from the paper, so the puzzle cannot be solved without exceeding the implied boundary of the dots. Thus it teaches the wisdom of "going outside the problem in order to solve the problem."

Horn and Zuckerman's *The Guide to Simulations/Games for Education and Training* describes, in over 400 pages, many commercial games for T & D use.

"The Prisoner's Dilemma" (often called "Win As Much As You Can") is used to develop collaborative skills. University Associates of La Jolla, California, have published two series listing many such games: *Handbook For Group Facilitators* and *Structured Experiences for Human Relations Training*.

When people participate in games, many behaviors manifest themselves.

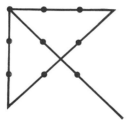

Fig. 10.4.

A simple didactic game.

Some of these behaviors may be identified as contributive to or counterproductive to group goals. Thus games are sometimes used in organization-development programs as both diagnostic and training tools.

In some therapeutic training, games may be used for self-fulfillment and self-actualization. Characteristic of this trend are the "New Games," epitomized in the activity of the New Games Foundation. Their motto is "Play Hard. Play Fair. Nobody Hurt." As one might imagine, new games stress the experience of playing—not the winning. They encourage creativity, and urge that the players stay in control of the game rather than get under the control of the rules of the game. Thus players may take an old game, change a few rules—and develop what they call a "new game." Winners and losers are rarely identified; if people keep score, it's usually in their heads and on no visible scoreboard.

Typical of the New Games is "Dho Dho Dho," an exercise in risk-taking or in chest-and-breath-development—it all depends on how the players wish to use it! Two teams play "Dho Dho Dho," and there is a physical baseline which they cross as their peril . . . and one at a time. A member who crosses the line into "enemy territory" must continue to utter the phrase "Dho Dho Dho" until back home. Failure to keep speaking means capture; thus the breath development. However, anyone tagged by an invader still uttering the phrase must join the other team. Winning isn't the object, so the game ends whenever the groups agree that it has served its purpose—in exercising risks, maintaining breath, or just plain having fun.

Of course games can be used to develop specific skills, for example, to develop spontaneity and thinking on one's feet. The "Long Tale" helps with these goals. Someone launches a ficitious story, gets it to critical point, and then points to another member to take over. This game can also help develop active listening skills; if you aren't listening you can't possibly pick up the narrative with a relevant "next chapter." Self-disclosure can be encouraged by a kind of "Fruit Basket Upset" game in which people must change places when leaders (or fellow participants) call out such challenges as "Do you find your present work assignment challenging?" or "Do you feel that you are getting something out of this training?" or "Do you feel that your ideas are being heard by the group?" or "Do you feel uncomfortable revealing how you feel about these questions?" All who answer "yes" must hurriedly exchange places.

But often the new games are invented by the players themselves—and always the rules of new games can be changed whenever the players agree. The games are ended in the same way. A description of many new games appears in *The New Games Book of 1976* by Doubleday and Company, one of their Dolphin books. That volume contains directions for 60 games in the New Games tradition.

Whether the instructor uses new games or traditional games, the motives tend to be greater involvement. Thus light games sometimes appear right after lunch when some competition—even some physical activity—can help regenerate the body functions.

Clinics

Clinics, in learning designs, are sessions in which learners devote their energy to solving a given problem. Clinics thus use the discussion format. They are helpful in developing problem-solving, decision-making or team membership skills. If the clinic is to be truly useful, participants must view the problem as real or relevant to their own jobs. It should provide for inputs from all students so it meets the adragogic or facilitative criterion of using learners' experience and valued skill to expanding their capabilities.

The second edition of *The Training and Development Handbook* (McGraw-Hill, New York, 1976, p. 34-35) says that the group "usually confronts real-life situations in order to establish a manner and method which makes them more successful." It points out that field trips, role-plays, and demonstrations form the basis of this diagnosis. Reith, the author of the chapter which discusses clinics, suggests that members of the clinic need to share a common interest. All this implies that a clinic might address a real-world situation, come up with a real solution—and still be a learning experience. That can happen, of course, only if the problem-solving processes are examined concurrent to and as part of the clinic.

Critical incident

Critical incident method also identifies and analyzes actual participant experiences as a basis for better understanding real problems, or for expanding insights by analyzing the "critical incidents" in the careers of the participants.

The rationale is that all experience can be a source of learning—but that some moments are of such critical impact that they significantly mold future behavior. Concentration on these incidents permits a generalization about a far greater sampling of relevant experience than instructors can supply.

The critical-incident method varies slightly from the clinic or from just having participants write up their own case studies. It doesn't ask them to identify problem situations for class analysis—but rather to describe the details of an incident which "changed their lives." Sometimes known as the "peak-experience" approach, this method is used extensively in upper management or executive development programs. The critical-incident approach enhances the validity and perceived relevance of the course content because the incidents come from the learners themselves—and are perceived to have great value.

Fishbowls

"Fishbowls" constitute another special kind of discussion. The title comes from the structuring, where at certain phases some of the discussants sit in the center (the fishbowl!) to discuss the issue. Other members observe this fishbowl, and will eventually take a place in it themselves.

Fishbowls may be used as instruments for analysis of group processes, or as instruments to control the content of a topical discussion. Technically, the method works about like this:

1. Choose a vital subject.
2. Prepare six to eight catalytic questions for the moderator.
3. Assign or draw numbers for all participants.
4. Arrange chairs into an inner ring and an outer ring.
5. Place participants with the odd numbers in the inner ring.
6. Even-numbered participants take seats in the outer ring.
7. Designate one inner-ring moderator to use the questions in arousing and maintaining the discussion.
8. Tell others in the fishbowl (inner ring) that their role is to keep the discussion going—but to limit their inputs to no more than one minute per input.
9. Appoint the outer-ring members (even numbers) to different roles, with people specifically assigned to observe:
   - The number of times each person speaks.
   - The number of times the discussion drifts to other topics.
   - Who interrupts, and who is interrupted
   - Facial and other nonverbal communications.
   - Disagreements: with and by whom?
   - Any conclusions about the subject or the processes.
10. At the appointed time, stop the fishbowl and feed back the data gathered in step 9.
11. Repeat steps 7, 8, 9, and 10 but with the even-numbered people in the fishbowl and those with the odd numbers assuming the observer roles.

Used in the manner described there, the fishbowl is clearly more concerned with group process than with course content. If instructors wish content to be the focus, they can divide the group into small buzzgroups, each of which discusses all of the catalytic questions. Each group also designates the sequence in which its members will participate in the fishbowl. At the appointed time, the first fishbowl starts. Only fishbowlers may speak, but if they misrepresent their group a "caucus" can call them back for short re-instructions or for a change of representative.

When fishbowls take this form, participants can acquire both the content of the discussion and skill in reflecting group opinions. To ensure this last learning for all trainees, the instructor must watch time limits carefully to make sure that all students serve as representatives in the fishbowl for a useful period of time.

T-groups

Laboratory training (through T-groups) has been a major thrust in training and development for the past two decades. It is controversial. For one reason, the behaviors it encourages are often self-disclosure and openness. These are behaviors which many people feel the oganization's real world ultimately punishes. Others attack "sensitivity training" (what T-groups and laboratory training amount to) because of some of the excessive activities which have taken place in actual training sessions.

The word "laboratory" helps explain the method. The T (for Training) group may be given a task, or even instruments—but the feedback and thus the learnings focus entirely on group processes and interpersonal relations. This provides insight into how groups behave. How one behaves as an individual, how one's behavior is perceived by others, and how one influences the group. Such insights tend to be so personal that they exist almost totally in the affective domain.

Since the T-group is conceived to be a leaderless unit, success depends very, very heavily upon the skill of the process observer. To serve in this role an instructor needs special upgrading. A typical part of the process feedback in laboratory training is observing the emergence of leaders, the failure of other members to achieve leadership, the impact of each comment and behavior upon other members and the entire group. The feedback tends to grow progressively more personal. Sensitivity training is not for amateurs!

Hot roleplays

Hot roleplays are used to resolve issues which arise in the dynamics of classroom processes. This type of roleplaying differs from structured roleplays in that no instructions are given to participants; it is a spontaneous outgrowth of the classroom dynamics. Thus hostilities between members, characteristic behaviors of students, deep misunderstandings, or blockages of group processes can become the content of a spontaneous, "hot" roleplay. The only instructions are those which come extemporaneously from the instructor who decides that the best way to get the issue out into the open is to use a hot roleplay.

Hot roleplays can become psychodrama. In this usage, the purpose is therapy. Psychodrama should be undertaken only by trained psychologists. Dr. J. L. Moreno did a great deal of psychodrama while living; now his widow continues the work. There are institutes of psychodrama, and recent publications explaining theory and technique. *Psychodrama, Theory and Therapy,* by Ira Greenberg, is available from Behavioral Studies Press.

Words like "Alter-Egoing" or "Magic Shop" or "Magic Wand" appear as titles of forms of hot roleplaying. The Magic Wand might work when a participant says, "If I could just tell that so-and-so what I really think!" The instructor hands the participant a pencil or a pointer and says, "Okay. This magic wand gives you the power to do just that. I'm So-and-So. Tell me off!" Magic Shops are similar: "You're in this magic shop and you have enough money to buy anything you see. What can I get for you today?" Or there are Empty Chairs. The roleplayer fills them imaginatively with someone with whom communication comes hard—and starts communicating.

Such applications tend to be therapeutic, but not all hot roleplays have therapy as their objective. Keener insights into how one appears to others can result from Alter-Egoing. For example, during class activities one participant might rather consistently "put down" others in the group. The process observer, after such an overstatement, might try to let the overstater see the impact of that behavior by a comment like, "We're all really pretty damn stupid, aren't we." Or again, "old-timers" may repeatedly preface their remarks with "In my 27 years with this outfit." If the observer feels this is causing others to resist the old-timer, the observer might say, as a kind of echo, "I see you telling us that without your seniority we can't make proper judgments." These examples may be crude, but they explain why this method is known as "hot" roleplaying. When participants Alter-Ego each other as a structured exercise in sharing perceptions, the heat can get downright tropical!

OD data gathering

Organization development data gathering uses a great many "hot" interventions if feelings are impeding the collection of "cooler" data. Feelings may be so deeply suppressed that the consultant feels lesser methods will never uncover them. A common technique is Organizational Mapping, in which people take a position reflecting such things as their relative influence, or their relative comfort with other members of the group.

Another method is "Polling" in which a paper-and-pencil instrument is used so members can indicate whom they perceive as most and least influential, or most and least helpful, or most and least cooperative—or most and least anything else the consultant feels would be helpful data for their renewal effort.

"T-Shirting" or "The Library" also reveal perceptions about how members of the group relate to group goals and to one another. In T-Shirting they decide what the inscription should be on each other's T-shirts. Typical products of this exercise are "There Must Be A Better Way," or "I Am So Smart I Make Myself Sick," or "Tomorrow Has Been Canceled Due To Lack of Interest." In The Library, book titles are assigned to each member: *In Cold Blood, Once Is Not Enough,* or *The High and The Mighty* were products of one such intervention.

Another form of data gathering is the compilation of "Do More/Do Less" lists. Every member prepares a list for every member, headed with two titles: "I wish you would do more of this" and "I wish you would do less of this."

These polling activities are really searches for metaphors in order to get at the truth of perceptions. The metaphor can also be physical, as in "physical representations."

Neurolinguistic Programming (NLP) observes eye movement and other unconscious physical behaviors to identify patterns of thought and feeling. This is highly technical data gathering and analysis, requiring the services of a trained specialist.

"Maps" require people to position themselves in a row (and agree that they are properly sequenced!) in relation to things like relative influence, power, flexibility—any issue requiring clarification and resolution. A tougher map reflects working relationships: in a furniture-less room, you are to stand near people with whom you enjoy working, away from those with whom you feel friction. This process itself is revealing! Explanations about why you are where you are can lead to open identification of problems and action planning to overcome them.

By their very titles these methods declare that they are unusual . . . not a part of the ordinary instructor's repertoire. They assuredly do not come up very often in day-to-day classroom situations. But they are there, available for that small percent of learning situations where the new behavior is highly threatening. Such methods become especially useful when personal blockages in group dynamics make it impossible for the learner to take initial or significant steps toward new insights and new behavior.

GROUPINGS OF METHODS

The well-rounded lesson plan in T & D programs will undoubtedly involve more than just one method. Variety is an important ingredient in adult learning experiences.

Certain standard groupings of these methods have proved useful to T & D specialists.

Consciousness raising activities cover a whole range of group and deeply introspective exercises. Many forms of meditation are taught in management, executive, and supervisory programs: Yoga in the Executive Suite is no longer an absolute rarity.

Health and wellness has entered the organizational purview, with special staff and consultants helping people learn a range of personal behavior from better diets through physical exercise to self-hypnosis. Aerobics, wilderness survival treks, or addiction programs with their wide range of interventions would all be part of this consciousness raising group.

The sources of these methods offer an interesting contrast: there is the research of Neurolinguistic Programming and Whole Brain Creativity—and then there is the mysticism of Eastern culture that jet-age transportation and electronic communication make available to everyone.

Job Instruction Training (JIT) is a four-step process designed to train one worker to do one job. It was developed during World War II as an efficient method to get quick worker replacements and maintain production in critical war efforts. It involves a lecture, a demonstration, a performance try-out, and a critique. These are usually called the "Tell, Show, Do, and Review" steps. There is more to it, like making the worker comfortable, begin certain learners can see the elements of the demonstration, and redoing those steps which don't come up to standard. But even with these embellishments, Job Instruction Training is an elegantly simple way to achieve efficient, productive learning.

Learner Controlled Instruction (LCI) has come into prominence in very recent years. It is often called "Open Classroom," but should not be confused with those wall-less learning centers in which educational materials are stored for rather random access by permissive instructors—or for highly rigid use by Hitlerian teachers. In true "open classrooms" learners actually control many of the basic decisions of the learning process.

Learning objectives, for example, may be assigned, or delegated to learners. When learners establish their own objectives, they secure guidance from the staff and negotiate a "contract" which will define the test of achievement. The contract is thus a description of what the learner will be able to do at the end of the learning. It is usually accompanied by a "learning map" which outlines the resources and activities which ought to contribute to that achievement. These are best when they are collaborative products of both the learner and the instructor or instructors. Maps tend to include a list of many activities; reading, discussion, demonstrating, watching films, creating some design or product.

LCI systems delegate as many as six decisions to the learner:

- The objectives,
- The pace of the learning,
- The sequence of the learning activities,
- The methods,
- The materials to be used in the learning, and
- The evaluation of the learning achievements.

It is quite possible to delegate only some of these decisions. Any such delegation is a form of andragogy and a step toward Learner-Controlled Instruction. LCI, as Roger Harrison notes, is especially useful when the learning needs to "radically avoid the creation of dependency relations" and/or when an objective is to strengthen the learner's initiative. (*Simulation and Games,* March 1977, p. 74)

Conferences tend to be gatherings of people from a given profession, and the activities within a conference can range from lectures through discussions to actual clinics or workshops.

Workshops are often announced in organizational training programs. More frequently workshops are public affairs, attended by personnel form a number of organizations. True workshops are extensive clinics, addressing a specific problem and hopefully resulting in some sort of product. Typical products are action plans, policy statements, or *bona fide* materials which participants can use when back on the job. For example, workshops on training methods might cause participants to spend class time creating the descriptions for roleplays to be used in programs "back home." They might go home with the write-ups for case studies, or with the design for the pieces of a jigsaw. A workshop on problem-solving may very well produce the action plans for solving a number of the realworld problems the participant has processed during the workshop. A letter-and-report-writing workshop can produce drafts of answers to current letters, or outlines or key sections of a report due soon after the workshop ends.

Seminars in graduate schools mean that members of a class undertake individual research responsibilities on some phases of an announced subject. They then report their findings to other seminarians. In industrial contexts the word has been considerably distorted. It is often used to describe highly structured learning designs—and just as often used to describe a parade of lecturers who speak on varying aspects of a central theme. Such parades are more properly designated as colloquies. However, that word appears less and less in the advertisements.

A *symposium,* according to a dictionary, is a convivial party (after a banquet) with music and conversation. It's hard to see why T & D specialists see the symposium as a useful format—at least if they abide by that definition. In actual practice most T & D symposia tend to be colloquies . . . collections of opinions on a subject, or formal meetings at which several specialists deliver short addresses on a single topic or on closely related topics. If that's what happened at a symposium you attended, take your pick: Were you at a symposium, a colloquy, or just a panel?

SUMMARY

Asking what method to use for a training program is like asking a physician what instrument to use for surgery. It all depends on the nature of the operation! Fortunately the contemporary T & D specialist, whether a designer or an instructor, has a vast range of instruments from which to choose.

CHAPTER

HOW IMPORTANT IS TEACHING TECHNIQUE?

GENERAL CONCEPTS

In *The Imperial Animal,* Tiger and Fox make a wonderful comment about the nature of teaching: "We have a propensity to learn. We also have a propensity to teach. These combine to make the teacher-student relationship a very satisfying one. That it often is not may very well be that . . . what is primarily a social relationship has become a technical transaction." (p. 152)

If the instructor-learner relationship is reduced to nothing more than a technical interchange, that is indeed sad.

Nonetheless, anybody who teaches or leads conferences knows that there are "little things" you can do to make the experience more successful. Those "little things" are called technique.

In a sense, the instructor manages a series of stimulus-response (SR) patterns. These SR dynamics involve several relationships: interaction between the learner and the program content; interaction between one learner and other learners; interaction between the learner and the instructor. Tiger and Fox feel that the last one is least important, that "Students learn best when their attention is wholly on what they are doing rather than on the teacher." (p. 167)

THE INSTRUCTOR'S USE OF OBJECTIVES

A most useful instrument in the instructor's professional toolkit is the list of learning objectives. We might look at it this way: instructors need some way to focus the attention of all learners on one single concept. What better focus than the goals of the learning? How do instructors bring this about? At the very first class session, people sit down with a list of the course objectives. They discuss the meaning, the impact, and the importance of applying each one. This gets their attention where Tiger and Fox want it: "on what they are doing." Some instructors go further, emphasizing the objectives with visual aids. Such visual statements may:

1.   Help control discussions. When students see the printed words they tend to filter their comment by asking "Is it appropriate?" In this case, a visual reminder by the learning objectives helps them make a good decision.

2.   Help smooth transitions from one segment to another by providing a "road map" of the total course design.

3.   Increase the value of "process" sessions by causing learners to ask themselves what they have achieved and what remains for them to learn.

4.   Give new focus and emphasis to the goals, reminding learners why they are in the training.

If there have been pre-training conversations between students and their immediate "boss" about the learning objectives, the instructor can: (1) mention that, or (2) refer back to written notices about the program, which ought always to feature the learning objectives very prominently.

The objectives are useful in other ways as the program continues. They can serve as a reasonable control when students wander from the subject. A discreet inquiry about how the comment or activity contributes toward the goal will either bring learners back to a profitable path—or show the instructor some exciting new dimension of the learning experience! When learners cannot see the relevance of class activity, instructors can help establish that relevance by analysis of the objectives. When giving themselves feedback about their own progress, the only real reference point learners have is comparing their present ability to the ultimate objectives.

At the end of the program, a list of objectives is most useful. In quiet, introspective moments all learners can evaluate their own achievements for each objective. A group discussion can refocus on the desired behaviors and how they can be applied on the job. Action planning which relates to learning objectives has sharper direction than mere general resolutions to "do good things."

Let's summarize: because the objectives are so useful, professional instructors use them as a technical instrument. They insist on pretraining communications at which learners (and hopefully their bosses) set expectations by analyzing the objectives. They hold early discussions using the objectives to refine those expectations and to clarify questions; they revisit the objectives at intermediate "Quaker Meetings," open discussions in which learners can explain how they feel about the program and their progress. They summarize at the end by looking at the objectives as a way to check the learners' sense of achievement, to double-check that all material has been covered and all goals met, and as a way to focus on on-the-job application.

ONGOING MEASUREMENT

Instructors use periodic feedback as an effective way to motivate their learners.

Whenever possible, they provide some early "pre-test" activity which lets all the learners discover where they are in relation to the ultimate goals. Experienced instructors tend to avoid the word "tests." They point out that this is really a "diagnosis," or a way to "find out what we already know and what we already can do." In this sense, the pre-test may be called a "baseline" or an "index" of the learner's beginning "inventory."

If the same pre-test instrument is used again later in the program, learners get an ongoing sense of their accomplishments.

If parallel instruments are used for a final (or "terminal") examination, learners have concrete evidence that they have indeed met their learning objectives. The point is that the instructor must always key the measurement and feedback in with the objectives.

There are instruments for affective as well as cognitive goals. Agree/Disagree questionnaires can show how people have changed their positions on issues central to the program. There are, of course, no "right or wrong" answers in measuring feelings. For example, these samples from a questionnaire on womanhood:

Indicate whether you Agree strongly, Tend to agree, Have no opinion, Tend to disagree, or Disagree strongly with these statements:

- Marriage is an institution which primarily benefits males.
- Job vacancy notices should not mention sex.

- ● Women should receive preferential treatment right now as an indemnity for past discrimination.
- ● The charge that women are over-emotional is a male smokescreen.

These are not used in programs about Women's Liberation; rather they are used when the learning objectives involve values, communication styles, or mental flexibility—what the ASTD Competence Study calls "Intellectual Versatility."

Ongoing measurement need not use paper-and-pencil formats. They can be performance try-outs, such as assembling or repairing an instrument, troubleshooting a machine, or performing a mental regimen—like successive steps in an assertiveness model or a rational problem-solving process. Again, the important thing is to relate the measurement to one of the learning objectives. Thus there is great value in checksheets on which learners score their own performance on details of the task they are learning to master.

QUESTIONING TECHNIQUES

Questions are an important instrument for professional instructors. They employ questions as routine devices for maintaining communication; they may even use questions as a control device for "troublesome" students. Let's examine the use of questions in greater detail.

Directive questions can review factual material and help learners discover new insights. Examples: "What is the square root of 144?" "Give an example of horizontal loading as opposed to real job enrichment."

Reflective questions can double-check feelings, can consolidate issues and insights. Example: "You feel then that your own job is confining?" "Am I correct in sensing that you feel we've explored this topic more than enough?"

Open questions cannot be answered "Yes" or "No" or with facts. They are thus useful in probing for feelings and in testing a learner's inventory. "How do you feel about the Equal Rights Amendment?" "What do you know for sure about how adults learn?" When good instructors sense latent apathy or hostility, they tend to use open questions. In both one-on-one and group sessions, open questions can communicate a concern which allows apathetic or negative learners to redirect their psychic energies.

Besides knowing when to use each type of question, professional instructors master some other questioning techniques.

First, they avoid the "Any questions?" trap. To ask a class "Are there any questions?" rarely produces anything at all—much less cogent interrogation! So professional instructors stimulate with carefully planned provocative questions which:

- Elicit specific opinions or feelings,

- Require an examination of all sides of an issue,

- Permit a learner to share a relevant valued experience, or

- Arouse sufficient interest that the answers trigger related questions from the class.

Maybe after instructors positively reinforce student-initiated questions, the "Any questions?" question will produce a flurry of questions. But by-and-large, students ask questions when: (1) the class activity stimulates them to do so, (2) they feel reinforced for asking, or (3) they are stimulated to ask another question because the instructor asked a good question in the first place.

Professional instructors have learned not to interrupt pondering students with follow-up questions. They wait for the student to respond. The follow-up (or "tandem") question usually stems from the instructor's desire to help the student. It rarely works. If the initial question has been well-conceived, students will need a few seconds to think. Let them do so. Asking another question, or rephrasing the old one, just gives them two things to think about. One was enough! This is especially true when learners are having trouble formulating their answers. Instructors just add frustration by rephrasing or changing the question. A wonderful cartoon captures the learner's viewpoint on this; the exasperated student exclaims, "Just when I thought I had the answer, I forgot the question!"

Experience also teaches instructors to ask the question before naming the respondent. Why is this important? Because it permits *all* the students to decide how they would answer. If not called upon, they can check their intended response with the one given—and be ready to participate if it is incorrect or incomplete. Such covert involvement keeps them "attending" the entire session; it avoids the daydreaming potential which comes when they have been excused from answering a question by an instructor who asked someone else before even asking the question. Because all students "attend" all the time, they are more apt to enliven and enrich the discussion by comments or questions of their own.

Experienced instructors call on students in an irregular, unpredictable sequence. They don't go around the room in clockwise or counterclockwise patterns. They don't go down the alphabetical roster. Students who do not know when they will be called on tend to answer every question in their own minds.

When students ask questions, professional instructors usually give the asker the first chance to answer. Why? Because the instructor may feel this will allow the learner to grow in self-confidence. Or because it will let askers discover answers of which they are capable, but which they may be ignoring for the moment.

As a second choice, instructors like to redirect a student's question to other class members. This keeps attention on the content rather than on a dominant instructor. It provides a helpful way for adults to invest their existing inventory in the learning process. It gives the instructor useful feedback about where the students are in their progress toward learning goals.

A poor third choice is for the instructor to answer the student question. There are, to be sure, times when this is appropriate, but only if:

1. The question deals with course logistics (only the instructor knows those answers), or

2. The questioner specifically asked for the instructor's opinion (and then it's "maybe"), or

3. It is appropriate or necessary to color the discussion by revealing the instructor's opinion, or

4. The class has been totally unable to come up with a right answer, and

5. A search elsewhere would delay processes beyond the value of the question.

That seems like a lot of times when instructors may legitimately give answers, but those "iffy" cases don't come up very often!

Professional instructors use questions to "get a discussion going." In *Teaching Tips,* W. J. McKeachie warns against asking questions which obviously have only one right answer. Discussion questions, he says, "Need to get at relationships, applications or analysis of facts and materials." He also identifies a need to frame the questions at a level of abstraction appropriate to the class. "Students are most likely to participate in discussion when they feel they have an experience or an idea that will contribute." (p. 54) Directive questions (with one right answer) are useful for review—not for stimulation.

GETTING ATTENTION VERSUS GETTING INVOLVEMENT

Instructors who seek dominance and attention rather than learning would do well to seek employment in the lecture hall, the pulpit, the theatre, or the night club rather than in the classroom.

The issue for instructors is, "Do I want to cause learning, or do I want to make a great impression?" Although the two are not incompatible, they are by no means synonymous.

Another way of looking at it goes like this: "Do I want to do all the work myself—or would I like the learners to do some of their own work by getting busy in learning activities?'' Real trainers and real instructors want to stimulate, not overpower; they want to facilitate, not to deprive or smother.

That being the case, questions which elicit thought, and activities which involve learners, replace startling statements and flamboyant stimuli.

Yet "centering" or "polarizing" techniques are necessary. They change attention from the previous topics of concentration to the reality of the learning. We have previously mentioned two ways to "center": reviewing objectives, and questions. Andragogic designs stress the importance of learner involvement in any centering method.

A traditional method has been to have the class "get acquainted with one another." This is especially common when participants come from various parts of the organization and are assumed to be strangers to one another. It's hard to know precisely what such introductions accomplish unless the class activity will use a great deal of interrelationships between learners. Since andragogic designs *do* depend upon this interrelating, the method of introducing is a technical activity deserving some attention.

A typical get-acquainted activity has each person stand up and share something biographical: name, position, seniority, family data, hobbies. Such disclosure lectures are often punctuated with lots of "uhs" and "ers" and awkward silence. They are usually accompanied by great waves of anxiety. One actual participant was so benumbed by this exercise that he literally couldn't remember his own name!

Thus creative instructors seek and use more creative yet more relaxing methods of handling introductions:

1.   "Dyadic Introductions" allow two members to share data together in a very small "community" before they introduce each other to the members of the entire group.

2.   The "Zip game," is useful is you have good evidence that the group is too "laid back" and will not take the training seriously. The first member gives the usual data: name, position, and one other personal detail, but speaks only to one person. That second person then adds a personal dossier before introducing the first person to the third learner. The third person adds personal details, and introduces the first two people to the fourth learner. This "snowball" and repetition continues until one introducer forgets a fact. The forgetter says "Zip," asks for the missing data, and starts all over again. The game is over when everyone has successfully introduced everybody else.

3.   "Cocktail Parties" provide everyone with a nameplate and a predetermined amount of time. They are given a goal to meet as many other participants as possible and to remember names and data which will help them help each other during the program.

4. A variation uses "sandwich boards," large placards worn across the chest. On this board the participant prints data for others to read and ask about or discuss. Name, home town, place of work, position title, and hobbies are typical content. A more active format has the sandwich board left blank; then when another person asks a question, that other person inscribes the answer on the sandwich board. The notion here is that the act of writing the data onto the board will help the memory.

Any of these introduction activities should help participants relate effectively to one another during the remaining learning action. In their *Structured Experiences for Human Relations Training* series, Pfeiffer and Jones describe many other ways to get group members involved and acquainted.

The goal behind all these introductions is for every participant to get acquainted with everyone else. That objective needs to be made very clear when the activity is announced and launched. If they are purely ritualistic, they become sterile. It is useful if the instructor explains convincingly that getting to know one another at the beginning helps a lot in achieving learning goals.

USE OF REPETITION

There is a mistaken notion that sheer repetition assists learning. Sheer repetition may assist memorization—but that means it's useful only in achieving knowledge. Repetition doesn't help much in comprehension or the other more advanced cognitive and affective objectives. Repeating a psychomotor behavior can provide the "practice that makes perfect," but even as we say that we should discover something else about the principle of repetition: It's repetition by the learner that pays off—not repetition by the instructor!

Repetition by the learner helps the "imprinting" process, memorizing key words, or perfecting psychomotor skills through drill. For other types of skill, repetition is most valuable when it's "repetition with a difference." That explains the value of having learners themselves put ideas into their own words . . . of hearing other learners express it in varying phrases. Their unique phrasing is original to each, and it gives learners "ownership" of the idea. It lets them personally adapt a stimulus so they are comfortable with it; it allows them to hear the same concept different ways from different people.

When drill takes the form of problems or simple case studies, it also offers repetition with a difference. Principles are applied repeatedly, but in different contexts or with different ingredients. Such drill permits repetition at the "application level," and reduces mere repetition of theory to a practical, useful activity.

For example, merely repeating "two times two is four" again and again is a sterile exercise. Asking how many children there are in a house with two families each of which has two children improves the experience accompanying the drill—and the ability to retain and apply the formula. There is real value in educational use of the literary device of "incremental repetition," or "repetition with a difference."

Many instructors like to provide too many examples for the most deliberate learners to complete. In this way all students get repeated drill—the fast ones just get to repeat the process more frequently than the slower students. By varying the complexity, this procedure also permits greater adaptation to the individual differences within the class.

THE INSTRUCTOR'S PHYSICAL BEHAVIOR

The days are pretty well gone when people thought instructors must look "imposing" in order to be in charge of a learning experience. Nor is there any very good evidence that distracting mannerisms distract learning. Audiences may notice such mannerisms in speakers, so maybe instructors who lecture a lot should be concerned about their gestures—but professional instructors who use more experiential methods can be less fastidious.

Even so, there are things to consider. Instructors who hide behind the furniture may not impact on the class as clearly as those who are "out front." Things like desks, podiums, or platforms send subtle messages that the instructor is something special. They establish barriers which impede two-way communication.

A fair amount of movement is probably desirable. That's easy to do if students are steadily involved in doing things themselves. Instructors just naturally move around the room, counseling and monitoring and reinforcing. The obvious technique is to remove focus from the instructor's physical activity by placing focus on the student actions.

Physical activity often involves the use of visual aids. Professionals don't obscure visual aids by standing in front of them. They locate themselves where they can point to the visual display and still maintain responsive eye-contact with learners. When there are questions (or even puzzled faces!) the instructor thus receives feedback and responds to it. Users of projected visual aids avoid getting "in the spotlight." That lets them avoid creating any shadow-plays on the image; it avoids printing the display in three-color process across the instructors' backsides.

If the visual aid is an outgrowth of class activity, it tends to have more impact and more learner involvement. Some instructors refer to these as "real-time" visuals. A real-time visual is the display that gets posted on the chalkboard, flipchart, or overhead projector as a result of student inputs. Or it is the schematic developed "on the spot" in response to a class inquiry. It is the "jerried up" model students created just because curiosity or interest prompted such energy.

When instructors develop such impromptu visual aids, they should observe a few fine points of teaching technique:

● They clean up as they go. Thus whenever a new inscription doesn't relate directly to one which is already there, good instructors know that it's time to erase and start all over.

● They try to make visuals, not mere "verbals." They do more than merely write *words* for people to look at. They find symbolic ways to express concepts and relationships. They have learned how to make stick figures of the human body, and how to do one-point perspective drawings.

● They have mastered a technique for printing speedily, legibly, and uniformly. Fig. 11.1 shows a system which tends to produce reasonably professional lettering in rapid time. (Another nice thing: it's legible, too!)

RELATING TO STUDENTS

Instructors, says Dr. Carl Rogers, should be "as concerned with their relationship with students as they are about the content of the course." This doesn't mean that they stand up in front of the class and immediately seek affection.

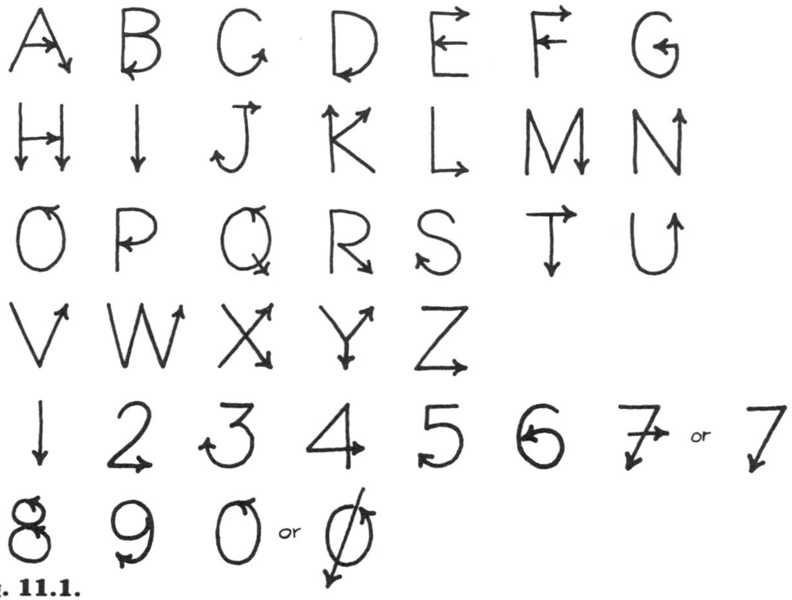

Fig. 11.1.

Unskilled ego-centered instructors do that. Nor does it mean that instructors win popularity contests—or that they confuse comradeship with a useful instructor-learner relationship. It does mean that they *care* about the relationship. That, in turn, probably means that they care about the learners . . . that they care enough to make certain that every one of them achieves all the desired learning objectives.

In a somewhat oversimplified way, this means that instructors consistently look for student behaviors to reinforce positively. Why? Because instructors know that people will tend to repeat behaviors for which they feel "rewarded." Thus when a student gets part (but not all) of a correct answer, the instructor commends the correct part—then follows with a question which encourages the learner to improve what's wrong or to add what's missing. The essential technique? To form the habit of doing this; to develop skill in locating "what's right"; to find out the private, unique personal "rewards" each person cherishes.

Beyond—or better, *before*—positive reinforcement comes letting students know that the program means business . . . that they are accountable for learning. This can be implied in the initial discussion about objectives. However, it's likely that this important message should not be implicit: it's wise to make a statement that when one is in training, the organization expects that learning will occur "just as our organization would expect you to complete your regular tasks if you were on the job today instead of here." Above all, the message that learning is a serious business is communicated by instructors who themselves are businesslike and professional.

This does not mean stiff formality or coldness. As Kohl points out in *The Open Classroom,* "A teacher has as much right to be angry, frustrated, impatient, distrustful as students and should let them know that . . . Only when a teacher emerges as another person in the classroom can a free environment based on trust and respect evolve." (p. 81)

Does this mean that instructors have little responsibility for self-control? Of course not. Judiciousness is a part of being businesslike. And that brings up the issues of language, personal appearance, and humor.

There is always a temptation to "do as the Romans do." In modern organizations the Romans nowadays are using lots of words which only a few years ago were considered to be in bad taste. No definitive studies prove this next point; but it does seem that when the instructor's language becomes too informal or profane, students lose respect for the learning experience. Conversely, stilted formal language can impede learning. Students may not know what those big words mean. An instructor's display of an extensive vocabulary can discourage or even humiliate learners. Yet some technical words are big words, and they are absolutely necessary. Instructors need not apologize for using jargon; it's the only correct word, and professionalism must involve a concrete, specialized vocabulary. Similarly, some earthy words are the only ones which precisely convey the feelings. Perhaps the moral is just this: use technical jargon and slang when it is accurate, necessary, and comfortable— but don't do either too much! The excesses, not the words themselves, are what may impede learning.

The instructor's clothing is unimportant as long as it doesn't call attention to itself, and so long as it is functional to the activities of the session. It would be ridiculous to wear a shirt and tie for a demonstration in the grease-pit of the service station. It would be socially uncomfortable to wear cut-off jeans to a conference involving upper management in the Board-Of-Directors room! Organizational norms usually tell instructors what to wear. Recent years have seen some changes in these norms. In the 1970s it became normal for men to wear slacks and sportshirts or leisure suits while teaching; pantsuits, or skirts and blouses have joined dresses as normal attire for women.

Humor is another thing. Like language and clothing, it involves the issue of taste. Since taste is an individual thing, humor isn't very universal in the learning world. The danger is that when one is "being funny," nobody will laugh. That silence can make an instructor mightly lonely! Since nobody can really define humor, only a few ground rules are much help to instructors. One vital criterion: the humor must be relevant to the topic or the immediate situation. Jokes seldom work if brought in just to let the instructor say something funny. Another important point: the joke should be kind, not scornful. It should not ridicule a person or a group. Next, the joke should be new to the listeners. It's difficult (if not impossible) to be sure that a relevant story hasn't made the rounds. So smart instructors follow the rule: if there's even a glimmer that this is an "old clinker," forget it! Finally, the joke should be short. They need not be one-liners, but nothing kills humor so much as embellishment. Added details belabor the point; adapting a story to local conditions is often painful; pretending that it happened to someone in the room seldom adds to the hilarity—it usually just makes the situation awkward and amateurish.

If instructors focus on learner needs, classroom dynamics make for pleasant, exciting relationships. However, there are such things as problem students. What does the instructor do when trainees refuse to invest energy in learning? . . . or when a trainee consistently distracts others?

Sometimes this takes peculiar twists. Maybe a student talks a great deal, consuming valuable class time and distracting other learners with irrelevant ideas. What's the "desired behavior"? Longer periods of silence, right? Reinforcement theory would urge the instructor to listen for significantly long periods of quiet. After such silence, the instructor should give the student a chance to do something pleasant—even if that "something" is to talk!

There's a general rule: "Never interrupt a talking student." Well, the case of the over-talker may be one exception. Instructors may have to remind such "chatterers" that time is limited—just to protect other learners. If instructors can send such messages in private counseling sessions, or at breaks, so much the better. That avoids calling the entire group's attention to the problem. But as a last resort, an instructor may need to be a timekeeper!

What about "the mouse," the student who talks too little or not at all? The instructor may get mice to "attend" with these techniques:

● Open questions, seeking opinions or feelings, produce answers which are easy to reinforce.

● One-on-one conversation, at breaks or over-the-shoulder may establish rapport and allow the instructor to reinforce private comments so the student will want to talk to the entire class.

● Small groups may be more comfortable for "the mouse" and make it easier for the instructor to "eavesdrop" and commend something about any input from the quiet one.

Then there is "the parrot" who talks an appropriate amount, but always quotes someone else, goes the party line, or avoids expressing any original idea. Instructors need to listen for the first trace (or "successive approximation") of originality, praise it, and call the attention of the entire class to the uniqueness of that idea. Special techniques include:

● Probing with open questions;

● Asking them to give Pro/Con analysis of a cliche'd opinion;

● Having them imagine what opponents would say in rebuttal to a bromide they've just expressed; or

● Having them work with others (and eventually alone) to find metaphors for the views they parrot or the theories, models, or processes the class is studying. For example, a computer might be "Otto" because it's so automatic; in one factory they call their robot "Clyde the Claw." Dr. Ned Herrman, in developing the right (or creative, intuitive) brain, urges metaphorical activity.

Parrots are troublesome to convert to creative contributors, but they are less disruptive to the group processes than "the mules" who take exception to everything said by instructors and anyone else:

● Again, Pro/Con analysis helps, making sure that the mule is required to contibute to both sides . . . and is reinforced for the "both-sidedness" of their analysis; or

● Paying very little attention to their negativism eventually helps mules who only seek attention.

Confrontation is probably a "No-No!" because the attention it involves may be perceived as positive reinforcement by both the mules and the rest of the class. If it must be done, the confrontation should probably occur privately, and must focus on the negative behavior—not degenerate into a debate about one of the issues raised by the mule in class.

"The donkey" is different from the mule; the donkey is treated like a jackass by other class members. When this happens the instructor is tempted to be a "rescuer," and in doing so may set up polarization with the rest of the class. It may be better to:

- Ask other trainees to find value in donkey's class comments;
- Patiently and privately analyze all the donkey's behaviors in order to find their real strengths which can be used to solve problems faced by the class or small teams;
- Use donkeys in low-visibility functions, as timekeepers or secretaries, which eventually lead to high-visibility roles like reporters or discussion leaders;
- Carefully watch for one really good insight that even their detractors will admire; and
- Remember always that the kidding may grow out of affection—and even when certain it doesn't, interpret any reaction you make to the derision *as if it did stem from affection.*
- In really dire cases, deal privately with the big kidders and ask them to "cool it."

In all these cases, reinforcement theory helps. If instructors can find no behavior to reinforce positively, then neutral reinforcement at least prevents the situation from worsening.

What does that mean? Merely doing nothing to encourage the undesirable behavior. For example, during discussions one trainee consistently wanders from the subject. The instructor merely says, "I see" or "Yes. Who else would like to comment?" or "Oh." There should be no further inquiry, no insistence upon an explanation. Or again, a trainee takes exception to many key principles. Rather than argue or draw attention to this, the instructor gives a minimum response: "This may become clear later," or maybe the instructor says nothing at all. The less attention to the behavior, the more likely it will disappear.

But that can be a slow process, and it isn't always easy to do. Furthermore, ignoring troublesome trainees may destroy the business-like atmosphere that supports other learners. How much heckling can you tolerate from a satanic "devil's advocate"? How long can noisy splinter conversations be allowed to distract? What is your obligation to get some activity from those who refuse to participate—even to do the performance tryouts?

At such times private counseling is probably necessary. Away from the classroom pressures, instructors may discover mistaken expectations or hidden reasons for the poor performance. They may help learners discover that the two can have a profitable relationship in reaching behavioral objectives. Some confrontation, gentle or forceful, may be necessary. There may even be occasions when the instructor must request the trainee to drop the program.

We need to distinguish between two behaviors: ongoing appropriate reinforcement and discipline. The first process is inevitable; the second is only rarely necessary in organizational classes or conferences.

When do adult instructors need to discipline adult students? Very, very rarely. Professionals agree that discipline is necessary only when their authority is being challenged. Now this doesn't mean each time the learner questions the correctness of data, or the tasks, or the processes. It's only when there is open defiance . . . only when the gauntlet has been thrown down so clearly and so persistently that the instructor can no longer function effectively with other learners. Instructors must deal with such an impasse, and discipline is one way of doing so.

Discipline in organizational training does not mean punishment. There is no authority for (and less sense in) making them "stay after school" or stand in the corner. Instructors can't give forty lashes or draw-and-quarter trainees. Verbal tongue-lashings are about all most instructors think of as available disciplinary action.

In *Dare To Discipline,* James Dobson points out that, "Once it succeeds, defiance becomes the logical recourse." (p. 106) Since instructors will never be able to please all their students on every issue, failure to deal with defiance means that the defiance will recur. Dobson points out that "Discipline and love are not antithetical," (p. 29) and that adherence to a standard is an important element of discipline. (p. 104) In organizational T & D, trainees who do not invest minimum effort in the learning process are not doing their assigned work. Why not return them to their regular workplace, with an explanation through regular channels?

If policy prohibits such expulsion, then isolation of the problem students as much as possible may minimize their ravages on other learners. When there are early signs of defiance, instructors may schedule individual or "small team" activity. This gives the defiant one less visibility, and therefore less reinforcement for the defiant behaviors. It also provides a chance to observe individual behaviors; instructors who do that often find the cause of the defiance, or the "private reinforcer" to use on the belligerent learner. Above all, the instructor has a closer contact because of the smaller group—and thus has a better chance of discovering something to reinforce . . . some successive approximation of constructive participation in class activities.

On rare occasions several problem students appear in the same session. Isolation is probably the most effective strategy after positive or neutral reinforcement have failed. Instructors don't want the negative ones to infect the more positive learners, so they seat troublemakers at the same table and assign them to the same buzzgroups. This doesn't solve the real problem, but it limits the scope of the damage such students can inflict.

Another solution which doesn't solve anything is direct eye-contact with the troublemakers. It doesn't reinforce their negativism, and it makes their behavior less public—but it probably throttles their energy, encouraging later, more active insurrection. It is useful only as a stopgap before private consultation when the instructor can get at the real root of the problem.

Incidentally, when people talk inappropriately, instructors might well use more directive questions: specific people are asked to reply to factual inquires. These offer more containment, and are appropriate when control rather than facilitation is necessary. But it's wise to remember that control is necessary only when other techniques have failed—and that it rarely becomes the central need in organizational T & D systems which have communicated and maintained a businesslike policy about learning. It is even less necessary in classes and conferences where teachers are facilitative and andragogic . . . where they remember B. F. Skinner's statement: "Only when the good will and affection of the teacher has failed as a reinforcer need we turn to the use of aversive stimulation." (*Technology of Teaching,* p. 20)

SUMMARY

Sheer technique will not produce great instruction. Truly great instruction will not be fatally impeded by clumsy technique.

However, an instructor's attention to little details can sharpen and intensify the dynamics of the learning activity. This means that the stimuli applied by the instructor will be sharper and more productive. That sharper stimulation in turn permits a greater interaction between the learner and the course content, between peer learners, and between learners and instructors.

In professional instruction, learning processes are not blurred by an instructor's awkwardness or amateurism. The stimuli are adapted more quickly and more productively if the instructor is a professional. That professionalism is often based on the mastery of a few teaching techniques.

CHAPTER

WHAT SHOULD TRAINING ROOMS BE LIKE?

THE INFLUENCE OF THE T & D OFFICER

Should we perhaps call them "learning rooms" instead of training rooms? Or should we stress the word "environment?" That is an increasingly popular word, and the more we learn about learning, the more environment seems to be a significant factor in bringing about behavior change.

On the other hand, maybe the semantics are unimportant; maybe Horace Mann was right: maybe all we need to have a training center is a log, someone with a question, and someone to help find the answer.

Besides, it may seem that architects make all the decisions about the rooms we use for our training programs. Things like the modularity of the structure, costs, and building codes determine key decisions like dimensions and ceiling height. T & D officers may easily feel "out of it" when it comes to these key decisions.

However, T & D officers can influence architectural decisions when buildings

185

are in the planning stage; instructors can do a great deal to adjust the physical environment during training; everybody in the T & D function can observe key criteria when selecting hotels, motels, or conference sites.

CRITERIA FOR LEARNING ROOMS

Different kinds of learnings require different environments. For example, if contemplation and introspection are involved, then calm and quiet seem necessary. If the learning requires movement, lots of open space is a must. Even so, there are general criteria. Experienced instructors will tell you they want flexibility, isolation, lighting control, capacity to accomodate computer equipment, and ventilation. Each of them is important enough to rate individual discussion.

Flexibility

If instructors or course designers had to settle for just one quality in learning rooms, chances are they'd opt for flexibility.

Flexibility is an understandable criterion if you just stop to think about the wide variety of methods professional T & D specialists employ nowadays. Within a single room—probably within a single afternoon—class activities may vary from watching a filmstrip to fishbowling, from using a computer to appearing on a video camera, from taking part in a discussion to roleplaying, to doing a bit of meditating. Naturally the instructor wants a room that can quickly and easily be rearranged.

Thinkers like Isaac Asimov tell us that computers will improve the human IQ, giving us the Rogerian utopia of learning how to learn. (*Modern Maturity,* February-March 1984, p. 38) Naturally the instructor wants a room which is wired to accomodate both the computer units and the videotape network with which they will probably interact.

Flexibility has several dimensions. A major element of flexibility is size. Cramped quarters don't give the needed flexibility, or that sense of growth-potential needed for the learning experience. One way to estimate the adequacy of a room is to calculate the square-feet-per-participant. Such calculations need to allow for chairs, tables, access, and capacity for course equipment. For "theatre type" sessions, nine or ten square feet per person is about right. Of course, this arrangement limits one to "tell-and-show" presentational types of methods. Classroom set-ups (rows of chairs, probably with arm-tablets) require 15 to 17 square feet per participant. Conference arrangements place learners at tables, and require 23 to 25 square feet per person. The table should allow at least 30 linear inches per person. It should also provide 18 to 24 inches of depth. This permits learners to spread their papers and learning materials during workshop activities.

For that reason, tables that are 60 inches long are excellent: they offer the minimum working dimensions for participants, but they can be easily shifted to new arrangements. Such flexibility doesn't apply to the six-foot tables often ordered for training rooms. The six-foot table offers an additional hazard: the temptation to crowd three people onto each side! It follows that tables 60 inches by 36 inches permit two people to sit at each side, providing both adequate table-top space and face-to-face seating for two-way communication during discussion and team task activities.

Plenty of space is a "must" if buzzgroups are to work simultaneously in a learning center—and there's much to be said for their visible proximity to one another. The synergism produced by such nearness vanishes quickly (as do lots of precious minutes!) if the groups must commute to nearby break-out rooms. Besides, how often are these rooms truly "nearby"?

What does this imply for the total dimensions of the learning room? The Rocky Mountain Association of Meeting Planners recommends these specifications in *Training*, July 1976:

For this type of activity	*Provide these dimensions*	
Conference	23–25	square feet per participant
Classroom	15–17	square feet per participant
Theatre	9–10	square feet per participant
Meals	11½–12½	square feet per diner
Receptions	8½–9½	square feet per guest

Another way to check adequacy of the dimensions is to base distances on the width of the screen used for visual presentations. Several critical judgments may be based on that single distance:

●   The distance from screen to the last row of seats should not exceed 6W, or six screen-widths.

●   The distance to the front row of seats should be 2W, twice the width of the screen. Participants who are nearer than that may be expected to experience discomfort and fatigue.

●   The proper width of the viewing area is 3W, or one and one-half widths from a centerline extended perpendicular to the screen through the viewing area. If this criterion is met, no one will be farther to the right or left of the screen than 1W.

These figures (quoted or extrapolated from an article by Raymond Wadsworth in *American School and University Magazine*, October 1971) indicate that another element in flexibility is the proportion of the room.

Optimum width-to-depth ratio is three to four according to Dr. Gerald McVey, quoted in *A User's Look at The Audio-Visual World* from the National Audio-Visual Association. The closer a room comes to this ratio, the more appropriate it will be for visual presentations.

Davis and Hagman of the National Conference Center advocate a room " . . . as nearly square as possible." They argue that square rooms bring people together "psychologically as well as physically." They continue by saying, "Both sight and sound, vital factors in verbal and nonverbal communications, are facilitated." In no case, they contend, should the length exceed the width by more than 50 percent. (*Training,* July 1976, p. 29)

An added virtue of either of these ratios is that the room can be changed on a functional or daily basis. The wall which is "front" today can be the side or rear wall tomorrow: in fact, any wall can be "the front" except the one with the door by which people come and go—and even that can be the focus of a small buzzgroup when the class is divided into teams, which tend to create their own "environment." Of course, while learners concentrate on what they themselves are doing, the whole idea of "front" becomes passé and meaningless.

In any event, astute instructors "reorient" the classroom every day or so, allowing students a new perspective, causing them to take seats in different positions and beside different people. That is often healthy: those with impaired sight or hearing can privately solve their problem, and everyone gets acquainted with more of the rest of the class.

If the screen is permanently mounted on the wall, that wall tends always to be the front. It needn't be. At sessions with no visual presentation, tables and chairs can face a different direction. This shift gives a "different feeling" and subtly underlines the theme that during training, change is the name of the game.

A special note: When that screen isn't being used, keep it rolled up. Participants inadvertently bump into, scratch, puncture, or otherwise deface screens; dust has a bad effect on any type of screen surface. Stored screens avoid these abuses.

Ceiling height is important. Anything under 10 feet poses problems for instructors and conference leaders. The screen should be high enough so learners in the rear can see it "above" and not "around" the heads of people in front of them. Experts urge that the top of the screen be as high as possible. Don't measure ceiling height from the center of the room. Enclosed airducts and indirect lighting lower the ceiling alongside some walls. Screens must then be placed too low, or away from the walls. This reduces total useful square-footage in the room.

Acoustical engineering is a special technology, beyond the range of most T & D officers. However anyone can check a few things. Carpets should be a low pile, nonabsorptive. Ornamental ceilings and crystal chandeliers are good. According to Cyril M. Harris of Columbia University, they provide excellent "diffusion" and produce a desirable "sound decay curve." (*The New Yorker,* Nov. 8, 1976, p. 63) T & D officers can influence such details when designing new training centers; T & D specialists can check these features when selecting rooms in rented or leased facilities.

Dr. Gerald McVey, Associate Professor of Educational Media and Technology at Boston University, urges careful consideration of student chairs. They should have relatively flat seats, slightly dished in the buttocks area, about 17 inches from the floor. He recommends an inch of padding, plus a slight padding for the back. The back should be slightly curved, with major support in the lumbar area. Parts which contact the learner (seat and frame) should be constructed of material which does not conduct heat or cold. If desks, or tablet arms, are included, the writing surfaces should be slightly inclined and about 27 inches above the floor.

Davis and McCollon point out, in *Planning, Conducting and Evaluating Workshops,* that "Adults are people who have relatively large bodies subject to the stress of gravitational stimuli . . . Most experience discomfort when they sit too long in hard chairs. Chairs that are too short or too narrow are worse. Some adults fall asleep in chairs that are just right." (p. 20)

Isolation

Isolation is another criterion. It doesn't mean that learning rooms are soundproofed and windowless—though those conditions sure do help! Soundproofing has an obvious value. Windowless rooms are excellent for visual presentations. They offer minimum distraction and external noise; there's less hazard from temperature shifts.

Isolation also implies that the room is sufficiently removed from the workplace so the learners know they are in training. If the proper policies prevail, such isolation can take place within a few feet of the workplace. Bosses of trainees should understand that when their employees are in training, the instructor is "the boss" and that all messages to trainees are routed through the instructor. Many organizations state policy clearly: nothing except personal crisis in the trainee's immediate family will be mentioned to trainees during learning sessions. They sometimes call this their "thousand-mile rule." Work-related messages or requests will not be delivered to trainees during the session unless the content is so critical that it would cause the manager to call the trainee back to the duty post were the trainee a thousand miles away!

Isolation can also be achieved by policy. Many organizations establish and enforce the "Work = Learn" philosophy which simply means that while employees are enrolled in training, what the company expects of them is that they acquire the behaviors outlined in the learning objectives.

This philosophy may be implemented by policy, or rules such as "Hands Off," "King's X" or "The 1000 Mile Rule." The logic is that messages designed for trainees are either personal or work-related.

Personal messages are either critical or delayable; a crisis in an immediate family requires immediate delivery, but less urgent messages will be delivered from a central spot at the end of the training hours.

Work-related messages are also either critical or delayable. "Critical" is defined in one of three ways:

1. "The work can't go on without this trainee, so I must pull him or her from *the rest of the program!*"

2. "The work can't go on without information from this trainee, so I must request they be informed at the next break."

3. "This requires action/information so significant that I would pay for a person-to-person collect call myself, and therefore I must request delivery at the next break.

(But next time I have trainees, I'll make sure we do a better job of training their temporary replacement!")

It is significant that: (1) only family crises justify calling people out of training; work reasons must be serious enough to withdraw them from that training; (2) in most organizations, no work-related messages may be delivered before the start of the training day, and (3) the procedures are all predicated upon the belief that the learning is important enough to deserve the employees' undivided attention.

When organizations establish and enforce these policies, they note immediate drops in the number of "urgent" trivia that once destroyed the isolation that accelerates effective training and development.

Effective isolation is further achieved by a policy communicated before reporting to training: Instead of performing regular duties, for the period of the training trainees are expected to achieve the objectives of the program. "Learning" is their work.

Thus isolation is both physical and psychological. Considerations in achieving isolation range from getting far away from highways, airports, and loud plumbing to getting away from the boss!

Lighting control

Lighting control is a prime criterion for visual presentations. Although total darkness is required by only a few visual media nowadays, excess sunlight can dampen the sensory impact of even the most colorful films. As we noted when discussing flexibility, windows are thus something of a liability. (Some folks protest, saying it's unnatural to be away from the sun that long. But instructors who work in windowless rooms report that sunlight is usually available at coffee breaks, at lunchtime, or when the session breaks for the day!)

One dimension of lighting control is the ability to eliminate light; another is the ability to diminish it by degrees. The advantages of rheostat controls are obvious—especially if there are several. In some designs, different learners will be doing different things simultaneously. Thus, if the instructor can have bright light in one portion of the room and dim light in another, multi-method designs are easily executed. When the screen must be placed near permanent light fixtures, there's trouble. If there aren't rheostats to dim them, or switches to eliminate the light, then a ladder and a quick twist become the instructor's problem-solving materials!

For normal student note-taking, 30 to 50 footcandles are minimum. Some people, as the National Conference Center staff, recommend 70 footcandles at desk level. Dr. Gerald McVey notes that when taxing visual tasks are part of the student's activity, 100 or more footcandles should be available. This means that there should be lots of lumens available at worktables when participants work with minute diagrams or precise visual discriminations.

Within any learning room there is a potential problem of glare. It can best be prevented by removing naked lamps or glossy surfaces. Trainers who inherit rooms with glaring lamps and windows should install shades and drapes. Trainers who rent public rooms with glossy tables should insist on tablecloths. (By the way, here's a tip. When arranging for rented rooms: be sure to insist that there be a tablecloth for each table! Otherwise, when you go to move the tables to fit the changing activities of the design, you'll find that the cloths don't come out even . . . and waste lots of time adjusting the ashtrays and water glasses and pitchers.)

Lighting control involves more than merely dimming and directing illumination. The computer has become an essential tool of the interrogative mind. Electrical wiring that will accomodate computer equipment is thus imperative in the contemporary learning room.

Computer Assisted Instruction (CAI) Equipment

We are living in the age of the silicon chip. It allows us to have calculators no thicker than credit cards, gives us automobiles that tell us to buckle up, allows manufacturers to produce personal computers so inexpensive that most families, and certainly most instructional media departments, can have one. In some school systems, primary school children are being introduced to microcomputers (or is it the other way around?). Some children are using microcomputers to learn—and growing numbers of universities require computer literacy, or a computer itself, as an entrance requirement.

This reality will have an ever increasing impact on the training and development field: each year the work force will absorb a new graduating class nurtured on microcomputers. Therefore, using microcomputers as at least part of the training department's instructional media inventory will become a requirement.

This may not please old-time "stand-up" trainers, but it is the new reality, and even old-timers must learn new training technologies. The microcomputer will not go away. Since microcomputers reduce learning time and improve the retention factor, they not only are "nice," they do their work well. Trainers are accepting this reality the way film makers have found that video has an important role in the communication of moving pictures.

The computer has brought its own extensive vocabulary. T & D specialists need to know that "hardware" is the machinery itself: processing units, a keyboard for input, a cathode ray tube (CRT) for output and input, and printer for output. "Software" involves the programs compatible with this hardware. T & D classrooms need to accommodate this hardware. Indeed, certain rooms may be designated "Resource Centers" housing videotape libraries and playback units, and computers for use with Computer Based Learning.

Let's quickly examine some terms: Computer Based Learning (CBL) or Computer Based Training (CBT) are the umbrella terms for everything that involves the use of computers for learning. Under that umbrella we have:

• Computer Assisted Instruction (CAI) refers to the direct instructional involvement of a computer with the learner or trainee.

• Computer Managed Instruction (CMI) covers the role that computers play in managing the training function. It includes record keeping, testing to see if the trainee has met his or her learning objectives, and determining the sequence of instructional activities trainees will follow based on their individual requirements.

• Computer Supported Learning Resources (CSLR) refers to the database or pool of information available to trainees by using the computer. Electronic "for further study" if you will.

Let's now talk about CAI, Computer Assisted Instruction. CAI simply refers to those situations where the trainee is interacting with the computer to achieve learning to improve skills. The computer is used to make learning easier as well as to test the trainee to see how well he or she is doing. Those test results are retained by the computer, and can be passed on to the facilitator to determine the trainee's progress.

What are the most common uses (or modes) for CAI? First, there is the *tutorial mode*. Information is presented to the trainee. The trainee is then asked questions and his or her answers are compared to the answers programmed into the computer. Feedback is given to the trainee, and if the answer is correct, the trainee will go on to the next learning segment. If incorrect, the information will be repeated in the same way or another way. The complexity and originality of any program depends on the abilities of the person who authored or created that program. One of the objectives of the tutorial mode is to approximate the techniques and responses of a live instructor working with a trainee one-on-one.

The second mode is *drill and practice*. This can be most easily compared to the use of flash cards to build speed and efficiency in learning certain information. In school it might be used for math or language instruction; in training it would be used for learning technical terms or procedural steps.

Next comes the *discovery mode*. Here the trainee is presented with a problem which must be solved through trial-and-error. It expects the trainee to think and analyze situations, and come up with solutions. The discovery mode is also called the problem-solving mode.

Fourth we have the *simulation mode* where the trainees undertake real-life situations and make the same decisions they would make if faced with those situations. Any errors have no real-life consequences but they sharply underline the learning. The marriage of computer to videotape offers incredibly exciting simulation for learning; a mannequin for CPR training is one example. Another is simulation for aircraft pilot training. The trainee crew can sit in a classroom which duplicates the cockpit. They see what is happening on a TV screen which becomes their window. Thus, they see what is happening or would have happened as a result of their decisions, even smell the acrid odor of a fire they could have averted had they taken proper corrective action when the computer generated the first symptom of the "fire in engine #1" program.

The *gaming mode* uses games to facilitate and stimulate learning. It is most useful in turning some dull, rote learning into a game where correct answers are worth points or some other reward is given by the computer.

A sixth mode of CAI is *modeling*. A model is developed in the computer; then by changing a variable in that model, the trainee can see what effect it will have. Modeling is used to teach trainees systems or processes, and the effect that a change in that model will have on the rest of that system or process.

Why does CAI work? Basically, CAI is grounded in the studies of behavioral psychologists. People who are rewarded for a good response will continue that good behavior. CAI offers rewards to people who give the correct answers. Such rewards involve self-satisfaction, and the "privilege" of being allowed to go on to the next learning activity. Additionally, feedback is instant. We all remember the excitement (if we thought we did well) when an exam was returned by a teacher. CAI retains this excitement and does so throughout the entire learning session. Through this use of immediate feedback, CAI creates its own energy, and if learning is not taking place, it helps the trainee overcome the hurdles by teaching the information again.

CAI is fun. Learning does not have to be drudgery, and using computers builds a bridge on which drudgery can become entertainment and entertainment can become learning.

Last, CAI is effective for adult learning situations since it takes into account differences in individual learners. People can work at their own pace. They do not have to succeed or fail based on group standards. A person who needs more time to learn is still learning. Adults appreciate and thrive on the opportunity to pace themselves or to select their own path through a program of instruction.

The reality of the marketplace is that there are available off-the-shelf or "canned" programs on a billion subjects—but not all programs or courseware will fit every computer. Since all software is expensive to develop—especially educational courseware—developers naturally work on programs for the widest possible market. As a result many courses are left commercially undeveloped, and must be created in-house by programmers hired to do the job. These people must not only by good programmers, they must be equally good instructional designers. Regardless of the skills of individuals who create in-house courseware, it takes time to write, test, debug, and distribute.

The cost of developing CAI depends on the programming skill of the training staff, the knowledge-readiness of the Subject Matter Expert and their ability to work together. A "high-side" estimate by Jeremy Main (*Fortune,* October 1, 1984) cites $2,000 to $20,000 per instruction-hour. He adds, ". . . makers of interactive systems say they can reduce the time it takes to finish a course by 25% . . . increase retention by 50%." This may very well be another "high-side" claim unless field-testing in several methods proves those results.

Computer hardware is advancing in leaps and bounds; software is achieving greater compatibility with many computers, so increased numbers of programs can be used on hardware from increasing numbers of manufacturers.

Computers are here to stay, an exciting and valuable resource for organizational T & D.

Ventilation

Ventilation is another criterion for learning rooms. An additional argument for high ceilings is that when the temperature goes up, so does the heat. But high ceilings will not guarantee good ventilation. Experienced instructors will tell you that ventilation is a "lose-lose" situation. "You can't please all the people any of the time—or any of the people for more than about 15 minutes at a time!" These old-timers say they prefer to keep things a little on the cool side: they'd rather have people alert than asleep!

A more scientific statement, again from Dr. McVey, says that when room temperature is between 68 and 76 degrees Fahrenheit (20° to 25° C) and relative humidity between 30 and 60 percent and air velocity is 12 to 25 feet-per-minute, "heat exchange between people and their environment generally takes place without discomfort." Most adults seem to be most comfortable when the temperature is between 73° and 75° F (22.5° to 24° C) and the relative humidity is about 50 percent. Current interest in pollution and anti-smoking movements has prompted many instructors and conference leaders to establish "Smoking" and "No Smoking" areas. This reminds us that Dr. McVey feels that ventilation is achieved best by keeping the air moving—and that if you must err, you should err on the side of coolness.

Let's emphasize that point about keeping the air moving. T & D officers who are getting new learning rooms would be wise to see that there is proper equipment to provide the minimum air velocity of 12 to 15 feet-per-minute.

There are some special problems associated with projection equipment. Many projectors generate lots of heat. It isn't that the machines make learners all that uncomfortable; it's that the efficient operation and their longevity is affected if the heat continues while the machines are in storage. Dr. McVey gives these guidelines for storing such equipment and material:

If housing	Keep the temperatures °F	°C	And the relative humidity
Film projectors	65 to 70	17.8 to 21	25 to 40%
Film	Below 80	Below 26.7	25 to 60%
Audio tape	60 to 90	15.6 to 32	20 to 90%

In summary, by checking rooms for compliance with those four criteria—flexibility, isolation, lighting control, and ventilation—the T & D specialist is more likely to be in quarters where learning can easily happen. Beyond the room itself, there are some things instructors and conference leaders can do to make room arrangements conducive to the participation planned for each module of the training.

ROOM ARRANGEMENT

Flexibility is such a vital criterion for the training room because instructors will need to rearrange the furniture so it fits the variety of methods they will be using. The more andragogic the learning design, the more varied the furniture arrangements. This implies that the furniture will be moved—and quite often.

Even if the functional activities of the learning design don't demand a rearrangement, there are several reasons for changing the furniture from time to time:

● Individuals are given a new perspective on the activity by sitting in different parts of the room.

● Individuals get better acquainted with more of their peer-participants when they move around from time to time.

● Handicapped individuals are not consistently and permanently punished by being great distances from the screen or from the speakers.

● Small cliques do not arise. (There's nothing wrong with cliques per se, but in some cases they can become problems by forcing their norms or their agenda upon the entire group.)

The various functional arrangements often found in T & D learning rooms may be analyzed according to their facilitation of two-way communication. In this analysis we will look at them on that basis, starting with the least encumbering arrangements and proceeding to the more formal plans . . . plans which control rather than encourage free-and-easy communication between participants and communications between participants and the instructor. Finally, we'll consider arrangements which "deformalize" those rigid arrangements.

The un-furnitured circle in Fig. 12.1 is probably the most democratic and unencumbered of all arrangements. There is no status symbol denoting a leader, and every participant has direct sightlines to every other participant. Since there is no table between participants, each person is in a sense "totally revealed." Subtle nonverbal communications are possible. This arrangement is typical for T-groups and sensitivity training, for data gathering sessions in organization-development programs.

This circle (Fig. 12.2) is uncluttered, but there is a clearcut leader. Consider this as a grouping for a brainstorming session. One person is in control, partly because of the standing position and partly because of a "scepter of authority": the pencil and the flipchart or chalkboard.

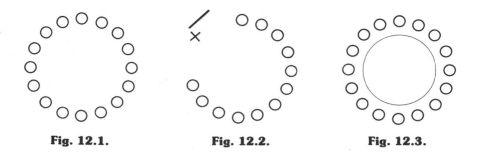

Fig. 12.1.   **Fig. 12.2.**   **Fig. 12.3.**

When the circular table is used (Fig. 12.3), participants still have direct access to each other, including facial nonverbal communications. Remember the Paris peace talks? . . . when the nations argued relentlessly about the shape of the table? It apparently *does* make a difference! Informal studies show that there will be more conversation and shorter inputs, and that more members will participate, when the same people sit at round rather than at square tables!

Instructors can always arrange rectangular tables into various rectangular patterns. The square arrangement (Fig. 12.4) produces several noteworthy effects. Participants are now seated in rows, the first step toward formality. In rows (as opposed to arcs) nobody can see the faces of all the other participants. Depending upon where visual aids are placed, one side or another may become the "head" of the table. An interesting sidelight: informal studies show that a gap in the center, as shown here, retards participation. A solid table (Fig. 12.5) seems to encourage conversation. With a "hole in the middle," some people don't speak at all, and some who do speak tend to talk for longer periods of time. It would thus seem that when instructors want more control, they should arrange the tables around a central "void." For more democratic conversation, the tables should be joined to form a solid unit. This holds true with any rectangular arrangement.

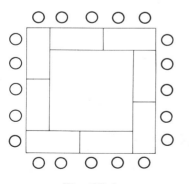

Fig. 12.4.

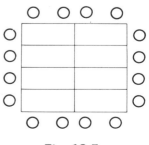

Fig. 12.5.

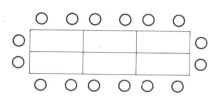

Fig. 12.6.

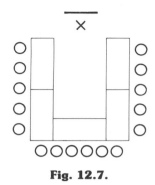

Fig. 12.7.

If the rectangle becomes long and narrow (Fig. 12.6), there are longer lines. Thus even fewer people can communicate face-to-face with their peers. The positions on the short dimension of the table are often identified as "leadership seats." Could this be because the father sat at the head of the table? Indeed, even when no leader is appointed, members along the sides tend to look to the end positions, expecting people seated there to dominate.

You'd probably win the bet if you wagered that more Management Development conferences use the "U" (Fig. 12.7) than any other arrangement. It has a sense of the "senate" with equality of membership—but no doubt about who is presiding. It is frequently effective, even though it does have a formality and a constraint on participants. Since there are just three rows of people, a great many participants are blocked from viewing the faces of their peers.

Although some clutter results from placing people on the inside of the "U," as in Fig. 12.8, such placement does open up more visual contact and bring the entire group into close physical proximity. That proximity cannot be ignored; the farther apart members are from one another, the more reserved their behavior—and the greater the control.

Whenever rectangles are used, the participants should be encouraged (or forced by the nature of the activity) to take distinctly different positions every now and then. If name cards exist, they can be shifted regularly. When such a practice is to be used, it's a good idea to start it at the first break or the first lunch break. This lets participants know that mobility is the norm for the entire program. Most instructors encourage participants to move on a voluntary basis in addition to the moves made with the name cards or the varying activity.

Simply "softening" the shape of the "U" can make considerable difference in the participants' ability to see and communicate with one another. With the

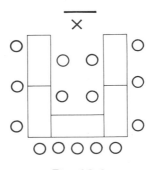

Fig. 12.8.

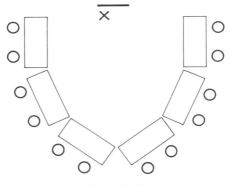

Fig. 12.9.

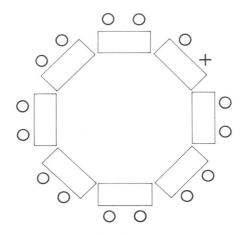

Fig. 12.10.

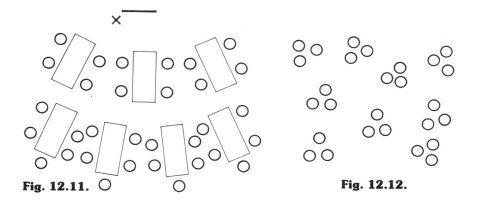

Fig. 12.11.   **Fig. 12.12.**

conventional "U" there are only three rows of students. By placing the tables at an angle, as in Fig. 12.9, the long rows are broken into numerous shorter rows and participants' mutual sightlines are improved.

Tables can also be arranged in circular or semicircular patterns (Fig. 12.10). An advantage is the return to the "arc." More people are able to see the faces of more peers than they can in some rectangular arrangements.

Cabaret arrangements, like the one in Fig. 12.11, facilitate the establishment of buzzgroups for team tasks, games, or individual study. A cabaret setting is especially useful during workshop or programmed instruction modules within longer programs. Each table can be designated for a particular activity. At the same time, sight lines and the proximity of learners encourage free exchange of ideas. Discussions involving the entire group can occur as easily in this arrangement as in any other. The instructors can easily assume a position of authority, yet can just as easily move among individuals or teams when they are working at tables. The cabaret plan reflects an informal, flexible type of learning environment.

The scattershot method (Fig. 12.12) may seem extremely haphazard. It actually permits quick change of learner focus and produces tremendous investments of learner energy. It works very well in multiple roleplays, two-person team tasks, or highly synergistic action training. When necessary, participants can quickly form larger groups. The scattershot arrangement produces high interpersonal and intergroup communication. It's bad for notetaking, but the scattershot grouping is designed for experiential training when notes are rarely necessary.

The "classroom" set-up is almost the opposite. As shown in Fig. 12.13 it reminds us of academic classrooms—and is a bit undesirable. When students occupy chairs with arm tablets, the arrangement does have great flexibility. It's easy to shift to scattershot groupings and to break up the "military" rows of seats found in most "schools."

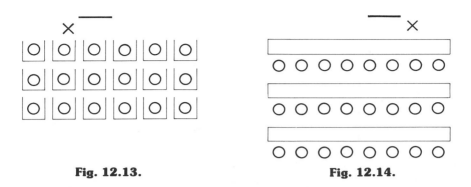

Fig. 12.13.   Fig. 12.14.

Organizational "classroom" arrangements (Fig. 12.14) usually feature rows of tables. These indicate that there will be considerable control by the instructor. The rows limit face-to-face communication by participants, unless they twist a lot; it's hard to talk to anyone save the instructor or to the people right beside them. Unless there is ample room between the rows of tables, instructors cannot easily access individual learners to review progress with problems or projects. There is a barrier against forming natural groups for team tasks. There is no easy way for instructors to provide private or semi-private counseling.

An antidote for these limitations is a wide aisle between each row (Fig. 12.15).

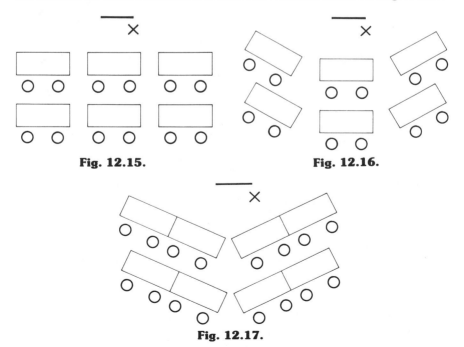

Fig. 12.15.   Fig. 12.16.

Fig. 12.17.

If seating is restricted to the recommended two-at-a-table, instructors can have access to every learner without undue "nearness" of other participants.

Converting the rows to arcs, as in Fig. 12.16, will enhance the learners' ability to communicate with one another. They can more easily see each others' faces, and the lines are bent—so the total environment seems less structured and less rigid. This "chevron" or arched arrangement isn't seen very often, but it's a useful plan in square rooms or in rooms with the recommended 3 : 4 ratio.

The modified chevron in Fig. 12.17 permits a great deal of cross communication among participants without too much twisting and turning. Instructors are still able to access all parts of the room.

It goes without saying (but probably should be said anyway) that whenever possible the more formal arrangements should be set up so the main entrance is *behind* the learners. In such formal, presentation-type situations, control and focus are hard to maintain when participants are periodically stimulated by the arrival of the mid-morning coffee—or those outsiders who ignore the "Do Not Disturb" sign hanging over the doorknob!

SUMMARY

A "place to make learning happen" need not be a grand room, elaborately furnished. It needn't be equipped with the latest electronic equipment, media machinery, and fancy control panels. Those things facilitate the mechanics of the support systems of learning. They shouldn't be ridiculed—but in themselves they don't guarantee learning.

A room where learning can happen is flexible—quickly responsive to the group's need for a new arrangement. It is isolated, so learners never doubt that their mission is to learn. Lighting and ventilation are not obstacles to maintaining that focus on learning.

But above all the room permits the creativity of the instructor to put things where trainee-participants can quickly use them as tools for their learning processes.

CHAPTER **13**

WHAT ABOUT
VISUAL AIDS?

THE PROPER ROLE OF VISUAL AIDS

When visitors arrive at the Training Center they quickly learn a lot about the T & D officer. If a short early chat ends with a visit to a classroom, learning is the apparent focus. What is the focus if (as often happens) they visit the audio-visual center?

Perhaps the A/V paraphenalia is the apple of the officer's eye. Perhaps it's where the budget is chiefly invested . . . or the easiest place to prove that the T & D department is keeping up with the Joneses: after all, there is wonderful and justifiable new "hardware" like videotapes which interact with computers—and even with learners!

Maybe it's just that all this hardware is easier to see than are the programs or the policies. Certainly TV studios are more glamorous than lesson plans or job aids. Maybe the A/V Center is like the chrome and plush upholstery on a sleek automobile, a symptom of affluence and enlightenment.

Affluence is a questionable credential, but utilization of contemporary media is commendable. The key word is "utilization." Elaborate systems are not necessarily better than simple ones. As Martin Broadwell says, "Many training directors who are new to the field of training view the multi-media razzle-dazzle and . . . come to believe that if a little visual aid is good, a lot must be better." (*Training,* October 1970)

The point is that visual support for a learning system is good if it causes learning to happen—bad or unnecessary if it doesn't. Asking what visuals are best is, as Broadwell suggests, just like asking what tool is best. It sort of depends upon what you're trying to fix, doesn't it? We noted the same thing in selecting methods.

And that takes us to the selection process.

HOW DO YOU SELECT THE MEDIUM FOR YOUR MESSAGE?

The decision to use any form of visual support should come rather late in the design process. As Ronald Anderson says in *Selecting and Developing Media for Instruction,* requests like, "We need a video tape on . . ." or "A slide-tape unit should be made for the course in . . ." replace one problem with another. (p.9) Designers and instructors resort to visual aids when they must . . . when learners cannot be expected to grasp the concept without visual aids—or when the learners can grasp the idea so much more easily if there is visual support. To fit the media decision into the entire design process, let's look at a model freely adapted from a design by the National Audio-Visual Association in the *User's Look At The Audio-Visual World.*

The process chart in Fig. 13.1 reflects one basic principle: that the decisions about what audio-visuals to put into the system must grow out of earlier decisions about the output. One sure way to inhibit efficient learning is to design the learning experience around an available "pet" medium. There's a suicidal fallacy in the logic that exclaims, "We've got all this great new video equipment: two cameras and a monitor in every room. Let's put the management training program on tape!"

In their same *User's Look,* NAVA suggests that "The best medium for a specific application is simply 'the least costly one that works.' Making that decision is a mix of pragmatism, experience, and showmanship." Expressing the decision in rather greater detail, NAVA says that the steps look like those in Fig. 13.2.

Let's spend a moment expanding step 3 of Fig. 13.2. Identify requirements. What are some of the considerations involved at this step of Fig. 13.2.

Well, one issue is that of motion. Does the objective involve concepts, or does it involve processes? Unless your learners must master some process in which

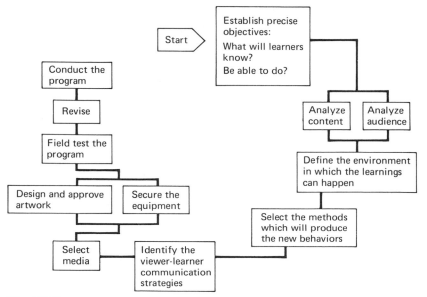

Fig. 13.1.

Process chart for choosing audio-visual material. (Reprinted by permission of The Industry and Business Council of the National Audio-Visual Association.)

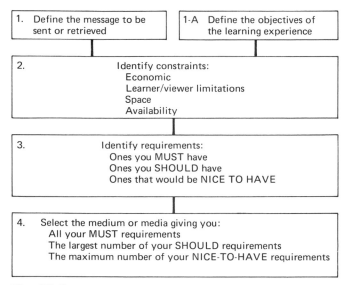

Fig. 13.2.

Decision guide. (Reprinted by permission of The Industry and Business Council of the National Audio-Visual Association.)

parts or psychomotor behaviors are involved, still pictures may be just as effective as motion pictures. If the processes are interpersonal, and emotions are prominent, it's nip-and-tuck. Will they learn better by watching compassion grow on the face of the characters in a case study, or will static photographs say it effectively . . . so the facial expressions register for a longer period of time?

What about color? At the end of the lesson, are learners supposed to distinguish between colors—as, say, between pink and cerise? If that's the objective, then colors are a *must* requirement.

Let's take another look at step 3. Remember, it requires that we use some judgment about criteria:

To distinguish between a *must* and a *nice-to-have* requirement, let's go back to teaching a process. If the process is the operation of a machine, motion in the medium may be a *must*. However, if the graduate learners will not control the machine, but rather merely observe it, then motion isn't critical. It is probably just a *nice-to-have*. Take another example: We've decided to demonstrate the interpersonal processes through case studies. Because we want to "ease into" roleplaying, the first cases will be put onto film or videotape. Should that be back-and-white or color? Well, color would be *nice,* but scarcely a *must.* Under certain circumstances, added stimulation from color could be counterproductive.

What about sound? Once again, it all depends upon whom and what you're teaching. Sound adds nothing to people who cannot hear! Suppose the trainees are learning to operate a complex piece of equipment. The noise of the machinery on the sound track could obliterate the voice of the narrator giving the instructions! On the other hand, audiotapes accompanying good diagrams of the controls could be a most appropriate way to send the content to the learner. Or consider this example: The objective is to detect irregularities in an engine before the problem becomes serious. What better medium than sound? Just try to draw a picture that will help your learners discriminate the good from the bad condition!

Another issue goes something like this: "Should we use pictures, simplified drawings or schematics, facsimiles, models—or the real thing?" Here again the choice of medium is ultimately dictated by the defined behavioral objective—plus constraints of cost or availability. But the first test is, "What must we have in order to permit the desired learnings?" Youngsters will never learn to drive by looking at pictures of automobiles—but simulators are quite effective for certain skills which go into the total driving process.

Ultimately the training aid must permit what the psychologists call "generalization." They're talking about the perseverance of the desired behavior in the world outside the learning room. Driver training furnishes a good example: the student may learn how to give all the proper signals in the classroom (even in the simulator) and then forget it entirely when first driving under pressure "out on the highway." The flight-attendant-in-training may be able to balance the meal trays perfectly in the training center's mock-up of the aircraft. Then these same attendants toss food around in alarming ways when the trip is running late, and encountering turbulence, and there are two "pinchers" in the aisle at Row 17! No photograph can recreate that environment!

AUDIO-VISUAL EQUIPMENT

When T & D officers get to the subject of machines (called "hardware" or "equipment" by professionals) they face several questions:

- What kinds of equipment are available?
- Where there are competing media, what's the advantage/disadvantage of each?
- Are there special maintenance requirements?

Let's look at some of those issues by examining different kinds of equipment.

Screens

Screens will be required if T & D programs use any kind of projection.

A basic decision is for "front" or "rear" screens. Front screens use a projector placed in or behind the audience. Rear screens require projection from a room behind the screen or in a portable unit. Rear screen arrangements use mirrors to place the image on a screen between the projector and the viewers.

For front viewing, screen fabrics may be beaded, lenticular, matte white, or super bright. Beaded fabrics are very light and have a high light return.

Lenticular (silver) screens reject stray light, but present problems for students seated at angles to the screen. Matte white gives comparatively low light return, but is most accurate for color and sharpness. "Super bright" screens are so bright that they can sometimes be used out of doors—but even more than the lenticular, they are subject to fall-off in clarity for side viewers.

Rear screens may be made of glass, a plexi/acrylic, or some flexible fabric. Large screens in permanent locations tend to use glass; small mobile units rely on the plexi/acrylic or flexible fabric. Glass offers easy cleaning and good sound isolation; the other two types are unbreakable and lightweight . . . easy to carry around.

Any screen is a target for dust when not in use. Glass can, of course, be washed; but any other type screen will last a lot longer and give much better image if owners keep it rolled-up and stored in a place that's free from moisture, heat, and dust.

When positioning a screen in a classroom, try to keep the most distant viewers nearer than six times the width of the screen. Try to keep the nearest two widths away so they'll avoid eye fatigue. When buying a screen, check to see how it's attached to the roller. Lightweight staples won't do the job if your screen will make many trips up and down!

Projectors

Projectors can give you movies or a variety of still-picture forms. The advantage of the motion picture is, of course, that it can depict motion when that's necessary for the learning—as in a process of interpersonal "dramas" used in case studies or models in human behavior training. Modern motion pictures inevitably offer sound.

Industry sources today say that A/V users probably spend more of their money for 16 mm projectors and films than for any other kind of equipment. The unit costs are higher than less sophisticated projectors, and film costs correspond. Copies of commercially produced films run from $150 to $450 per copy. The cost of making home-produced films runs as much as $2,500 to $3,000 per minute for colored movies—$1,650 for black-and-white. Some feel these estimates err on the conservative side. One specialist, Barry Hampe, has developed a checklist for estimating the cost of a given film. Hampe says the checklist is eight pages long! (*Training*, July 1976, p. 19.)

A major interest to the T & D specialist is the threading in the projector. Totally manual threading lets the operator match the film to a path printed on the side of the projector. Manual channel threading permits operators to open up a path for threading and removing the film by pressing a single lever. Automatic loading lets operators insert the film into an entry slot and watch as the machine itself routes the film through its proper path to the take-up reel. Of course this feature is popular with most operators—unless the film gets jammed somewhere on its inaccessible track! Automatic loading permits a more professional "set-up" time when the equipment is used by employees not specifically trained to operate 16 mm equipment.

Some 16 mm projectors have an "analysis" capability allowing the film to move through at varying speeds. For learnings involving careful analysis of manipulative or machine processes, this feature could well be worth the extra investment.

Few motion pictures appear good in lighted rooms. Thus the light output of the projector is important. NAVA's *Audio-Visual Equipment Directory* explains that it's unreliable to equate light output and wattage. It suggests that buyers concern themselves with "lumens" measured at the screen, not with wattage in the projector.

When buying a 16 mm projector, the T & D department is making a considerable outlay of cash. Important criteria are portability, durability, sound and picture capabilities—and don't overlook quickly available local service! When your projector breaks down (they don't very often; but like Murphy's law, they do it on days when you're trying to impress the board of directors!) . . . anyhow, when they do need service, you don't want to wait while the repairman waits for your turn before starting to drive out from some distant metropolis.

Motion pictures are also available through the videotape media. Inexperienced purchasers of video systems (no matter how long they have been in the field of training) would be smart to get professional counsel for this buying decision. The entire field of videotaping is so new that there are "crest of the wave" developments about every six months.

If there is any single rule of thumb it is this: Don't commit to a videotape capability until you are certain you will use the medium enough to justify the purchase price—plus the ongoing cost of operators. Many T & D audio-visual centers today look like the "equipment storeroom" of so many public schools: hard to locate and cluttered with cobwebbed audio-visual equipment. In the case of T & D departments, the most expensive and the dustiest are often those glamorous video cameras that were going to do so much when purchased. Good forecasting and creative thinking in how to apply video equipment can prevent such dysfunctional outlays of monies.

But the alternative is equally disturbing; buying on a hit-or-miss basis produces incompatability between parts of a larger "system" . . . produces needless duplication of certain elements. If ever a "systems approach" is in order, the installation of a videotape facility is such a time. In its *User's Look at The Audio-Visual World,* NAVA summarizes: "Get professional help early in the process. It's one way to avoid the rough road all too many buyers have travelled . . . 'A trail cluttered with the bones of gear overbought and underutilized.' That 'underutilized' is no accidental adjective. When you invest in a videotape system, be certain that it will be the medium for *many* messages . . . that you have access (or a staff that can produce) tapes for many programs . . . for a good many years to come." (p. 37)

When T & D specialists use still pictures to assist the learning process, they may choose from several forms.

The 35 mm slide projector is perhaps the most common still-picture projector, though overhead transparencies and filmstrips are growing in popularity. One need not be a T & D specialist to acquire experience with 35 mm slides and projectors. This equipment is a basic vehicle for the family pictures one shows to relatives when they visit and to neighbors when one returns from vacation.

When T & D departments purchase projectors for steady A/V activities, they want to be sure of sturdiness, reliability, freedom from jams, and ability to handle several mountings: cardboard, metal, glass, or plastic. They are also concerned with quietness of operation, and capacity of the magazine to handle all the slides for a showing. (Sometimes it's smarter to replace the magazine during the showing than to buy magazines with enormous capacity; they often jam after slide mounts warp or fray!)

Is a remote "trigger" available? They are *nice-to-have,* but not always *must* requirements.

Most projectors still require a darkened room. (Some instructors consider this their big disadvantage.) Thus the ability to change magazines or to operate the machine in the dark is of some concern.

Since portability is one great asset of the 35 mm medium, the equipment will probably be used in lots of settings from tiny rooms to cavernous ballrooms. It's shrewd to buy several lenses (including zoom) for these varieties of size in room and screen. A projector case should be used, or secured; dust is always a great inhibitor to successful, easy operation.

Filmstrips are preprogrammed 35 mm slides, linked to an audio narration and mounted onto a continuous film. They are thus less flexible, but more self-contained, than the usual 35 mm presentation. There are several options available in the sound presentation: records, cassette, and reel-to-reel. Each of these three options presents the further alternative of manually or automatically triggered advance to the next frame. Some 16 mm filmstrips are available.

When the content of the material is rather stable, and when geography or time separates the classes, the filmstrip offers attractive packaging. T & D specialists who want to avoid dropped trays with scattered slides, out-of-sequence visual presentations, or bulky shipments—well, they like filmstrips.

Overhead projection is appealing to instructors or conference leaders who like to face their class, or to inscribe or "build up" the image as they teach. The very name "overhead" implies that the screen will be at some height. Modern architectural passion for low ceilings means that lots of overhead projections actually take place at eye level—thus defeating one great advantage of this equipment. Perhaps there is a real world hand-off here: if you give up on the height you overcome the problem of keystoning (the top of overhead images are usually wider than the bottoms!) and students with aching necks . . . but you inherit heads which get in the way of other learners' eyes—and of instructors who get in the way of all of them!

Of course there are solutions for these visual interferences. Chairs can be so arranged that all students have a direct line of eye contact to the screen. Instructors can stand near the screen or be seated near the projector.

Fortunately, the overhead projector isn't a very sophisticated machine: it seldom outwits its human operators, and maintenance is relatively easy.

And there are other advantages. This type of projection works well in a totally lighted room, so learners can see what they are doing at their own tables or what they're writing into their own notebooks. Transparencies are generally easy to make. If the more enduring ozalid equipment isn't available, rather inexpensive heat-transfer systems can produce projectuals for as little as 50¢ plus the cost of designing the artwork. A serious warning needs to accompany this ease of making transparencies! It's tempting just to take a page out of a manual, or some tiny-print form, and run off a transparency. Lots of instructors do this—and think they have created visual aids. Unfortunately lots of trainees look at the results—and are throughly confused about the images on the screen. These duplications of bad designs are distracting, eye-straining monsters that discourage learners from ever again looking at the manual or dealing with the form they're supposedly going to master with the assistance of the visual aid.

An opaque projector is an altogether different machine. It uses a solid page of print, and requires no transfer to the "transparent" state as do overhead projectors. It is thus all the more tempting to quickie, cluttered, impossible-to-read projection! Nonetheless, it's one machine that helps in those special cases where intricate drawings must be examined in detail. It is sometimes used as a way to project drawings onto a large chart, which can later be displayed before the class. Standard opaque projectors require a darkened room.

For any operator of projection equipment, a few commonsense operating practices apply. These would be the behavioral objectives of an A/V operators' training program! At the end of a successful checkout, the A/V projectionist will:

- Carry spare lamps with the equipment for all projectors,
- Carry extension cords to all presentations,
- Dust any glass surface (lens, projector "stage," or screen) with only the softest of cloths,
- Keep hands and sharp pointers off the surface of any projection screen,
- Read the instructions at predetermined periodic intervals—but at least before each trip away from the home base, and
- When equipment won't work, check first to see that it's plugged in! (Seriously! Significant numbers of "house calls" are completed satisfactorily

when highly paid technicians merely check the plug-in, the ON/OFF switch, or the circuit breakers. The operator had forgotten to check these elementary things.)

Video*

In the last ten years, technology has brought video into the American home— and into the training and communications departments of businesses and organizations. A wide range of format, quality, and price is available to any company joining this revolution.

What exactly is video?

• First, video is the electronic re-creation of images which are stored on magnetic tape similar to the tape we find in audio cassettes. Video allows instant playback of images just taped, while film requires a laboratory process to see what was filmed. (Film, both movie and still, involves chemicals, not electronics.)

• Second, video is a medium which allows us to communicate information by using motion visuals. In that sense it is similar in its use to film, and thus does not really put us into new communication territory. Video, however, has opened up the use of motion visuals to a much wider range of users than film ever did. Use of video is quite simple, and the instant feedback shows the video user how easy it is to get a decent image on tape. Tape is easier to work with. With inexpensive video formats, one can do a better job than one can with super 8-film.

• Third, video is a method of producing visual support for a training program; putting a bit or most of the program on tape has become a viable alternative to slides and overheads.

• Fourth, video is a method of showing training programs to the trainees. Such distribution can be anything from playing a tape once to a roomful of people, or sending that program out to a thousand branches across the country. Such tapes may show lectures, or little dramas (cases and roleplays), or non-motion visuals, like slide/tape shows. Any program produced on film can be distributed on tape: graphs, charts, still photographs with explanatory narration.

In short, a company which sets up a video production and distribution facility can still effectively incorporate any other production medium into the new video medium.

Let's look at video hardware and some basic costs. The video format refers to the tape width. The wider the tape, the more expensive that format becomes,

---

* The author gratefully acknowledges the contribution of Peter R. Schleger to this section.

but also the better the quality of production. The home video format is ½" VHS or Beta. Since the two formats are not compatible, most people stick to one or the other. The tape is housed in small plastic cassettes. Using home video equipment, a company can spend about $1,500 in equipment and be ready to make a program on video tape.

Since ½" tape and equipment don't usually give acceptable quality for wide distribution, most companies produce on a larger format and transfer to ½" for distribution. This works well since ½" cassette players are the leading playback machines.

The standard industrial production format is ¾" "U" format or U-matic. ¾" tape is housed in cassettes that are about four times larger than the ½" cassettes. This makes them heavier to ship, and more expensive, which is one reason that ½" is a popular distribution format. ¾" production ranges from broadcast quality—depending on the equipment used—to reasonably low-budget productions. ¾" production equipment starts around $7,000.

Another popular current format is 1" "C" tape, which is 2 reel-to-reel format, reserved for high-budget work. It is also used by broadcast television. Most organizational video will not be involved with the 1" format, and its six-figure production equipment.

One consideration when getting into video is the expectation of the audience. Most large organizations prefer not to send out sloppy programs made on inexpensive equipment; they have an image to uphold to employees. A small organization (say a four-outlet retailer) cannot afford the video "polish" that comes with expensive equipment and highly-trained production staff; the programs it will produce will have a different look from those produced by the major corporations.

The "biggies" will hire professional actors and use a full production crew; the retailer might use real employees and the crew might be no more than one person doing all the work. The giants might have full 1" computerized editing at their disposal; the retailer may use the T & D specialist to edit while the shooting proceeds. However, if both programs are designed, written, and produced with equal care, who can say that the learning impact on the employees in those retail stores will be any less than the impact of the big-budget show on the people at the giant firm? One need only recall Hollywood features that cost millions and became critical and economic disasters, or low-budget features which swept to critical acclaim and financial success. The *Marty/Cleopatra* syndrome exists in T & D videotaping too!

An organization can decide to use video as a training medium without making an investment in production equipment, facilities, or staff: it can use freelancers with equipment or hire a production house. Playback equipment can be easily rented. Everything is available in all formats to meet every budget.

Even after the purchase decision is made, it can be implemented slowly. A camera and recorder can be purchased, but editing can still be taken to a post-production house. A video manager can be hired full-time, and freelancers brought in to assist with the shoot. A studio is not necessary: equipment is portable and can be taken on "location" to the executive's office or the assembly line. When studio space is needed, it can be rented. Taking that video plunge need not be complicated or expensive.

Video is not going to be a cure-all for bad training or poor supervision; it is only a tool to enhance good training. Furthermore, video does not magically become the best medium for every training need. Sometimes one slide of a chart or diagram projected on a large screen can be much more effective than a video program on the same subject. For detailed training of step-by-step procedures, video might be a good introduction, but hands-on training and a well-thought out manual are requisite to that training need. Each training situation requires analysis to determine the most appropriate and instructionally valid medium for visual support.

Video training can be broken down into two types: linear and interactive. A linear video program has a straight line structure. It has a beginning, a middle, and an end. It is usually shown without stopping, and there is no chance for the audience to interact with the program. There may be stop tape points to allow for questions, but once those questions are answered, the tape continues to its conclusion.

Interactive video implies control by the trainees as to what they will see next on the screen. Trainees are asked to make decisions or answer questions at times specified by the program. A question answered correctly sends the learner to the next instructional sequence. A question answered incorrectly will take the learner back to the point where the correct information was originally taught or present the data in a different way. Interactive video programs may also offer the trainee a choice of subjects to learn. In sophisticated forms, it can analyze student responses over a portion of the program and select the next stimuli to reflect that analysis.

Interactive video allows trainees to learn at their own pace, and can repeat information as often as it is programmed to, or it can tell the trainee to ask for assistance from a facilitator.

The video portion of an interactive video program can be stored on video tape or on a video disc. The disc is the more popular format since it searches for different parts of the program very quickly. The video is taped on broadcast quality ¾" or 1" formats since a quality picture is important for the disc. Then the taped program is transferred to a disc.

Writing programs for interactive video require diligent pre-planning to account for every frame and branching decision. It is an expensive program to produce. Computers control the interactivity. There are ever-changing technologies in video:

- One company has a new piece of equipment which allows discs to be "mastered" in-house.
- There is new high-speed, high quality ½" video. It is not expensive, with prices equivalent to broadcast quality ¾" production.
- Cameras are becoming smaller and better.

Though we automatically think of linear video for groups, there is no reason why interaction can't involve group discussion as well as individual decision; it just takes longer and serves different learning objectives: group process as well as course content.

Astute T & D officers carefully study the marketplace when it is time to make any decision on buying video equipment. However, when they need video, they get into it. They know they will never, ever own state-of-the-art equipment for more than a few weeks. The state-of-the-art is always improving.

One rich application of video tape is as a feedback vehicle for learners in class—particularly of performance try-outs in the form of roleplays, simulations, or try-outs of psychomotor skills. Video feedback obviously offers convincing data; the performance is there for the learner to see and believe, not just to hear about from a fellow student. Not only is this more convincing, it is more thorough; it contains non-verbal behaviors and subtleties of diction and vocal inflections.

Yet while such feedback is very useful to the receiver, it can be a colossal bore to others; as with any redundant replay of what went on in class.

To overcome this problem, astute instructors use one or more of these antidotes:

- Carefully note critical events; tab their number on the timing record and playback only those moments.
- Give participants checksheets with several areas to analyze; have groups of them watch for and provide feedback on just one area at a time—then shift.
- Schedule the review in small groups, or by individual, so that not everyone has to watch everything a second time.

The moral is: if all the class will *learn* something from reviewing the tape, fine; otherwise plan on each learner reviewing only the personally "learningful" segments.

Audiotape

Audiotape has become very common in recent years due to new interest in self-study and remote learning. All types of workers engage in self-study on or off the job. Managers or salespeople want to learn while driving between calls; executives listen to tapes on new issues while being driven to work in the company limousines. Such activity has emphasized the audiotape—especially cassettes—as the medium for acquiring knowledge.

Obviously this medium is most suited to the cognitive or affective domains. However audiotapes can be linked to visual presentations in effective "mediated" programs which teach people "how to" perform psychomotor skills.

A basic decision in adopting an audiotape program is the type of tape: Reel-to-reel? Cassette? Cartridge? Two common criteria in the decision are "What do we have available?" and "How long is the message?"

If you choose cassettes, the length is indicated in the number of the item you buy. C-30's give a total of 30 minutes of message, 15 minutes on each side. Thus a C-120 will play for two hours, 60 minutes per side. The difference is achieved in the thickness of the tape. Thin tapes can wind within the standard cassette housing and thus be longer, giving a longer message.

If you use reel-to-reel, and wonder about how long the reels will play, the NAVA *Audio-Visual Equipment Directory* publishes a table showing how long certain tapes can play at given speeds. For example, from p. 435 of the 1972–1973 edition:

Length of tape (feet)	Playing speed in inches per second (IPS)			
	$1\frac{7}{8}$	$3\frac{3}{4}$	$7\frac{1}{2}$	15
150	15 min.	$7\frac{1}{2}$ min.	$3\frac{3}{4}$ min.	$1\frac{7}{8}$ min.
300	30 min.	5 min.	$7\frac{1}{2}$ min.	$3\frac{3}{4}$ min.
600	1 hr.	30 min.	15 min.	$7\frac{1}{2}$ min.
1200	2 hrs.	1 hr.	30 min.	15 min.

Cartridges imply a continuous playback capability, since the tape is "looped." They come "eight-track," which moves more rapidly than do tapes in cassettes. The continuous feature is most desirable for display and exhibits. In T & D applications it permits initial "start up" by learners who approach a teaching machine or student carrel.

Playback quality is important if the audiotaped program is to sound professional. The secret is in the speakers and the amplifiers of the playback equipment. To sacrifice the quality of the speakers is to impair the ultimate stimulation for which the audio presentation was designed. If the programs must physically move about an organization, then "durable" and "lightweight" are good adjectives to keep in mind when buying audiotape equipment.

Some audio programs rely on records. Playback machines should have a strong drive motor. Astute buyers ask for life statistics and endurance warranties. Good speakers are equally important. Some buyers want variable speed—not quite the same thing as multiple speed. Variable speed allows the machine to operate at any speed—a requirement when tonal analysis is necessary. Multiple speed playback units permit use of the standard speeds; 33⅓, 45, or 78 are most common. Multiple speed is a *must* requirement for the T & D specialist. Even though the T & D department may have adopted one speed for everything it produces, it will want to review (and possibly purchase) programs recorded at another of the standard speeds.

Boards

Chalkboards, flannelboards, magnetic boards and flipcharts form a battery of very simple equipment which works extremely well for visual stimulation. Practically anything that can be put onto overhead transparencies or 35 mm slides or filmstrips can be put onto any of these media. We take them so much for granted that we sometimes forget they are media—available with little cost or effort to help us in stimulating and clarifying visual processes.

There is other "special equipment."

Models

Models cover a wide gamut of complexity. Some are merely designed to replicate small subsystems of machines or hardware used by the organization. These are for demonstration by an instructor—and hopefully for inspection and manipulation by the learner. Others are actual machines—specially marked so novices can handle the training aids—which Ron Anderson calls "real things."

Simulators

Simulators run through an even wider gamut of complexity. Simple paper mock-ups of mechanical devices, life-size photographs which duplicate a life-like atmosphere (as of an airplane cockpit or a submarine) to computerized simulations of total environments. Sales counters, autos, airplanes, and submarines are typically simulated by T & D departments. The cost of these simulators varies from a few dollars to several millions of dollars. An airline can better afford to pay three to five million dollars for a simulator than to remove a twenty million dollar aircraft from scheduled service, or subject it to abnormal flying conditions. The computerized flight simulator can react to any set of circumstances the instructor "instructs" this training aid to perform. The word "simulator" doesn't come lightly when applied to such sophisticated training aids; the learners are in an environment which dynamically duplicates the real world and which alters in direct relationship to their actions. It permits learning "the consequences" in a machine which produces the ultimate reality. Thus the "generalization" is presumed to be complete: the learner has tried out the new behaviors in a world which precisely duplicates the real world in which the organization says the behaviors must survive.

One could learn a great deal more about the audio-visual field, and in some large T & D departments there are A/V specialists who do that—and nothing else. If asked for the big secrets of successful operation, they would probably stress:

1.   The medium is selected *after* the message and *after* the learning objectives. When media selections come first, that is because of the constraint of available media—or because some "nut" is forcing a fad upon a program, its designers, and the unfortunate learners. But no matter the reason, when media considerations come first, the designer may use a less-than-optimum medium. This sometimes must happen. Example: there is no other equipment available—but it's not the most professional utilization of media.

2.   Durability and portability are important criteria. Why? Professional utilization in T & D activity can be demanding upon equipment. Normal household standards aren't always adequate for the repeated use and heavy travel demands made by busy T & D departments.

3.   A close working relationship with local vendors and salespeople is a great asset! These professionals can tell the T & D specialist about new equipment, about effective new maintenance procedures, and about suitable repairs.

But no matter how sophisticated the equipment or the specialist, the ultimate effectiveness of audio-visual material is its contribution to learning. That means that there must be "software" . . . films to thread in movie projectors . . . transparencies or slides to project . . . filmstrips to project . . . slapons or drawings to put on the boards. Let's look at a few simple principles of visual presentation.

PRINCIPLES OF VISUAL PRESENTATION

Effective visual aids adhere to certain criteria.

First, a good visual aid is *unified*. It makes just one point; it contains nothing irrelevant to the learning for which it was designed.

Second, it will be *simple*. That's a bit different from unified. Simplicity implies that the message is told in the fewest possible symbols, pictures, or words. There is no clutter. If a picture of one tree makes the point, why show two trees?

Visual aids should be *accurate*. There should be no unexplained distortions or

Fig. 13.3.

Distortions and missing relationships.

missing relationships. Look at Fig. 13.3. To a person who had never previously seen an apple or a house, the learning would be that they are the same size. The person who had never before seen a human would have a definite misconception of our visual apparatus!

Next, visual aids should be *colorful*. This doesn't mean merely that they escape the parameters of black-and-white presentation, though that is a part of it.

The "colorful" criterion implies a certain intensity—especially for key figures or key words. Let the lighter tones (the tints and pastels) serve as background; let the things learners are supposed to remember appear in stark, vivid colors. But this criterion also implies that there should be a restraint on the number of colors in any one display. Unless "profusion" is the theme, the visual aid shouldn't use up the entire spectrum—nor show the full range of colored pens and ozalids available in the A/V tool kit! Let such variety express itself through an entire program, but restrain the number of colors on any single visual display.

Even when there is a wide array of colors in an entire program, consistency in color is important. There should be a reasonable and reliable consistency in the symbolism of the colors. Since we think of red as a STOP signal and green as a GO cue, some designers like to show the "correct" way in green or against green backgrounds. If blue is used to show the upward flow of communication on one slide, then blue should also be used to show similar flow in successive slides.

When colors are selected for psychological impact, Keith Craven (*New Dimensions,* No. 2, 1974) recommends these guidelines:

Use red for warm, stimulating effect.
Use blue for cool, sedative, depressing effects.
Yellow gives warm, capricious, sunny overtones.
Green is for pleasant, healthy, growthful messages.
Orange is stimulating.
Purple sends messages of dignity and reserve.

Visual aids should be *legible*. That means they're "readable" and that the images should be big enough to be seen. Colors can add to, or hinder, legibility. Robinson P. Rigg, in *Audiovisual Aids and Techniques,* distributed in the United States by Olympic Film Service of New York City, presents these guidelines:

Viewing distance	Height of lettering used on screen or display board
8 ft.	¼ in.
16 ft.	½ in.
32 ft.	1 in.
64 ft.	2 in.
128 ft.	4 in.

Rarely do class situations find learners as far removed from the screen as 64 to 128 feet. However, at conferences, T & D professionals would do well to check the image height to make certain they are meeting something like minimal professional standards. This same source suggests guidelines based on screen widths:

If the farthest viewer is seated	Then the minimum height on 9″ × 12″ artwork should be
4 screen widths	0.12 in.
6 screen widths	0.18 in.

As we've noted, viewers should never be seated farther away from the screen than the 6W (six screen widths) mentioned in that table. On page 144, Rigg offers an extremely useful template showing the actual minimum image size for use in creating artwork for projection.

Keith Craven suggests that legibility and *visibility* are two different things, and that color can contribute to visibility. He quotes Bustanoby's *Principles of Color and Color Mixing,* which rates 20 color combinations for their visibility. From best-to-worst, they are:

Black on yellow
Black on orange
Orange on Navy blue
Green on white
Scarlet red on white
Black on white
Navy blue on white
White on Navy blue
Orange on black
White on black

White on bottle-green
White on scarlet red
White on purple
Purple on white
Navy blue on yellow
Navy blue on orange
Yellow on black
Scarlet red on yellow
Yellow on Navy blue
Purple on yellow

Warm colors (reds, yellows, oranges) will appear larger to the viewer than the cooler blues or greens. A light color appears brighter against a black background than against white. Strongly saturated colors seem to have more weight than pastels, and are used widely in small areas balancing large pastel areas. Obviously, pastels are inappropriate for the key words or images of a visual presentation.

Frederick J. Haines contends, in "Coping With Color: Easy When You Know How" (*Video Systems,* July/August 1976), that all flesh colors are yellowish; only the brightness varies among European, African, and Oriental skins. Thus blue, the complement, is a useful background—the one seen most often on television news broadcasts! Haines urges the producers of videotape productions never to start filming without previewing the set colors.

Just to be practical, we must add *portability* as a criterion for effective visual aids. It is less critical in those T & D departments which operate out of a single training center—but it certainly applies to scattered operations! Even in central quarters, there are probably instructors who can testify to the importance of portability. Remember, the heaviest equipment can be made portable with the judicious installation of a few wheels!

Finally, the visual aid should be *visual!* If that sounds silly, here's what it means. There is some small evidence that seeing a picture and a title simultaneously produces better retention than seeing them separately. But there is no evidence that seeing and hearing a word simultaneously produces comprehension. In other words, just printing words on a training aid doesn't make a *visual* aid . . . only a verbal aid. Let's take an example. We're trying to teach a country child what a skyscraper is. We say the word and then we show the word on the screen. The child may know the word—but how about the concept? How could any child, given that visual aid, envision the towers of Manhattan!

This isn't meant to imply that abstractions and unfamiliar concepts aren't subject to effective visual aids. Quite the opposite. If ever a learner might profit from an effective photograph, that "skyscraper" concept is a perfect example. But it's the picture—not the word—that causes the insight.

When visualizing concepts, the designers can let their creativity have full play. They can think in analogies—like trees representing growth . . . maps to show that there are alternative highways, options in the problem-solving process . . . Sherlock Holmes as analyst for the data-gathering phases. They can think in contrasts. Thus day and night, smiles and frowns, plus and minus may become visual themes underlying and reinforcing the concepts of the printed words. Creative A/V designers can, in short, prevent the visual program from being nothing more than a bunch of words thrown on the screen, slapped onto a flannelboard, or revealed on the flipchart!

PARTICIPATIVE POTENTIAL IN AUDIO-VISUAL AIDS

Our study of learning theory nowadays stresses the importance of adult learners taking an active part in the learning processes. How can that apply to the use and design of audio-visual materials?

It's immediately apparent that media like videotape offer unlimited ways to involve learners, who can take part in simulated conferences, speeches, teaching assignments, roleplays. They can design "cases" to put onto tape. In all these they can replay for self critique or group analysis.

T & D specialists have been getting their learners involved in making tape recordings of roleplays and presentations for a good many years. This medium has been an effective device for giving learners feedback about what they have accomplished and what they need to polish for further improvement.

When they use models, instructors face a choice of doing all the manipulating themselves—or of getting the learners immediately involved in handling the parts, assembling, disassembling, or operating. The latter method is clearly the more participative, the more andragogic choice. Unfortunately, it is not clear that this is the choice most instructors make most frequently.

But it is less likely that the T & D specialist can think of ways to get learners involved with the other forms of audio-visual presentation. This unlikelihood does not make it impossible. Overhead transparencies do not need to be "fixed" and complete; they can leave room for participants to add answers, steps of a process, items in a list. They can be made "mobile" so pieces can be moved and assembled into patterns. The entire transparency can carry the findings of a team project; it can communicate a student's design for a form or a process, thus forming the basis for a report to a class and for a class analysis.

The pieces of the "jigsaw" to be moved around on the stage of an overhead projector might be the elements in a process (decisions and actions) or the

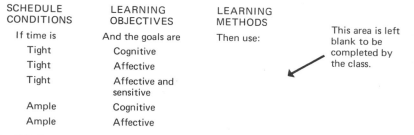

SCHEDULE CONDITIONS	LEARNING OBJECTIVES	LEARNING METHODS	
If time is	And the goals are	Then use:	This area is left blank to be completed by the class.
Tight	Cognitive		
Tight	Affective		
Tight	Affective and sensitive		
Ample	Cognitive		
Ample	Affective		

Fig. 13.4.

A sample visual aid.

departments of an organization, or the members of a department. Participants can then arrange these elements into different patterns and discuss each. Similar jigsaws can be assembled, analyzed, and reassembled on magnetic boards or flannelboards.

Any visual aid can contain questions or elements which make it subject to questions from the instructor or from the class. For example, a list of variables for making decisions can appear on the visual aid; the class can then work out the appropriate action to take for each combination of circumstances. Fig. 13.4 shows an example. In this case, the instructor would supply the combinations on the visual aid; the students could work out the answers for the third column. There is no reason, of course, why participants couldn't use a discussion to generate the key variables—and from that create their own visual aid as a control and stimulus device to assist their learning process!

In *The Modern Practice of Adult Education,* Malcolm Knowles identifies an A/V "Experience Cone" (Fig. 13.5). As this adapted version indicates, some media are inclined toward abstractions, concepts, and generalities; others toward concrete experience. The continuum between these two points represents the "scale of sensory experience" for the learner.

SUMMARY

How important is audio-visual support for the learning process? What is the best medium for your message?

Individual learning objectives and special learning environments and the personal styles of the instructor determine the answer to those questions.

But let's just consider one last comment from Martin Broadwell in his "The Use and Misuse of A-V" (*Training,* October 1970): "Let's dispel a misconception we all blame on the Chinese, who really knew better. Ever heard, 'A

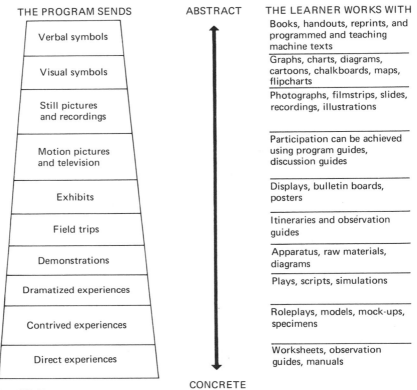

Fig. 13.5.

Continuum of A/V experiences. (Adapted from the "Experience Cone" in Malcolm S. Knowles, *The Modern Practice of Adult Education.* Used by permission of Association Press.)

picture is worth ten thousand words,' or something else close to that? . . . A big point is missed by failing to add the word 'good' before 'picture.' Ten million words are better than a bad picture.''

WHAT'S SPECIAL ABOUT TRAINING AND DEVELOPMENT BUDGETS?

INTRODUCTORY ISSUES

Training and development officers prepare budgets about the same way any other manager prepares budgets—with a few special considerations.

Of course, the items they include in the budget are training-related—and there is always the issue of trainee salaries. Do they show up in the T & D budget or in the budgets for their regular department? Then there is the ambiguity of forecasting performance problems which haven't yet happened! How can anybody possibly forecast the cost of solving a problem which hasn't yet revealed itself, much less been scoped? Then finally, there is the sensitive issue of trying to assign dollar values to human performance, a process which frequently frightens many people and which usually angers many humanists.

This urge to demonstrate a return on the training investment is not new—but it is certainly growing in intensity. In 1969 Malcolm W. Warren wrote, in *Training for Results,* "Most organizations expect a training manager to provide a reasonably accurate cost estimate of future training actions. A few also expect an estimate of return on investment." (p. 89)

In the years since 1969, many T & D officers have probably amended this to read "A *great many* expect an estimate of return on investment." More and more T & D officers are learning that their job security (to say nothing of their own satisfaction with their achievements!) depends heavily upon their ability to calculate the cost of performance deficiencies . . . and the cost of correcting them.

In short, good T & D budgeting puts the T & D dollar where the organization will find the biggest return on its investment.

To some degree this implies a change in the way T & D officers talk to top management about the T & D function . . . in the way they "sell" their services. As Warren also points out, "The data must be in terms useful to the organization. The trainer who reports the value of training programs in terms of final tests is not likely to be telling management much about its return on investment."

Therefore in this chapter we will look at some general "rules of thumb" for planning the volume of T & D activity. Next we will consider a process for computing the cost of performance problems. Then to determine whether training is or is not a cost-effective activity, we will finally look at formulae for computing the cost of training.

By doing these things, we will have answered our question, "What's special about Training and Development budgets?"

GENERAL ESTIMATING POLICIES

How much of the organization's total budget should be invested in T & D activities?

For normal operations, most organizations allocate between 1.5 and 2.5 percent of their total employee salary cost to T & D. Of course there are some exceptional cases. New plants will need much higher allocations for their first six months. When a totally new product or service is introduced, the allocation may double for anywhere from three to six months. Unusual organizations, like the numerous new high tech firms, and unusual departments (such as Research and Development or the T & D department itself) should probably budget from three to four times the normal allocation.

Then there are unusual circumstances where offices or entire plants may shut down for training. Plant start-ups, retooling, new product lines, installation of totally new processes or procedures, a new management team . . . all these might require training as a precursor to production. Such shutdowns mean extremely high costs: 100 percent during the training period. However, budgets are usually annualized, so the ultimate costs are more normal, though somewhat swollen.

The same thing happens when a distressed department uses organizational development. The T & D officer should budget (or counsel the client to budget) at least five times the usual training allocation. Ten times may be more realistic for the duration of the intervention itself. After all, the major energy of the top-salaried people will be devoted to analysis of their mission, structures, processes, and relationships. It's quite probably that eventually *all* employees will get involved, so there are periods where re-developing the organization, not production, is the focus. In this sense the OD intervention is really different from a shutdown only in the degree to which normal work continues.

Another unusual condition arises when an organization discovers almost too late that it has been neglecting its management development. It is not terribly rare for an organization or a department to discover that huge percentages of its management will be retiring within a very few years. The ensuing extra effort to train replacements demands extra budget allocations. The actual amount will depend upon the numbers to be educated and developed. It is not unusual, however, for such crises to require from five to six times the normal management development expenditures.

What implications do these figures have for the size of the T & D staff?

To answer that, we must look at the total organization and determine the numbers of people whose major contribution is training or developing others. We will (1) make no effort to determine whether they are T & D Department employees or line employees doing T & D work, and (2) consider the total manpower posts devoted to T & D, even though they may involve several people working part time to fill up one post.

In a study for his book, Warren found that the typical organization used about one T & D professional for every 96 employees. However he also found some organizations with only one T & D specialist for every 500 employees— and one with so little energy for employee growth that the ratio was one T & D specialist per 4,000 employees! Nowadays, with high technology required of more and more blue-, white-, and pink-collar workers, and with burgeoning life-long learning, T & D populations will predictably increase, both in raw numbers and in percentage of the employment roster.

Such data are useful only as "benchmarks" and must be augmented with reliable signals from the top of the organization. This is just one more reason why the T & D officer needs to be—and actually is—increasingly close to the people who make the major planning decisions. By both physical and organizational proximity, the T & D or Human Resource Director is indeed one of the strategic planners. In organizations where this happens, the number of T & D professionals may easily exceed the typical one-per-96 by two or three times.

But broad, sweeping plans and policies are ultimately validated and implemented by details, one step at a time. The discovery of a performance problem, current or imminent because of new programs, is the first moment the T & D officer is certain about the volume of work the T & D specialists will face. As a result, flexibility in staff size is highly desirable.

The variation between "highs" and "lows" isn't devastating. There is more than one way for the T & D staff to absorb the fluctuation:

● Since the T & D department needs more than normal allocations for educating its own staff, sometimes that can be slowed down to take care of unexpected peak workloads.

● People with T & D experience can be rotated into other managerial positions as part of their own education and development. When the peak occurs, they can be temporarily reassigned to the T & D project.

● Outside resources (consultants, contract instructors, or graduate students studying T & D in nearby universities) can temporarily augment the staff during heavy workloads.

● Temporary staff members, employed for a single project or a limited number of projects, can lighten a heavy workload. These people also learn a great deal about when to train and how to do it well; they are thus rich resources as strong allies in other parts of the organization.

Each of these is a useful option—but the best way to avoid unexpected peaks in workload is (repeat!) for the T & D officer to be in constant communication with the chief executives of the organization. This permits an early warning system that not only protects the T & D department against surprises—it also allows the T & D officer to counsel the executives about the real human resource costs of contemplated policy changes and programs.

The initial question from most T & D officers is, "What will it cost to run the department?" That can't be answered until there is an estimate about the number of performance problems that deserve solving. Not always, but usually, the basis for deciding whether or not a performance problem is worth solving is the cost-effectiveness. For this reason, the most pervasive budgeting question asked by the T & D officer is: "What will it cost this organization to keep employees performing at standard?"

A good specific question is: "What is this performance problem costing us?" The answers to that question are not always easy to discover—but they are usually there. Let's look at the process for getting the answers.

COMPUTING THE COST OF PERFORMANCE DEFICIENCIES

As we've noted, every employee performs a number of tasks. Successful completion of each task represents one accomplishment every time it's done. The unit may be a letter written, a shipment packed, a grievance handled, a decision made, a customer order, or an unhappy client mollified. When there is a performance problem, those accomplishments are either missing or substandard: the unit of satisfactory accomplishment is not there as an "output."

The formula for costing out performance deficiencies is to first determine the unit. The second step is to determine the cost of that unit. The third step is to multiply the cost-per-unit by the number of defective units.

Let's take a simple example. Sales agents consistently make errors in listing product categories at the cash register. Twenty percent of their daily total of 160 slips must be returned. That means we have 32 defective units each day, 160 per week, or 8,000 in a 50-week year. Our study shows that it takes an auditor 15 minutes to correct each error. Then supervisors are expected to follow-up, spending an average of 10 minutes making sure clerks use the proper code next time. If clerks earn $4 per hour, and if auditors and supervisors average $5 per hour, what are the salary costs to the organization?

Well we can calculate the cost by adding three elements:

15 minutes of auditor time costs one-fourth of $5, or $1.25.
10 minutes of supervisory time costs one-sixth of $5, or 83¢.
10 minutes of clerk time costs one-sixth of $4, or 66¢.

In making this estimate, we will ignore the time the clerk spent making the wrong entry. Nor will we try to compute the consequences, which are probably bad data in inventory control systems. We'll stick to the salary costs of the deficiency. We add the three amounts:

$1.25 + .83 + .66 = $2.74 per unit.

We know that on our entire staff we have 8,000 defective units per year, so we multiply 8,000 times $2.74. This tells us that the performance problem is costing $21,920 dollars annually. We won't know whether it's worth correcting until we estimate the cost of the training. It may be that it's better to install some sort of job aid for the clerks to check.

Not all units of performance are equally easy to cost out. For one reason, there are hidden costs. This means that the computation and analysis just to get the unit cost is more complex. For another reason, some units don't immediately reveal their costs. How do you put a price tag on the loss of a valued customer due to a rude employee? . . . on the loss of morale due to a flagrant misuse of discipline? . . . on the confusion resulting from a distorted or lost message from management?

T & D officers who *want* to cost out these apparently ambiguous deficiencies can do so.

"Wanting to do so" is the most important element. In the case of that lost customer it's possible to use standard figures: what's the profit from the average customer? How many do we estimate we lost due to rudeness last year? It's easy to multiply the two figures. Or the lost message: What are some typical deficiences which grew out of the loss? Maybe it's using an obsolete price list; maybe it's the overtime we had to pay because the swing shift didn't show up on time. The point is that where there is a will, there are data! In these days of computer-generated data, most management information systems provide more printout than people really want to have! Somewhere in that jungle of figures is just the precise fact needed to put a pricetag on a defective unit of performance . . . just waiting for the T & D officer who *wants* to track it down!

There are two significant notes of caution in this process:

1.   The figures used in computing the cost of performance deficiences must be seen as valid by the manager who "owns" the problem, and

2.   The data should generally be available through normal reporting channels rather than produced by channels designed only for this study.

As Warren cautions, the T & D function must be careful not to "make demands on the organization for data not otherwise required, or the expense of data collecting may exceed its value." (*Training for Results,* p. 99)

Nonetheless, when analyzing the cost of performance problems, one element appears in nearly all problems: the *time* wasted by the bad performance. It's a simple step to tie behaviors into time, time into salary. From those data one can compute dollars-and-cents salary costs. Material costs also tend to be available in other management reporting systems. When these two factors have been accounted for, the cost-per-unit is usually pretty well established.

Both the "flagrant misuse of discipline" and the "lost message" situation can be costed out by figuring a typical amount of time lost per incident—and then estimating the number of incidents. In bad discipline there is time spent in complaining, grieving, regretting, "getting even." Similar events can be traced, as we have already done, with the lost or distorted message problems.

Granted, the *real* loss may be neither time nor money. It may be esteem and trust and loyalty and job satisfaction. Nobody denies that these are valid as the real costs. But astute T & D officers don't try to put pricetags on these human values. Rather they make their point on what they *can* prove with the price tags that go along with the greater psychic costs.

The logic is this: "If we want to improve the quality of life around here, we can do so. What's more, we can justify it on a cost basis!"

The cost-effectiveness activity doesn't take away a thing from the humanistic enthusiasts; it merely permits the T & D officer to justify training and development as an economic investment. In doing that it also gives the data needed to make effective dollars-and-cents decisions about whether solving the problem is a sound investment—and if so, which problems are most damaging.

The point is that when T & D officers genuinely wish to do cost-effectiveness studies, they can do so. The data are usually there. The technology exists. To review, let's go through the steps of the process:

1. Identify a single unit of defective performance.

2. Calculate (or make the best possible estimate) the cost of one unit.

3. Count or calculate the number of defective units—usually for one year.

4. Multiply the unit cost by the number of defective units. This will give the annual cost of the performance problem.

Once the T & D officer, acting as consultant to the organization, has computed the cost of the deficiency, the next step is to compute the cost of the program.

COMPUTING THE COST OF TRAINING

Training is really a relatively expensive solution for performance problems. It contrasts sharply with the cost of other solutions:

1. Feedback is often a low-cost solution because the implementation mechanisms are so simple. They can frequently be installed even in large organizations for just a few cents per worker, following only a few days of design.

2. Job aids, once the task analysis is complete, can be printed for a few pennies or dollars. Once installed at the workplace, they can guide the performer as a substitute for training. (For very complex tasks or operations, they often supplement training as an effective post-training "handout" or follow-up.)

3. Job engineering takes longer and is more expensive to install because it requires thorough task analysis and involves enlisting management and worker support for the new distribution of tasks and responsibilities. However it is still often less costly to do this than to design, conduct, and evaluate the recurring training programs made necessary by "undoable" jobs which cause friction, stress, or boredom.

4. Contingency management is time consuming, and may require much greater expenditure during the analysis. However, new contingencies can be installed with relatively low costs—if the positive reinforcers selected for contingencies are integral to the work itself and not expensive external incentives.

5. Quality Circles may be costly to install, since they involve all levels of management and workers in an ongoing structure. That very involvement, however, has the "saving grace" of getting work done even while circle members are developing both interpersonal and managerial skills.

6.   Organization development, as we have noted, is costly in management time, but requires relatively few materials. Furthermore, it often involves relatively small numbers (albeit "costly") participants who represent the top of the salary scale. However, if it succeeds, the OD intervention should prevent many future performance problems.

Training is expensive because to budget for the *total* training program the T & D officer must include such items as program production, trainee costs, conducting the program, evaluation costs, and follow-up activities.

Salary and material costs during the design phase of a training program add up fast! Trainee costs (travel, materials, and salary) add up even faster; after all, there are far more trainees than there are instructional designers!

The T & D officer is concerned to control costs wherever and whenever possible. On one level this means that the monies which actually get spent are consistent with the monies budgeted for that purpose. On another level there is concern to keep each expenditure appropriate to its contribution to the entire T & D effort.

Malcolm Warren comments on such balances and control in *Training for Results*. He divides the training expenditure into "Support" and "Operating" expenses. Support costs include staff, equipment, special materials, travel, and "state-of-the-art" expenses. ("State-of-the-art" expenses are those costs of upgrading the staff in new technologies. As we've noted, the percentage of total time is abnormally high for T & D staff when contrasted to most other job classifications.) Warren feels that "Using total training dollars as a base, the minimum support cost should not be less than 10 percent of the total training dollars spent in the organization." (p. 95)

Another useful cost ratio comparison comes from the same source. Warren recommends a profile like this:

Development	35% of budgeted dollars
Operations	35% of the budgeted dollars
Analysis	20% of the budgeted dollars
Evaluation	10% of the budgeted dollars

As the number of trainees grows, the percentage allocated to operations will increase proportionately.

Production costs can be divided into two categories: Staff and Materials. Staff costs must include time spent in "front-end" analysis. This means the consultation about the real nature of the performance problem and appropriate solutions. It also includes the staff time spent in developing the materials used in the solution.

How much does "analysis" cost? What does it involve? Joe Harless, a major performance technologist, has pointed out that "An ounce of analysis is worth a pound of objectives." Other authorities have said that the analysis activity looks like this:

Planning	5%
Task analysis (defining the standard)	30%
Developing objectives	5%
Developing evaluation (criterion test)	10%
Validating test	10%
Developing materials	15%
Trying out the program	10%
Revising and retesting	10%
Publishing (or overseeing it)	5%

You may wonder at the low percentage of time given to "developing objectives." Consider, though, that this means merely casting the task analysis (or standards) into useful phraseology. The total time devoted to defining the desired learning really comes to 45 percent. It includes task analysis, developing objectives, and developing the criterion test. All those activities aid the process of pinpointing the desired outcomes of the training.

The "front-end analysis" detailed in that list includes some items which do not apply to non-training solutions. Nor does the list reveal how much of the *total* training cost goes to analysis.

A checklist documenting all the costs of training might look like this:

A Formula for Computing Training Production Costs

Item	Formula	Total
Staff Costs:		
Salaries: Consulting	Number of people times	
Designing	median salary times	
Conducting	number of hours on the project	
Evaluating		_____
Fees: Outside designers		
and consultants	Total fees and expenses paid out	_____
Travel: Tickets	Total from expense reports	_____
Other expenses	Total from expense reports, *or* per diem times number of days	_____
Overhead	Use standard organization figures; if none exist, use 100 percent of base salary	_____

A Formula for Computing Training Production Costs (*Continued*)

Item	Formula	Total
Materials:		
Film	Actual costs if purchased: $1,650 to $3,000 per minute to produce; $45 to $120 per ten minutes for prints	_____
Videotape	Prorated overhead from own studio, *or* Rental rate plus operator salary, *or* Staff salary median times number of hours	_____
Videodiscs	From $35,000 to $100,000 per hour	_____
Audiotapes	$50 to $200 per minute to produce $2.50 per print to duplicate $5 to $10 for commercial products	_____
35 mm slides	$15 to $50 per slide to produce 45¢ per print to duplicate	_____
Overhead transparencies	$30 to $100 to produce (includes artwork) 45¢ to $15 per print	_____
Artwork	Minimum of $1.50 per square inch to create	_____
Manuals and materials	Local figures; public or in-house printshop quotations	_____
Announcements	Local figures needed here	_____
Special equipment	Total purchase price; normally amoritized over 10 years	_____
	Total cost to produce the training program:	_____

The computations in this list were originally developed by the Office of Personnel Management in *A Training Cost Model,* published in 1972 when it was The United States Civil Service Commission. The astronomical videodisc costs occur, says Jeremy Main in *Fortune,* October 1, 1984, ". . . because it requires a production crew and cast." This expensive medium is used largely with interactive Computer Assisted Instruction. The other cost figures shown were reliable estimates at the time this book went to press. It's impossible to say what a changing Dow-Jones, or a fluctuating Price Index, or a money supply will have done to them by the time you read this chapter!

Development time depends heavily upon the format in which the training is presented. *A Training Cost Model* uses this formula to estimate the ratio between production costs and class time:

If the format is	Then figure this many hours of production for each hour of presentation
Technical formal courses	5 to 15
Self-contained for hand-off to other instructors	50 to 100
Conventional management development	20 to 30
Programmed instruction	80 to 120
Technical on-site	1 to 3
Computer-assisted instruction	Up to 350

Production costs are not limited to design. Instructors must also prepare to teach. This doesn't mean those minutes or hours spent the day before class—moving the furniture, setting up projectors, or putting paper and pencils at each learner-position. This refers to the instructors' activity in getting themselves ready to teach the program. In other words, it refers to eliminating their own D_K's about the particular program. The U.S. Civil Service estimates are based upon the length of the course. They go like this:

Does the course last	Then for each class hour, budget this many preparation hours
5 days or less?	3 hours preparation for 1 hour of teaching
Between 5 and 10 days?	2.5 hours preparation for 1 teaching hour
Over 10 days?	2 hours preparation per hour of teaching

Another approach to the instructor-preparation estimating involves the methods used in the program rather than the length of the course. When methods are considered, the estimates might be more like this:

If the methods are	Then for each class hour, budget this many preparation hours
A tell-and-show by instructor	5 to 10
Mediated tell-and-show	1 (to preview the program)
Group discussion	Less than 1
Action or experiential	1.5 (The instructor should *do* the role-plays, games, or whatever; then analyze the probable dynamics.)

When the program requires or permits a formal tryout period, there may be unusual travel and facilities costs. They are probably a good investment. Few training programs can be expected to move from the mind of the designer to the classroom without some revision and improvement. The same may be said when feedback mechanisms, contingency management or job engineering are the solutions to the performance problem.

Such tryouts bring another cost: the salary of the "test" or "control" population. T & D officers with "button-down" budgets want to charge those salaries to the production costs of the program.

That raises the entire issue of trainee salary. Should salary costs be considered part of the cost of training? This issue takes us to the budget for "conducting the training."

If T & D officers want rigorous proof that their programs pay their own way, they usually insist on including trainee salaries as part of the program costs. Even if there is no formal paper transfer of these funds, they want to know exactly what total amount of human resources must be invested in order to improve those resources. Some include fringe benefits; others include the downtime—production lost because the participant was off the job. A thorough cost estimate for conducting training looks like this:

A Formula for Computing the Costs of Conducting Training

Trainee costs: *Total*

Number of trainees (by paygroup) × median salary × training
hours   _____

Number of trainees × hourly fringe benefit charges × hours   _____

Travel costs: Total from expense reports, or median cost ×
number of trainees   _____

Per diem: Total from expense reports, or median allowance ×
the number of trainees × number of days   _____

Student materials: Unit costs × number of trainees   _____

Trainee replacement costs: Number of hours × median salary   _____

Lost production: Value-per-unit × the number of lost units, or
value-per-unit × the reduced production   _____

Faculty costs:

Number of trainers × number of hours × median salary   _____

Travel costs: Total tickets, or median × number of trainers   _____

Per diem: Total from expense reports, or median allowance ×
number of trainers × number of days   _____

Special equipment or services:

Rental of equipment: Total charges. If purchased, amortize over
10 years   _____

The cost of evaluating training may be considered as a distinct phase, or as items in the earlier phases. The important thing is to make the budget reflect the fact that evaluation does cost something. Documenting the costs further increases the probability that evaluation will be done—and that the total training budget will honestly reflect the total cost of training.

A document for estimating evaluation costs would probably look like this:

Cost of Evaluating Training

Item	Formula	Total
Salaries:		
Design:		
Selecting criteria	Number of hours × median salary	_____
Creating instruments		
Data sources:	Number of hours × median salary	_____
Graduates and managers		
Interviewers (if applicable)	Number of hours × median salary	_____
Data analysis	Number of hours × median salary	_____
Materials:		
Printing	Actual local costs	_____
Mailing	Units × two-way postage	_____
Travel (If interviews are used):		
Tickets	Actual totals	_____
Expenses	Actual totals or allowance × number of days	_____
	Total cost of evaluating the training:	_____

The total cost of the program is, of course, computed by adding the production costs, conducting costs and evaluation costs. As the next summary chart shows, it is also possible to compare and contrast programs by computing the cost per trainee, the cost per hour, and the cost per trainee hour:

Total Training Costs

Cost items	Dollars	Cost per trainee: Divide $ by number of trainees	Cost per hour: Divide $ by number of hours	Cost per trainee-hour: Divide $ by (number of trainees × number of hours)
Production costs:				
Staff	_____	_____	_____	_____
Material	_____	_____	_____	_____
Course conduct costs:				
Trainee	_____	_____	_____	_____
Faculty	_____	_____	_____	_____
Equipment/services	_____	_____	_____	_____

Total Training Costs (*Continued*)

Cost items	Dollars	Cost per trainee: Divide $ by number of trainees	Cost per hour: Divide $ by number of hours	Cost per trainee-hour: Divide $ by (number of trainees × number of hours)
Evaluation costs:				
Salaries	————	————	————	————
Materials	————	————	————	————
Travel	————	————	————	————
Totals:	————	————	————	————

HOW BUDGETING HELPS THE "GO/NO-GO" DECISION

By now it should be quite apparent that the budgeting process is another decision-making instrument for the T & D officer. To decide whether or not to pursue a solution to a recognized performance problem . . . to find more economical solutions—these questions can be answered by good budgeting practice.

For *every* performance problem, the T & D officer asks, "Is this problem costing a significant amount of dollars?" If the answer is "Yes," the next inquiry should be, "Can we solve the problem by investing fewer dollars than the problem is costing us?" That answer sometimes dictates a decision to live with the problem, or to consider less costly alternative solutions.

Schematically, the process looks something like Fig. 14.1. As the chart indicates, not all performance problems should be solved. The T & D officer has a major consultative responsibility to help management recognize this condition when it is true . . . to help invest the T & D dollars and energy in problems with the highest payoff.

It doesn't necessarily follow that all decisions rest on cost-effectiveness. There are certain occasions when the emotional strain of an unsolved problem is just too great to bear. The human beings involved with the problem cannot go on living with it—despite the fact that there is no economic loss from the problem. There may also be legal reasons for proceeding with training which is not cost-effective.

SUMMARY

In any event, the T & D officer must be concerned with the dollars-and-cents dimension of human resource development; those who ignore the economic

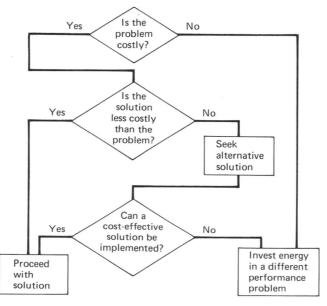

Fig. 14.1.

The go/no-go decision process.

impact of performance problems build their whole T & D operation on a shaky foundation. Continued refusal to confront the cost-effectiveness issue can jeopardize entire T & D departments—and even worse, whole careers. This is especially true during hard times, when we hear the lament "Training is the first thing to go around here!"

However, when T & D officers insist upon rigorous economic analysis of performance deficiencies, such budget cuts are minimized or eliminated. In organizations where T & D officers do solid, accurate cost analysis, training budgets tend to remain stable, even to grow when profits sag. Why?

If the T & D officer insists upon a cost-effective operation of programs that enhance productivity (and probably the quality of work-life while doing that!) then chief executives will probably consider T & D dollars as investments, not expenses. The prevailing philosophy is that dollars invested in human productivity will ultimately produce a more cost-effective operation, and therefore greater security for all the "human resources" in the entire organization.

CHAPTER **15**

HOW CAN
WE MEASURE
TRAINING AND
DEVELOPMENT?

REASONS FOR MEASURING

At least four people have good reasons for measuring T & D activities. Learners certainly want to know about their progress toward objectives. Instructors can intelligently modify and improve their own performance only on the basis of measurement of the learners' progress. T & D officers, knowing that learning is the product of their subsystem, have compelling reasons to measure. And finally, client-managers need measurement as an indication that they're solving or eliminating performance problems . . . getting something back on the training investment.

WHAT IS MEASUREMENT?

First let's distinguish between measurement and evaluation. Measurement is the process of gathering data; evaluation is the process of making judgments about those data.

Stated formally, measurement is the act of assigning numerals to processes or events or items, using some consistent set of rules. It is not necessary to measure in order to evaluate. That is to say, we can make judgments about the beauty of a landscape without measuring the distance between trees and clouds. However, if we wish to make sound judgments about an organizational operation, then hard data are necessary. We must count some objective evidence of conditions. Thus evaluation based on measurement has definite advantages:

• It reduces the possibility of disagreement between evaluators.

• It provides concrete feedback about what the program has achieved. If appropriately used throughout the training, it also provides continuous data about how the learnings are progressing.

• It permits positive comparison of pre- and post-problem status.

Evaluation involves making judgments about ideas, works, solutions, methods, or materials. It involves the use of criteria. (*Taxonomy of Educational Objectives*) When applied to determining the effectiveness of training, evaluation therefore would depend upon measuring the conditions caused by the problem, the progress made by learners in acquiring behaviors to solve the problem, the application of new behavior, and the impact of that application upon the problem.

Let's identify both measurement and evaluation in a typical T & D program. Suppose the Manager of Collections comes to the T & D officer, saying that the collection letters are pretty bad. "How bad are they?" asks the T & D officer.

"Here's how bad!" comes the reply. "We write 120 collection letters every day. We get some kind of payment from only 18. That's intolerable!" In this case there has been measurement. Someone determined the daily output; someone counted the responses. That's measurement. But the Manager of Collections commented, "Here's how bad!" and, "That's intolerable!" These are evaluations.

The process of counting should be integral to all T & D functions. Without measurement there is no positive assurance that the ensuing judgments are accurate. Without data there is no proof that a real performance problem exists. Without measurement there is no assurance that T & D efforts have really achieved their objectives . . . or that they have really paid their way by returning to the organization values in excess of the expenditures. A data base is essential to good decisions by the T & D officer. Measurement and evaluation are part of the "security system." Continued existence and future budgets depend on gathering relevant, accurate data on which to make intelligent decisions.

If we think of the acronym ME for Measurement and Evaluation, we have an appropriate symbol. "ME" is a selfish, first-person word. However it is wise selfishness to measure and evaluate at all phases of the T & D cycle (Fig. 15.1). Let's examine that process in more detail.

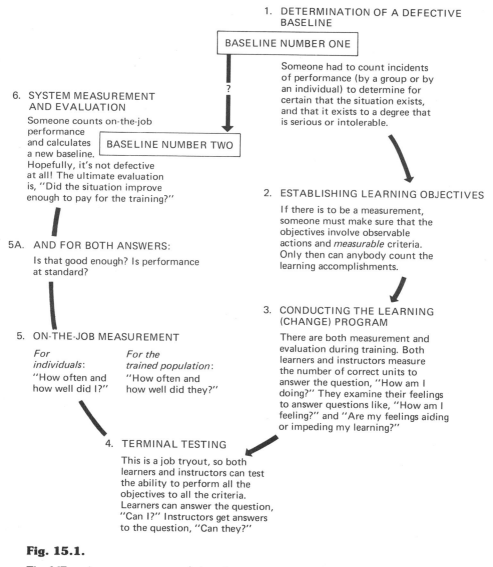

1. DETERMINATION OF A DEFECTIVE BASELINE

BASELINE NUMBER ONE

Someone had to count incidents of performance (by a group or by an individual) to determine for certain that the situation exists, and that it exists to a degree that is serious or intolerable.

6. SYSTEM MEASUREMENT AND EVALUATION

Someone counts on-the-job performance and calculates a new baseline. Hopefully, it's not defective at all! The ultimate evaluation is, "Did the situation improve enough to pay for the training?"

BASELINE NUMBER TWO

2. ESTABLISHING LEARNING OBJECTIVES

If there is to be a measurement, someone must make sure that the objectives involve observable actions and *measurable* criteria. Only then can anybody count the learning accomplishments.

5A. AND FOR BOTH ANSWERS:

Is that good enough? Is performance at standard?

3. CONDUCTING THE LEARNING (CHANGE) PROGRAM

There are both measurement and evaluation during training. Both learners and instructors measure the number of correct units to answer the question, "How am I doing?" They examine their feelings to answer questions like, "How am I feeling?" and "Are my feelings aiding or impeding my learning?"

5. ON-THE-JOB MEASUREMENT

For individuals:
"How often and how well did I?"

For the trained population:
"How often and how well did they?"

4. TERMINAL TESTING

This is a job tryout, so both learners and instructors can test the ability to perform all the objectives to all the criteria. Learners can answer the question, "Can I?" Instructors get answers to the question, "Can they?"

Fig. 15.1.

The ME cycle—measurement and evaluation.

SCALES OF MEASUREMENT

Skill in applying statistical methods is a great asset for the T & D officer who wishes to demonstrate beyond all doubt that T & D programs (not coincidence) have caused changes. Larger T & D departments employ such a statistical specialist. Smaller ones access similar experts employed in other parts of the organization. If the organization has nobody qualified to supply this statistical consulting service, outside help is usually available through local colleges or universities.

However, a great deal of effective measurement can be achieved without any professional help. Quite clearly the first step is to determine what you're going to measure. "Units of performance" is the inevitable answer in T & D measurements. The Manager of Collections counted letters written and payments received. A shop operation might count and classify such things as defective units, accidents, time lost due to accidents. Sales departments can count sales made, calls completed, volume of orders. In measuring management performance there are such things as grievances, decisions, counseling sessions, turnover, budgets planned, budgets adhered to—and above all, total production.

The next step is to select the scale to be used in the measurement.

Nominal scales are what we usually see in T & D measurement. They offer a simple "classify-and-count" process. Nominal scales permit the measurer to classify "satisfactory" and "defective" units. Such a simple scale permits only a limited analysis—but those limits are broad enough to tell T & D specialists and client/managers what they want to know.

From nominal scales we legitimately get totals, modes, and medians.

Nobody needs a lesson in how to compute totals, but modes and medians are technical terms. Let's define them: the mode is, as the name implies, the most frequent occurrence; the median is the exact center number in a series.

Thus if we measure the seniority of a group of trainees, our tally might look like this:

In service	Number of occurrences (f = frequency)	
Less than 1 year	++++	5
Between 1 and 2 years	/ / /	3
Between 2 and 3 years	/ /	2
Between 3 and 4 years	/ / / /	4
Between 4 and 5 years	/	1
5 years or more	++++ / / / /	9

The mode is quite clearly, "5 years or more of service," because more people fall into that group than into any other single group in the tally. The median seniority is, "between 3 and 4 years." Why? Because that group is the midpoint; there are as many trainees with less seniority (10) as there are with more seniority—also 10. That is, there are the same number of people on each side of the "median" category.

In nominal scales, when measuring the situation before and after a T & D effort, the mode and the median represent legitimate indices. An average, or mean, is not a valid index when using a nominal scale. Why not? To understand the reason, let's look at a different example.

Again we will measure seniority. We want to know how long the members have been with the organization before starting a team-building program. Let's have four members; one has been there two years, the others 16, 18, and 20 years. They have invested a total of 56 years, an average of 14 years. But not a single person has been there exactly 14 years! The mean is a delusive index; it does nothing to describe the real nature of the group.

Let's take another example to prove the point even further. Assume that you just became the T & D officer and are looking over the ratings given two recent sessions of an introductory management program. The previous T & D officer used a five-point scale to measure satisfaction with the course. You note that each session scored an average, or mean rating, of 3.15. This strikes you as unusual, so you compile a distribution tally of all the ratings for each session. Here is what your tally reveals:

Rated as	Session 1 (f)		Session 2 (f)	
5	// ┼┼┼┼	7		0
4	////	4	////	4
3	/	1	┼┼┼┼ ┼┼┼┼ ┼┼┼┼	15
2	/	1	/	1
1	// ┼┼┼┼	7		0
	N = 20		N = 20	

One look at the raw data shows that the two sessions were remarkably different in perceived experiences—yet the averaging shows them to be identical. All apart from the questionable practice of putting numbers on impressions, the tendency to average data from nominal scales is one of the more prevalent fallacies in educational measurement by organizational T & D specialists.

Ordinal scales are more useful in measuring such "invisible" elements as perceptions or values. Ordinal scales put items into a rank order. They tell who has more or less of something, or which values rank highest. For example, in determining training needs, T & D officers sometimes hand line managers a list of behavioral objectives, with instructions to rank them from first to last in "importance for your subordinates."

Or one might ask students in a Leadership Workshop to rank these five skills by putting a number 1 by the most vital, a 2 by the next most vital, and so on until you have placed a 5 by the least important skill:

> Clear communications   _____
> Counselling   _____
> Delegating   _____
> Time management   _____
> Problem solving   _____

Ordinal scales are extremely useful in post-training feedback. Graduates can indicate which of the acquired skills they value most, and so on down to a point where they designate "no value" in their on-the-job application. In such feedback, the ordinal and nominal scales can be effectively combined. Graduates can also indicate how often they have used each of the new behaviors. This can be done in one of two ways: feedback forms which are tallied on a short-interval basis, or perceptual ("to the best of your memory") estimates.

In the feedback sheet, a typical form merely lists the objectives of the training. Graduates check off each time they use the behavior. Such forms are submitted to the immediate "boss" rather than to the T & D department. After the boss has analyzed the on-the-job application, two things happen. First comes positive reinforcement and counseling. Second, the sheets are forwarded to the T & D department where macro trends can be established and analyzed.

To review: the tallies represent nominal scales; the rank-ordering is an ordinal scale activity. Ordinal scales also provide data which may legitimately provide medians and modes but not means.

Interval scales are used on such measurement tools as yardsticks and thermometers. As the title implies, they measure distances between phenomena; they measure intervals. Accurate interval scales follow one important principle: the interval between checkpoints is always exactly equal to the interval between other checkpoints. If the distance between the 11 and the 12 on your ruler isn't precisely the same distance as the interval between the 10 and the 11, your ruler is faulty. One degree of temperature on the thermometer must be exactly the same as another degree. If it isn't, you may be sicker than you think!

A major problem with past T & D measurement has been the frequent use of interval scales on which the intervals were not defined—much less equal. The typical end-of-training form measures accurately when it asks for opinions; it is only pretending to measure legitimately when it asks for numbers on a scale which poses as an interval scale—but which isn't. To compound the confusion, many T & D officers take the data from non-equal interval scales and average it. Remember the hypothetical case we examined about the two sessions of the same course with the same average score!

It is treacherous to use averages from nominal, ordinal, or interval scales as the basis of evaluative decisions about the learning, the program, or the instruction. Obviously, if different people perceive the distances between points in different perspectives, the numbers in themselves are unreliable. If those unreliable numbers (each of which means something different to someone else!) are averaged, the result can be only a mirage . . . a fiction . . . a distortion of what it seeks to measure.

When using legitimate interval scales, what legitimate mathematical functions may we properly perform? Modes, percentiles, and deviations are legitimate. So are means, *if* the intervals are fixed and equal. Since that list includes two new terms, let's examine the concept of percentiles and deviations.

Parents may have been told that their child is in the second quartile on a given achievement test. What does that mean? It means that of all the students taking the test, 50 percent were in lower quartiles—and 25 percent were in the higher, or top quartile. Quartiles divide a population into four groups of equal size. *Percentiles* are more precise. If a child is in the 99th percentile, 99 out of every 100 children earned a lower test score. Percentiles simply show a person's position in a population of 100.

Partiles are helpful to T & D measurers when comparisons are mandatory. Generally organizational trainers are not too interested in how one trainee compares to another. Rather they want to know how individuals compare with an established standard of performance. There may be times, however, when the "partile" of entire populations is significant. For example, before designing a program on a highly specialized subject, designers might want to know some hard facts about the potential students. If they knew quartile or percentile scores on standard aptitude or achievement tests, they could make better design decisions. Instructors forearmed with this knowledge could better respond to the group in discussions and in answering their questions.

More useful is the concept of *deviation*. It merely shows how far one unit deviates from the average unit. Deviations are not generally meaningful in themselves—only in comparison to other deviations. They cannot be calculated unless there is a legitimate average, or mean, from which to operate. When T & D measurers reach this level of sophistication, they are ready for the services of that statistical professional!

Finally, there are *ratio scales*. They can tell variability from an absolute condition. This implies the necessity of an absolute zero—a condition we don't get in developmental operations. Who can conceive a person with zero intelligence, or zero achievement? However, unless one is using a legitimate ratio scale, with an absolute zero, it is really improper to make evaluations such as, "Eve did twice as well on that as anyone else," or "Mary is picking this up beautifully. She did three times better today than she did yesterday!"

BASELINES: WHAT THEY ARE AND WHY THEY ARE IMPORTANT

When you're taking an automobile trip, it's nice to know where you are, how far you've come, and how far it is to your destination. Does that explain the reasons for pre-, post-, and intermediate-measurement activities?

Enlightened learning systems consider such measurement, accompanied by appropriate feedback, as integral to every growth or change process.

To measure progress toward a destination or objective, you must know where you started. "Where you start" is a baseline.

Baselines are imperative in pre-post measurement. Somebody needs to count the number of imperfect performance units. Probably someone should place a price tag on each defective unit. There need to be figures about such things as rejects, grievances, undecided grievances, customers lost—whatever key indicator can be identified as a reliable index of the problem performance. The process for establishing baselines is simple enough—but it isn't always easy to find that key indicator. In finding indicators, acceptance by the client management is essential.

The three steps to baseline measurement involve:

1. Defining in the most precise terms possible the object to be measured. This is that key indicator: tasks accomplished; faulty accomplishments; dollars spent; dollars wasted; time wasted; numbers of students.

2. Defining the numerical scale from which the number or measurements will be assigned.

3. Making sure that the measurement procedure is analagous to reality, and that it won't be contaminated by uncontrollable variables such as strikes, floods, depressions, new policies, or new procedures.

Baselines can be established for individuals as well as organizations. Perhaps one manager is giving a decision in only three of ten grievances per year. Maybe in a population of 30 managers only 63 of 256 grievances per year are settled; the rest are "kicked upstairs." The T & D officer wants pre and post baselines to justify and evaluate the program. Instructors and learners want individual baselines so they can set personal priorities and measure their successes. This is just a practical application of the $D = M - I$ formula. To measure deficiencies (what a trainee still needs to learn) one repeatedly measures the I (what the trainee now knows.)

INSTRUMENTS

A highway map and a mileage table help tourists measure their progress. In T & D, the tools of measurement are called "instruments."

Instruments for measuring learning involve some form of test, either by paper-and-pencil or by performance.

One obvious way to find out where an individual "is coming from" is to give a test on what that individual already knows. To sound technical, we call this "a test over the cognitive inventory"!

An increasingly popular way of doing this is to administer the criterion (or final) test, or its equivalent, at the first session. If this is explained properly, given in a goal-setting and diagnostic atmosphere, it need not be threatening. Actually, it can do more than measure; it can set expectations.

Such pretesting assuredly lets learners and instructors get a clear picture of what they don't need to stress—because people already know it. It tells what they do need to emphasize—because so few got it correct. But above all it gives *individual* diagnostic data! Learners can pinpoint the areas in which they must concentrate their attention; instructors know how each trainee performed, and where extra individual counseling will be needed. It is, in a sense, a practical application of andragogy: The experience (inventory) of learners is examined and becomes an early ingredient in the learning process.

If there are feelings about the content, or if the objectives are in the affective domain, the instrument must uncover the affective inventory. In such cases, several instruments are useful.

Agree/disagree (ADA) tests are easy for data-gathering, and can focus the learner on key concepts. An ADA presents crucial statements to students, who then indicate how they feel about them. It's a nominal scale, since the intervals are unequal. For example, a workshop for new instructors might use the instrument in Fig. 15.2.

Items in ADA instruments should be controversial enough to elicit a range of opinion. Eliminating the "No Opinion" option gives an even number of columns and forces respondents to "fish or cut bait" without sharp "Agree/ Disagree" decisions. The use of several columns permits: (1) a measure of intensity of opinion and (2) the possibility to graciously change an opinion as the learning proceeds.

Another instrument for getting feelings is a variation of the ADA test. Two

---

HOW DO YOU FEEL ABOUT THE INSTRUCTOR'S ROLE?

Here are a number of statements about instruction. You can show the degree to which you agree or disagree with each statement by checking your feelings in the column at the left.

STRONGLY AGREE	TEND TO AGREE	NO CLEAR OPINION	TEND TO DISAGREE	STRONGLY DISAGREE	
_____	_____	_____	_____	_____	1. The instructor is primarily responsible for motivating students to learn.
_____	_____	_____	_____	_____	2. No one has more responsibility for this motivation than the instructor.
_____	_____	_____	_____	_____	3. One mark of a good instructor is frequent use of visual aids.
_____	_____	_____	_____	_____	4. Lectures are efficient ways of covering lots of material if knowledge is the course objective.

And so on.....

Fig. 15.2.
Sample ADA test.

HOW DO YOU FEEL ABOUT THE INSTRUCTOR'S ROLE?

Here are some opposing viewpoints about what instructors should do. You can indicate whether you agree strongly (AS), tend to agree (TA), have no opinion (NO), tend to disagree (TD), or strongly disagree (SD) by a check mark in the appropriate column.

	AS	TA	NO	TD	SD	
Instructors have prime responsibility for motivating students.	___	___	___	___	___	Immediate bosses have prime responsibility for motivating students.
Instructors should be far above average in emotional control.	___	___	___	___	___	Instructors have as much right to be human and lose control as anyone else.
Student questions should be answered by the instructor.	___	___	___	___	___	Student questions should be referred to the class for for answers.
Student questions should be answered with another question.	___	___	___	___	___	Student questions should be reinforced with answers, not with other questions.

And so on...   And so on...

Fig. 15.3.
Variation of ADA test.

very different opinions are presented, with the students sharing their feelings on a nominal scale shown between them. Fig. 15.3 presents an example.

Another way to get at opinions is a "pro-rata" scale, in which students assign portions of an established number to reflect relative preferences. For example, you want to determine how managers feel about Occupational Safety and Health laws. The question might read:

Considering all the legislation with which you are familiar, what percent has had a GOOD effect and what percent has had a BAD effect on Society. You *must* assign a total of 100 percent.

GOOD _____ BAD _____

Now assign 100 percent again, but this time answer the question to show how you feel about the impact upon this organization.

GOOD EFFECT _____ BAD EFFECT _____

Another version of the pro-rata instrument might look like this:

Assume that you are using a numerical scale to appraise your subordinates. You want to indicate *the relative importance* of performance elements. You have exactly 100 points to assign to the elements listed below, and to two other factors if you wish to add elements which are missing. Remember, the numbers you assign must total 100.

Relationship with others _____
Dependability _____
Obedience _____
Quality of work _____
Quantity of work _____
Personality _____

_____ _____
_____ _____

Total: 100

This form uses a nominal scale, and data from it can legitimately be used to calculate modes, medians, and totals; such data reveal nothing about averages.

A Thematic Apperception Test (TAT) is really a psychological measurement tool. A modified form can measure learners' affective inventory. In TAT's, students write a story about a picture. Their stories reveal their feelings. The TAT has some interesting applications in T & D measurements. For example: learners might look at a picture of people arriving in a room. A sign by the door carries the name of the training program. By telling a story about the situation or the people, or by capturing the conversation of the people in the picture, trainees reveal their own attitudes about the program or about their attendance. In another example, the picture merely shows a group of people sitting in a circle. The instructions might read, "These people are telling each other what it's like to arrive for this training. What are they saying?"

By classifying the trainees' statements, instructors can learn a great deal about how participants feel. Do they mention course content? Or do they show social concerns, mentioning the other students and what instructors will be like? Do they reveal organizational anxieties? Things like "Why am I here?" or "My boss is the one who needs this!" or "Who ever heard of these instructors?" Instructors can also classify the data as "Approach" (comments showing inquiry, eagerness, anticipation, affirmation) or "Aversive" (reluctance, dread, fear, resignation). By repeating the same picture later, instructors can change the description to elicit interim or end-of-training data.

Many instructors like a "Team Effectiveness" instrument. Such devices come in several forms. The TAT version can ask trainees to discusss the way the people work together, and thus can reveal feelings which don't come out in open discussion. Another very simple method is to ask all participants to write down three adjectives to describe their feelings about the group. Usually they put just one word per small sheet of paper. The papers are shuffled and read aloud. During this reading other members and instructors can comment, or explain how they feel about the words—their appropriateness, their causes, the implications. It's often useful to tally these words so trends can be identified and acted upon.

More formal instruments can deal with specific dimensions of the group dynamics and learning activity. At periodic intervals, members respond anonymously, then collectively discuss issues like those shown on the form in Fig. 15.4. (Incidentally, if the need for anonymity persists, there's evidence the group isn't maturing). Note that there are seven positions. There's nothing magic about seven, but the odd number permits the participant to take any position on a continuum, including the neutral (center) position. When trainers wish to get a definite commitment, or pro/con data, they should use an even number of choices. That is to say, the trainee who selects "1" or "2" instead of "3" or "4" is making a statement of dissatisfaction: on a four-point scale, there is no middle number on which participants can express neutrality.

Instruments such as the TAT or Team Effectiveness scale will sometimes reveal feelings which don't come out in open discussions seeking to get at the same data. This doesn't mean that Process Analysis Sessions (often called "Quaker Meetings") are not effective. They are—and they should be used as ongoing, non-instrumented measurement activity. They help measure participants' feelings about their own participation, about their own progress, and about the program and the instructors. There is just one problem with instrument-less sessions: trainers have neither an instrument, nor assurance that

```
ANALYZING TEAM EFFECTIVENESS

Draw a circle around the number which best reflects your feelings.

                                    LOW                  HIGH
   1.  My freedom to express myself.    1   2   3   4   5   6   7
   2.  The extent to which my ideas     1   2   3   4   5   6   7
       and opinions are heard.
   3.  The way decisions are made.      1   2   3   4   5   6   7
   4.  The group's progress in pro-     1   2   3   4   5   6   7
       ducing desired results.
   5.  The way we manage our time.      1   2   3   4   5   6   7
   6.  The degree of trust and open-    1   2   3   4   5   6   7
       ness I feel in our group.
   7.  The extent to which I feel       1   2   3   4   5   6   7
       a part of the group.
   8.  The way we manage conflict.      1   2   3   4   5   6   7

   And so on...
```

Fig. 15.4.

Form for analyzing team effectiveness.

they've created an atmosphere in which participants freely express themselves.

Such feedback during the learning offers a most dynamic form of measurement. It provides data for decisions in dealing with people, with the group, and with course content. Because it involves the learners in that process, it motivates them to conscious investment of their energy in constructive ways.

Instruments or activities like Process Analysis, TAT, or ADA would obviously be no help in measuring progress toward psychomotor skills or cognitive acquisitions—but they might help explain and correct sluggish group dynamics in a program designed to reach such objectives.

The point is this: the instrument may fit either the objective of the program or the objective of the measurement. To measure learnings, the instrument should be appropriate to the domain of the learning objective. There are no precise guidelines, but the correlation shown in Fig. 15.5 is useful.

In the cognitive domain, paper-and-pencil instruments seem to prevail. They deserve a few comments. Adults are people who went to school—and as students in academic systems they took a lot of tests. They didn't like them very well, but they're accustomed to them. They are especially familiar with some of the quick-scoring formats like True/False and Multiple Choice.

Now if feedback is motivating, yet people don't like these tests, there's an

MATCHING MEASUREMENT INSTRUMENTS TO LEARNING DOMAINS			
FOR THESE DOMAINS ➤	COGNITIVE DOMAIN	AFFECTIVE DOMAIN	PSYCHOMOTOR DOMAIN
CONSIDER THESE ➤ INSTRUMENTS	Short answer: Fill in blanks True/False Multiple choice Matching Essays Can do/Cannot do	TAT ADA Essays Team effectiveness scales Can do/Cannot do	Performance tryout Manipulative games and exercises Can do/Cannot do

Fig. 15.5.

Matching measurements to learning domains.

interesting conflict of conclusions! It can be easily explained by the way in which the paper-and-pencil tests were conceived and administered. School-teachers so often devised "trick questions," or used so-called objective tests to enforce subjective opinions. So the entire testing process became a destructive game—not a legitimate vehicle for getting honest feedback. Example: "There is no Fourth of July in Great Britain." True or False? Of course there is; they just don't have a celebration. Another example: "The Instructor is the most important single person in the classroom." True or False. Well, that depends, doesn't it?

Not only were the tests tricky and arbitrary, they were often fed back in highly competitive forms: you got an "A," or you got an "F," or you were "in the lower quartile on a bell-shaped curve"!

In organizational settings we are rarely interested in "normal distributions" or competitive positioning of students. Nor are we primarily interested in the retention of information per se. We want to know that knowledge is there only to be sure that learners have a proper inventory before they begin to apply the knowledge.

Thus "factual recall" forms like True/False, Multiple Choice, and Matching have little relevance to most T & D measurement. Besides that, they're very tempting. The name of the game soon becomes for testers to outwit students or for learners to outguess the testers! Thus in true/false questions composers must avoid words like "always" and "never." (They usually end up with "usually" or "sometimes," which are equally transparent give-aways that the answer is true.) We can only be amused at some of the cognitive contortions required to write some multiple choice questions: one response is correct, two must be relatively reasonable (ingenuous but plausible) and one an out-and-out travesty.

If only learners did as much thinking when they respond as composers must do when they make up the questions! The chief advantage of such formats is not that they cause learning to happen (or even effective feedback!) but that they can be quickly scored.

If quick scoring is the requirement, then factual recall works rather better than the involuted True/False or Multiple Choice formats. There is little reason to think that you test less effectively if you ask, "In what year was the Constitution signed?" than if you ask:

> The U.S. Constitution was signed in:
> (A) 1775   (B) 1776   (C) 1777   (D) 1914

Such short answers require only a few seconds to score, yet they provide instructors with the direct nature of the learners' mis-comprehensions. Because a specific word appears on the exam paper, the instructor knows the direction of the learner's thinking and can better redirect it. Who knows what a student was thinking when the paper shows only a circle around "1914"? If the question composer hadn't prompted the student with four limiting choices, some might reply "1492." From that kind of error, learning can result!

Short answers have another virtue: When they are reviewed, the content is repeated yet another time. Too often reviews of True/False and Multiple Choice tests communicate only the codes. We've all heard conversations like this:

> "What's the answer to Number 12, Charles?"
> "False."
> "Good, how about Number 13, Elaine?"
> "I picked 'D'."
> "Good. How about Number 14?"

That could be a test about converting decimal numbers into octal expressions or a test about Maslovian psychology—and nobody could tell the difference from that kind of feedback session. It's nice to note, though, that the learners are reviewing the quiz. When instructors "correct the papers" themselves they deprive the student of some more learning—and one really useful part of the feedback.

Short answers measure actual mastery of the cognitive content; they cannot measure psychomotor skills. They also tend not to measure the learner's perception of achievements. For this reason many instructors find the Can Do/Cannot Do a useful form. It simply lets learners estimate their own confidence. They express whether they think they can or cannot perform the behavioral objectives. An actual example (Fig. 15.6) is used both during and at the end of a Managerial Communications course.

```
HOW ARE YOU DOING?

Listed here are the objectives of this training program. In the column at the left, you
have a chance to indicate your own sense of your mastery of each one.

  I CAN        I CANNOT
                              1.  Distinguish between open, directive, and
 _____     _____            reflective questions.

                              2.  Use each type of question spontaneously
 _____     _____            in conversation.

                              3.  Refrain from directive questions when
 _____     _____            probing for feelings.

                              And so on...
```

Fig. 15.6.

Sample can do/cannot do form.

POST-TRAINING MEASUREMENT

When the training ends, and the learners are ready to return to their work posts, the really appropriate measurement is a "terminal test" of their skill in performing all the course objectives. Such performance testing would undoubtedly enhance most T & D programs and better ensure effective results. Thus the final sessions may use simulations, try-outs of the desired performance, roleplays, or paper-and-pencil tests as both measurement and regular learning activities. If they are truly measurement tools, they probably should call attention to the achievement (or non-achievement) of each objective and each criterion. Such checklists become effective nominal scales. Learners can count their own achievements to measure and reinforce the learnings—and to redefine goals and skills not yet "mastered."

What happens too often is that students are asked to evaluate the training program. This is unfortunate at a time when measurement is what is needed and students are asked to make evaluations. Besides, the timing is bad. The data should have been part of ongoing measurement and evaluation throughout the program. Now, at closing, most participants just want to get home! If an evaluation can be made meaningful at such a moment, it is probably the learner's estimate of how much they have acquired (I can/I cannot) or how much they think they will apply the new learnings on the job. Thus the most effective instruments tend to get at questions like:

1. As a result of this training, I plan to make these changes in the way I do my work: . . . .

2. As evidence that these changes are producing results, I will be looking for these indices and/or symptoms of improved operations: . . . .

3. To feel completely confident in performing the new skills, I would like further help in . . . .

4. This training has shown me that I need future training in . . . .

5. When my boss "debriefs" me on this training, I will ask for special help in . . . .

6. The best feedback I can give myself about how well I am applying my new knowledge/skill is . . . .

7. If my peers or bosses hassle me about doing things in a different way, I will counter that by . . . .

8. In the future, when my peers are scheduled to attend this program I have just completed, I intend to help them get the most out of it by . . . .

Another end-of-training instrument which provides meaningful quantitative information for the learner, the instructor, the T & D officer, and client-management ties intended use directly into course objectives. A typical form is shown in Fig. 15.7.

It is significant that the instrument uses the behavioral objectives of the learning program, thus reminding graduates of their learnings and linking those objectives with the world of work by equating them to performance standards.

The ultimate impact of a T & D program can only be determined by measurement which occurs at some time after the training itself. Such measurement needs to get at the individual and the organization. With the individual the concern is the perseverance of the new behavior; with the organization, the focus is the impact of the accummulated behaviors upon the operation.

One effective way to measure the perseverance of the new behaviors in graduates is to ask all graduates (at an appropriate interval after the program) how often they are using the new skills. If the form leaves room for added comments, some affective data can be collected right along with the quantitative measurements.

One instrument for doing this is a mere tally on which the graduates make a checkmark each time they perform the new skill. There is obviously great value in asking graduates to do just that: the tally provides inherent motivation to use the new skill and triggers effective follow-up conversations between graduates and "the boss." It gives the latter a great chance to reinforce the new behavior before routing the tallies to the T & D department for quantitative measurement of the program's impact.

A more sophisticated instrument is shown in Fig. 15.8, with its right-hand column for perceptual data.

Obviously the captions for the vertical columns can be given different head-

---

HOW WILL YOU PUT THIS TRAINING TO WORK?

Now that you have finished this instructor training workshop, it's time to think about putting your learnings to use. Will you give us your best estimate by checking the columns at the right?

The behavioral objectives of the program are listed below. For each of them, indicate your intentions about applying that objective as you do your work.	I PLAN TO DO THIS				I DO NOT FEEL I ACHIEVED THIS OBJECTIVE
	ALWAYS	OFTEN	SOMETIMES	NEVER	
1. Prepare behavioral learning objectives for each lesson.					
2. Insist that the objectives involve observable actions and measurable criteria.					
3. Use some form of pretest to establish individual learner inventories.					
4. Use roleplays as a way to develop interpersonal skills.					
5. Use roleplays as a way to measure achievement of interpersonal skills goals.					
And so on...					

Fig. 15.7.

Sample end-of-training instrument.

ings in the instruments shown in both Figs. 15.7 and 15.8. A more specific version uses time-based terms like "HOURLY," "DAILY," "WEEKLY," "MONTHLY," or "NEVER."

The right hand "COMMENTS" column elicits more frequent and more specific data if phrased "WITH THESE RESULTS." Another version asks for an appraisal with headings that read:

I DO THIS ONCE EVERY				AND THE RESULTS ARE				
HOUR	DAY	WEEK	MONTH	AWFUL	BAD	SO-SO	GOOD	GREAT

A totally different approach is to avoid any "cueing" by mentioning the training objectives, yet to focus on on-the-job application of the learnings. Fig. 15.9 shows how this can be done in a relatively simple way.

DID YOUR TRAINING HELP YOU DO YOUR WORK?

Now that you have been back on the job for a while after completing the business writing program, we'd like to know how much you're using what you learned.

You'll remember the objectives of the program listed at the left. In the column at the right, will you indicate your use of each and give us any comments about how this performance standard works out in actual practice?

	I DO THIS				COMMENTS
	OFTEN	NOW AND THEN	SELDOM	NEVER	
1. State the purpose in the first paragraph.					
2. Use no more than 18 percent "big" words with three or more syllables.					
3. Keep average sentence length under 15 words.					
4. Use first names and first-person pronouns.					
And so forth...					

Fig. 15.8.

Collecting affective data.

Mail the forms to the superior, with instructions for the local manager to give them to the graduates and to collect them from the graduates. There are several important advantages to such a routine:

1. Graduates tend to put more importance on the measurement form when they receive it from their own "boss."

2. There is a greater return of the forms when the feedback is accomplished through regular reporting channels.

3. The conversation between the graduate and the immediate superior is stimulated.

4. Over a period of time, with repeated circulation of such measurement forms, the philosophy that training is supposed to produce a change in on-the-job behaviors is communicated and underlined.

POST-TRAINING FEEDBACK

Now that you have had a chance to apply what you learned in the effective counseling skills workshop, how is it going? We'd value your opinion. After you've filled in this form, will you talk it over with your immediate superior; then have it forwarded with the superior's comments to the T&D department? Thanks for helping us find out what happens when you use the training on the job.

I'VE DONE THESE THINGS THAT I FEEL GOOD ABOUT:	AND THIS IS WHAT HAPPENED TO MAKE ME GLAD THAT I USED THE NEW SKILL:
I'VE DONE THESE THINGS THAT I WISH I HADN'T:	THIS IS WHAT HAPPENED TO MAKE ME FEEL THAT THE NEW BEHAVIOR DIDN'T WORK OUT VERY WELL:

IF I WERE TO GET THE TRAINING NOW, I WOULD ALSO LIKE TO LEARN HOW TO

Fig. 15.9.

Sample form for self-selecting behavioral objectives being used.

Some T & D directors like to validate the perceptions of the graduate with parallel inquiry directed to the superiors themselves. When this is the goal, some simple changes of wording can provide a double check. Forms like the one we just examined (Fig. 15.9) can be sent to *both* parties: the graduates and the superior. The form for the superior then reads something like Fig. 15.10. You will note the extra question on the form for the boss. Some T & D officers like to route these inquiries to the boss's boss to send the message through more of the organization, and to increase the number of returns.

A FOLLOW-UP FOR EFFECTIVE COUNSELING TRAINING	
(Name)_____ has been back on the job about six weeks after attending the effective counseling skills workshop. You can help get maximum benefit from that investment and help us improve on future sessions of that workshop by completing this form and returning it to us.	
I HAVE NOTICED THESE BEHAVIORS THAT I LIKED:	AND THIS IS HOW I REINFORCED THESE IMPROVEMENTS IN PERFORMANCE:
I NOTICED THESE BEHAVIORS WHICH I DIDN'T LIKE:	AND THIS IS HOW I HANDLED THAT SITUATION:
I WISH THAT PEOPLE HAD ALSO LEARNED HOW TO DO THESE THINGS IN THE WORKSHOP:	
WHEN SUBORDINATES RETURNED FROM THE WORKSHOP, I REVIEWED THE TRAINING BY:	

Fig. 15.10.

Sample follow-up form.

How do you get people to return these post-training instruments? There are a number of approaches:

1. Route them "from" and back "to" a top executive in the client/user department. (That executive can re-route them to T & D);

2. Keep all the instruments as simple and time-saving as you possibly can;

3. As part of the "contract" for offering the training, insist upon agreement that the using department will distribute the instruments and follow up;

4. Arrange some contingencies:

- Letters of Thanks to random respondents.

- A personal "Thank You" to respondents you happen to meet in the halls or on your next visit to their area.

- Explanations that you will (or why you cannot) implement a graduate's suggested changes in programs.

- Incentives to managers who consistently forward the completed instruments to you: golf balls; pen and pencil sets; desk calendars; a new text on management technique, theory, or philosophy.

- A raffle of rather elegant gifts, with every completed response entitling the respondent and the boss who forwards the instrument to one token. A few organizations find such lotteries unacceptable; others regard them as standard events. Sponsors of lotteries point to increased returns and to increased enrollments in training programs!

- An award to the "Measurement Manager of the Year."

Measurement has some other effects. The very process of measuring tends to increase the use of the new behaviors. The feedback tells the T & D departments how well they are succeeding and where they are falling short. It also tells them whether the things they are teaching people to do are indeed reinforced in the "real-world" environment. In a sense, this measurement provides data which continuously validates and evaluates the legitimacy of training objectives.

But something else should happen too. The sum of the individual measurements should be used to determine a new baseline for each performance deficiency that caused the training. Then that sum should be validated against key indices. If the program was born because accidents in the Pocahontas Plant were too high, then the post-program feedback should reveal that individuals are practicing good safety behaviors. Finally, the post-training baseline should show that accidents are no longer a problem at the Pocahontas Plant. The ME cycle measurement should uncover new baslines for programs which have impact. Hopefully, the second baseline will differ from the pre-program baseline in desired directions.

SUMMARY

If any one element is more important than others in effective measurement, it is selecting the proper thing to count.

There's a significant dilemma there. If measurement doesn't count, if it isn't quantitative, then it isn't really measurement. If it counts the wrong things, it is inappropriate measurement. Teachers who count quiet learners as a measure of their success are really checking only their success as controllers—not as

CHAPTER **16**

HOW DO YOU EVALUATE TRAINING AND DEVELOPMENT?

PHILOSOPHIES OF EVALUATION

"We are all most talented as critics," muses a leading contemporary psychologist.

"Every country experiments with new programs, but none is organized to evaluate them, keeping the successes and throwing out the failures. We spend billions to explore innovations, and only a few dollars to see if they're worth anything." So says Donald T. Campbell in discussing "The Experimenting Society." (*Psychology Today,* September 1975, p. 47)

What Donald T. Campbell says has a double impact when applied to the T & D activity in many organizations:

- No real evaluation is attempted, and
- Existing evaluation is based on intuition, not on data.

When we evaluate without data we ignore a basic premise of the Bloom *Taxonomy of Educational Objectives:* that evaluation is the most complex of the mental skills, and can be done effectively only after some knowledge is acquired, comprehended, applied, analyzed, and, finally, synthesized.

Yet we have all known people who evaluate without any facts whatsoever! We have probably also known T & D evaluation systems which to the same thing! T & D officers who engage in such hazy thinking risk big headaches—and short tenure.

But few people agree about how training, development, and education should be evaluated. In this chapter we will look at several viewpoints about "right" and "sound" evaluation policies and procedures.

Malcolm W. Warren points out that evaluation is a " . . . double problem. Training must be measured both in terms of the training action itself and in terms of behavior outside the training situation." (*Training for Results*, p. 112)

"The most common reason for evaluation is to determine the effectiveness so future programs can be improved," says Donald L. Kirkpatrick in *Supervisory Training and Development*. (p. 88)

Next we read a T & D officer, indicating still another motive and another view: "Managers, needless to say, expect their manufacturing and sales departments to yield a good return and will go to great lengths to find out whether they have done so." The author goes on to comment that when it comes to training, however, they may *expect* the return, "But rarely do they make a like effort to measure the actual results." He regards this as fortunate for those in charge of training programs, pointing out that "such a philanthropic attitude has come to be taken for granted." But as the author pointed out, there is no guarantee that that attitude will continue. The conclusion? That T & D officers would be well-advised to take some initiative, "and evaluate their programs before the day of reckoning comes." (Daniel Goodacre III, in *Personnel*, May 1957)

What's the point of looking at these views? Well, for one thing, they're kind of fun. For another, they stimulate us to think of our own personal motives for evaluation. Is it Goodacre's nervousness, Kirkpatrick's urge for self-improvement, Campbell's social effectiveness, or Warren's "larger organizational" perspective?

Or do we opt for Campbell's counter-opinion: "We must never pretend that every program can be evaluated. It's a waste trying to study a new method if the participants don't think they've developed a better mousetrap." Now Campbell was talking about society, not T & D programs. But the parallel is discomforting. Do we possibly evaluate only when we feel the urge . . . only when we care a lot about the program?

It's pretty clear that all T & D officers need to establish a policy governing evaluation in their organizations. In 1975 Kirkpatrick wrote, "All training professionals *agree* evaluation should be done. That is as far as the agreement goes. When we try to define 'Evaluation' or determine *how to do it,* opinions and recommendations vary tremendously." (*Evaluating Training Programs,* Preface) Brethower and Rummler comment on the " . . . historical pitfall of training evaluation. That is, if a perfect laboratory type evaluation can't be done, the organization falls all the way back to happiness index." (*Improving Human Performance Quarterly,* Fall-Winter 1976, p. 113)

If this is an accurate evaluation of the evaluation situation, the best thing T & D officers can do is consider the several approaches shown here.

They then must decide which approach to use in their own organizations. The first step often really amounts to selecting the criteria on which the total effort of individual programs will be evaluated. The second step is to define processes.

Probably the logic would look something like Fig. 16.1. Such a process chart reminds us that the actual evaluation is just a small part of the measurement and evaluation process . . . of the ME cycle outlined in the last chapter. But making judgments about the success or shortcomings of a program is possible only when policy, criteria, and mechanisms have been established. The bulk of the process is concerned with measurement rather than evaluation. Future action, however, is based on the evaluation. After all, evaluation is making judgments about the data, not the data-gathering process.

The chart should help us understand:

1. That *evaluation begins in the design phase*—not after the program has ended. It often involves identifying baselines: operating indices that reflect the *status quo* and the future levels that must be achieved to prove that the problem has been eliminated.

2. That *evaluation costs something:* thought, time, money, energy. Evaluation, if legislated into T & D policy, must also appear in budgets and documentation of all programs.

3. The criteria on which T & D efforts are normally evaluated can be divided into three major categories:

- Contribution to organizational goals,
- Achievement of learning objectives, and/or
- Perceptions of the trainees and their managers.

EVALUATION BY CONTRIBUTION TO GOALS

T & D officers who are determined to be relevant to the main thrust of their organizations will opt for evaluation by contribution to goals. They see themselves as members of the problem-solving team. They are specifically con-

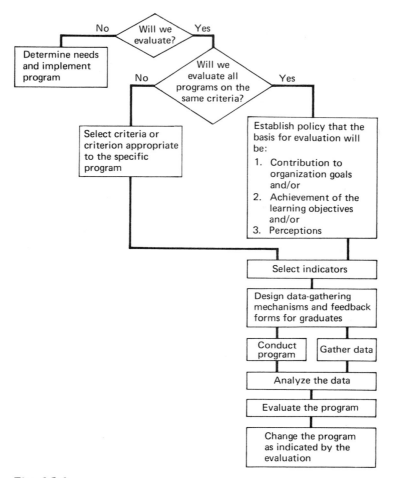

Fig. 16.1.

Defining evaluation processes.

cerned with the organization's performance problems. They prioritize training needs in direct proportion to organizational urgencies. They therefore want to know whether training has eliminated or alleviated those urgent problems.

To establish success or failure in this dimension, the evaluation must be based on quantitative data. Whether from fear or from a thirst for accountability, many T & D officers are no longer content to bask in the sun of the philanthropic management that supports training without proof of its contributions.

Quantitative data immediately suggests baselines: "How many defective units did the organization suffer before the program? After the program?" These are measurement questions. Then the evaluation asks, "Is this change sufficient?"

Recently a midwestern newspaper printed the dire headline: HALF OF STATE'S STUDENTS ARE BELOW MEDIAN IN READING SKILLS. Since that evaluation was based on the median, or midpoint, it's hard to see where else either half of the student could possibly be!

At any rate the data give no cause for alarm or rejoicing; that would be appropriate only if the *raw score* at the median were significantly higher than last year, or if local medians were frighteningly lower or deliriously higher than those in neighboring territories. As it stands, that headline is a specious evaluation.

Movement of significant numbers of trainees into higher modes or percentiles (or a significant change of the mode or median) provides evidence that changes have taken place. Very little knowledge of statistics is required when looking at pre/post profiles of student performance. Similarly, sound judgments can be made by looking at "before-and-after" charts showing system performance. If medians and modes changed significantly, there is evidence that the program helped the problem.

When the T & D officer or client/managers wish to prove absolute causality between the training and the improvement, they need to know that the differences between "pre" and "post" are statistically significant. For this level of analysis, a professional statistican should be involved. Only such technicians can answer the central question, "Are these changes well beyond coincidence?"

When profound numerical analysis is necessary, then the statistical consultant should be involved in the process from the very beginning. It is dangerous, maybe fatal, to wait until the data have been gathered. By then the T & D director may already have "booted" it in one or more of several ways:

- Necessary pre-training data are missing;
- The instruments asked the wrong questions;
- There was contamination in the measurement process;
- Key indicators are missing.

One mechanism upon which statistical experts may insist is a "control group." Even if you don't have a statistician insisting upon such a control group, you have important reasons for establishing one. This simply means that a part of the "defective population" will not immediately get training, or any other form of change program. They become the control group; those who are in the training are the "experimental group."

The reasons for control groups should be obvious. If the change takes place only in the experimental group, then there is some reason to credit the change program for the improvement. If, on the other hand, both the control group and the experimental group move in the same direction, evaluators must question the causal effect of the program. If they move in the same direction at the same speed, better drop the program. In situations like these, the professional statistician is a valuable resource for the evaluation process— valuable but not absolutely indispensable.

As indicated in the discussion of measurement, a critical element of such evaluation is identifying and selecting the key indicator. The evaluation process involves deciding how many units must be bad to require action—and what improvement must be achieved for the program to be adjudged successful. Among the indicators considered are:

Units of work per hour	Rejects
Units of work per worker	Backorders filled
Number of sales	Dollar value for backorders filled
Dollar value per sale	Tasks completed
Ratio of sales to calls	Percent of tasks completed properly
Percent of quota achieved	erly
Total dollar value of sales	Budgets submitted
Number of grievances	Budgets achieved within X percent of forecast
Percent of grievances decided	cent of forecast
Percent of grievance decisions sustained	Employee turnover
sustained	Inventory turnover
Percent of counseling problems solved	Machine downtime
solved	Number of disabling accidents
Total minutes tardiness	Cost of accidents
Total days absenteeism	Letters and reports completed
Number of absenteeism incidents	Percent of letters and reports
Scrap	which get the desired results

To make effective evaluations, the evaluation design must specify not only what will be counted, but when. This implies several measurements. Pre-training, post-training and post-post-training evaluations are indicated if the criterion is contribution to goals. The process should continue until management is satisfied that the problem no longer exists. That satisfaction results from matching data to predetermined, quantitative goals.

The T & D department evaluating its contribution to the organization must not ignore the standard operating indices already established. The baselines which reveal deficiencies are often the same baselines which are included in regular management reports. It is not always necessary to identify a new indicator. When a useful indicator is already part of regular reports, it is folly to invent new indicators! T & D officers who can find existing indices can "talk to management in their own language."

It is important to note that the program goals are not the same as the learning goals, or behavioral objectives. The latter tell what people will be able to do at the end of training; the former tell what happens to an operational index as a result of all those people doing all those things.

Let's take an example of collection letters: They aren't collecting much of anything. Our analysis shows that the collection clerks don't know how to write very well. It's a D_K. So we train them. One of the obvious learning objectives is that they will make a direct request for payment in the first sentence or within the first paragraph of any letter. Our baseline indicates that they were getting some money from 18 percent of their first letters. So we set a goal: that the training will more than pay for itself when they receive some payment from 70 percent of their first letters. They'll *ask* in 100 percent of the first paragraphs.

It's important that the objectives for the program are operational, not learning objectives. We might reasonably expect clerks to *ask* for payment 100 percent of the time in both letters and phone calls—but we could only reasonably expect the 70 percent *response* stated in our goals for the program.

When we have such operating goals, it's easy to evaluate the program. It either hit, exceeded, or missed the desired level of performance.

It is not quite so apparent at this point how to determine the precise quantities for the goal. Why 70 percent of the contracts? One possible answer is, "Because at that point the operation would begin to pay for itself. If we could get that standard of performance, the training expenditure would be cost-effective."

So now we see that another dimension of evaluation is the cost-effectiveness of the solution. The formula hardly needs repeating—but we'll repeat it anyhow!

> Cost of the performance deficiency
> Minus the cost of the improvement program
> Equals the cost-effectiveness of the improvement program

To apply this formula to any given program, T & D specialists must wear their very best consultant hats, identifying not only the key indicators but the cost of each unit. In the case of the collection letters, one might compute the total time spent in writing letters. That would give salary costs. Add to that the cost of materials and facilities. These data are always available somewhere in departmental budgets or records. By adding those totals together we get the total cost of letter-writing. To determine the unit cost we divide that total by the number of letters. The phone calls would be a bit more difficult to price. But it can be done. The phone bills are easily available, but the time costs could be more elusive. Some observation or work-sampling can give the needed facts: How much of their time do people spend on the telephone?

Similar logic and investigation can be used on those elusive management tasks which "nobody can measure." One can always estimate the time spent on tasks; one can always secure standard overhead figures for departments. And one can always find the "product"—that's how we knew we had a deficiency in the first place!

Thus meetings should produce decisions; grievance hearings should produce findings; counseling should produce changed performance. The way we knew we had a problem in the first place was that these products were too few or too faulty. Our evaluation merely asks, after we've counted and priced the new levels of productivity, "Is the change sufficient? Sufficient to meet the organizational goals? . . . Sufficient to pay for the training?"

When putting pricetags on human values, clever T & D consultants quickly point out to client managers that the ultimate pricetags may very well be psychic . . . inestimable elements like morale, human dignity, team-spirit. But they add, just as quickly, that these can come through programs which justify themselves on purely economic bases.

They are also careful not to jump to superficial indicators of changes in the operation. Things like "smiling faces," or "infractions reported by supervisors," don't indicate very much. Employees can learn to smile even when they're being rude or feeling miserable; supervisors can learn to look the other way.

Finally, clever T & D consultants err on the conservative side when putting price tags on performance deficiencies. After all, this is a process for evaluating the true cost-effectiveness—not for justifying the program. But some hard data on the "plus side" of the ledger or of a key operating index is necessary before one can applaud training programs on the basis of their contribution to organization goals.

EVALUATION BY ACHIEVEMENT OF LEARNING OBJECTIVES

If the output of training is behavior, then measuring and evaluating learning achievements is a logical basis for evaluation of T & D efforts.

What's a reasonable level of accomplishment? Conscientious learners want to demonstrate 100 percent achievement. Problem learners would settle for near zero. Professional instructors will tell you they "win a few and lose a few," but that they like to shoot for 100 percent. The fact is, you can't change all the people all the time. "You can't make a silk purse out of a sow's ear," as the adage goes. For in-house programs, where learning goals are totally consistent with standards, 100 percent is a reasonable target. It will vary considerably with different programs in different parts of the organization. It is considerably lower in public seminars where the goals may not be specific or reinforced by the management of the participants.

This type of evaluation requires that each learner be tested on each learning objective listed for the program. In very thorough T & D systems it will involve post-training measurement of actual on-the-job use of the new behaviors. Such double-checking shows not just that learners "can"—but that they "actually are."

To count the actual learning accomplishments is one step; to match them against predetermined targets is the second. Arranging the data in a visual display helps both the instructor and the ultimate evaluator. It's possible to build a simple matrix. Let's do that for the program on writing collection letters that we gave those clerks:

Objective	Trainee							
	1	2	3	4	5	6	7	8
Directly ask for payment	Yes	Yes	Yes	Yes	Yes	Yes	Yes	Yes
Ask in question form	Yes	Yes	No	No	No	No	No	No
Use first-person pronouns	Yes	Yes	No	Yes	Yes	Yes	Yes	Yes
Avoid thanking in advance	Yes	Yes	No	Yes	No	Yes	Yes	Yes
Set specific deadlines	Yes	Yes	No	No	Yes	Yes	Yes	Yes
Use less than 13% long words	Yes	Yes	No	Yes	Yes	Yes	Yes	Yes

Just a quick glance at such a display tells any analyst that something went wrong on the second objective: six of eight trainees cannot meet it. It also shows that Learner 3 has troubles: look at all the "No" entries. The chart should also demonstrate the value of periodic feedback and testing during the learning. Those trends could have been detected and corrected—in ways which would have benefited both the instructors and the learners.

Failures like those shown in the display bring up another evaluation decision: what to do about the "No" conditions? Retrain? Reappraise the objectives? Redesign the program? Take a look at the selection process?

The answer could conceivably be "Yes" to every one of those options. There are circumstances where any or all of those might be reasonable decisions to T & D evaluators. Let's look at the options.

Retraining makes some sense. Failure the first time isn't an unusual result for human endeavor. To reapply the original stimulus may produce different results. Maybe the mere repetition will cause different responses. Maybe there is some unidentified variable in the learner's life which will produce the desired learning the second time around. Instructors must be prepared to cope with individual differences. This may even mean reporting to management back on the job that certain "graduates" need special post-training follow-up. For example, a trainee may meet the qualitative criteria, but not the quantitative. Take apprentice machine operators: At the end of training they may be doing everything right—but just not doing it fast enough.

Sometimes organizations are too zealous. They expect too much. "Benchmarks" may be necessary, with certain criteria set for the end-of-training and tougher criteria established for later dates. Here's an example: Learners might be expected to complete five units per hour at the end of the training, eight units per hour two weeks later, and twelve units per hour after a month on the job.

If experience proves that nobody can meet these goals, then consider the second option: that the objectives need to be reappraised. Some might be evaluated as "just plain unreasonable." If sizable numbers of trainees, but not all of them, fail to meet the desired goals, perhaps individual tolerances could be established. If so, the training department must be sure to follow up with the immediate supervisors of all graduates who cannot perform to the expected standard.

When significant numbers fail to achieve any given goal (or set of goals), then a redesign of the program should be considered. When the "outputs" are missing, it's just reasonable to reevaluate the "inputs." Perhaps new methods, more drill, different visual aids will produce the desired learnings.

Finally, people may fail to meet learning objectives because they lack the needed personal or experiential inventory. Personnel departments and managers have been known to put people into jobs for which they were misfit. It follows, too, that people may be assigned to training programs which involve objectives they cannot master. Even capable people may bring "negative affective inventories." These bad attitudes can inhibit or prevent acquisition of the new behaviors. Good instructors can overcome some apathy and some negativism—but there is considerable question about how much of this responsibility ought to rest on the instructor's shoulders. Learners and their bosses have a responsibility for motivation too!

Which brings up a brand new option: accepting defeat in some cases. This means that sometimes the best thing to do is "give up" on certain individuals. It isn't that these people never could reach the goals; it's just that to produce the learning may be more costly than it is worth. That cost can involve energy and psychic pain as well as money.

When T & D specialists use such a display of achievement of learning goals, they may very reasonably evaluate: (1) the reasonableness of the goals, (2) the effectiveness of the training design, (3) the effectiveness of the teaching, and (4) the trainees' suitability to the learning assignment. (Did they belong in this program?)

A simple formula permits a quantitative analysis:

1. *Compute the potential:* Number of students multiplied by number of goals.

2. *Test individual achievements:* Test each student on each objective.

3. *Compute gross achievements:* Add all the "Yes" achievements.

4. *Compute achievement quota:* Divide step 3 by step 1.

Applied to the Collection Letter-Writing program, the formula shows:

1. Eight students times six goals equals a *potential* of 48.

2. Testing produced 36 "Yes" and 12 "No" results.

3. *Gross achivement* is therefore 36.

4. The *achievement quota* is 36 divided by 48, or .75.

This achievement quota shows that the Collection Letter-Writing program was only 75 percent successful in producing the desired behaviors.

Some T & D officers set achievement quotas for every program. In highly critical skills, 100 percent achievement is mandatory; 90 percent is more typical for most organizational training. (The remaining 10 percent can accrue on the job with proper supervisory follow-up.) Public seminars seldom establish achievement quotas; indeed they rarely use performance testing at all.

Achievement quotas, or performance testing, show what learning was accomplished. The same approach can reveal on-the-job utilization.

Graduates are asked if they apply the new behaviors, or to count the numbers of times they do so. When such post-training data are evaluated, some "shrinkage" is inevitable; 10 to 20 percent deterioration is not unusual . . . unless, of course, supervisors are properly trained in following up in ways which maintain the new behaviors.

EVALUATION BY PERCEPTIONS

Perceptions are hard to quantify, yet most T & D departments use perceptions as the data-base for their evaluations. And most T & D departments try to put numerical values onto the perceptual data used to evaluate.

It isn't strictly necessary to put numbers on perceptions. And we have already noted the fallacy of using "averages" for such numerical scales.

When you've asked anybody for perceptions, there are several things you can do to evaluate the data. First, you can count the positive and the negative comments. Next, you can classify the comments into inherent categories: the content, the instruction, the facilities, the appropriateness of the objectives.

When you ask a number of people for their perceptions, your classifying and tallying reveals a great deal about the program. You can take the things they write to answer an open question, and you can analyze those comments to identify trends.

Let's say that of 18 participants, five describe the classroom as "formal." Two use the word "claustrophobic" and seven say "stuffy," "annoying," "close," "tiny," or "marginal." You don't really need any more numbers to tell you that the facility is getting in the way of the learnings!

Such strong trends (in that case, 14 out of 18) are important when basing evaluation on perceptions. Minor trends should not be used as the basis for action. Nor should hotly worded comments. T & D officers would be wise to temper overstated comments like "The worst program I've ever been sent to!" or, "Totally irrelevant to this organization," or "The instructor is an egotist—out to get the students." Such reactions need to be treated as some judgments are at international skating and swimming competition: the highest and the lowest ratings are thrown out in the final computations.

Whenever one seeks perceptual data, there is an eventual "balancing phenomenon" in which comments contradict each other in almost equal numbers. For instance, 17 people will say that the program moved too slowly; 18 will say that it was too rapid.

What does this really tell an evaluator? Probably not that the program was either too slow or too fast, but that the design needs to provide more time for individual activity . . . for one-on-one counseling. That might allow all 35 of the commentators to feel comfortably in control of their own scheduling.

It might also tell the instructor that there is too little ongoing process feedback during the class sessions. When as many as 10 percent of any student body mention pacing problems, the instructor is probably not getting feedback soon enough.

This raises an important point: that professional instructors are getting perceptual data throughout the learning. They establish an atmosphere in which it is more than possible; it is inevitable! Instructors are clearly evaluating on perceptual bases whenever they adjust their instruction as a result of such perceptions.

It is doubtful that we learn more by asking participants to put numbers onto their perceptions. Scales like 5-4-3-2-1 tend to obscure facts of feelings, not to clarify them. Some participants use the scale backwards; others make a policy of "never giving a 5 or a 1." Such scales substitute numbers for the real perceptions.

Let's test this. Assume that we had used a five-point scale on that program when 14 of 18 participants objected to the facilities. We will also assume that they used the numerical scale to show their feelings. Chances are the "facilities" question would rate about 1.7, or at best 2.1. We know that we have a problem with facilities—but we don't know as much about that problem as we knew when our data include words like "close" or "stuffy" or "tiny," "pill box" or "claustrophobia." The adjectives and nouns are perceptions; the numbers are evaluations without data. Furthermore the specific words permit some active response by T & D specialists. It's hard to know what to do when the participants rate the facilities as "2."

There are several dangers when learners are asked to assign numerals to the general effectiveness of the program. Such numerical data can lead to unfortunate and devastating decisions. "Meaty" but unusual modules get taken out of programs. Competent, courageous instructors become showmen or mollycoddles in order to avoid low generalized ratings.

To do a legitimate evaluation of perceptual data, certain criteria should be met. That happens when the T & D officer faces several important issues.

First, there is the issue of the format of the data. We have already discussed that. Do adjectives which reveal the perceptions, and sentences which express ideas, tell us more or less than numerical codes of the perceptions?

Second, there is the mathematics used in preparing and analyzing the data. Perceptual measurement instruments tend to be nominal scales, no matter what numbers we attach to them. Thus using an average, or mean score, can only lead to fallacious evaluations. Only interval scales with absolutely equal intervals, or ratio scales starting from absolute zero, can justify averaging. Since one person's "3" is another person's "5," and since the distances between numbers are not even approximately equal, the typical numerical T & D evaluation form tends to distort rather than measure data which we are trying to evaluate.

Another issue is the nature of the question. If the instructor is to be evaluated on delivery, use of visual aids, personal appearance, and handling of student questions, then the evaluation should come from a professional. Surgeons don't ask their patients for comments on their scalpel techniques; wide receivers don't ask a spectator to evaluate the way they caught that pass. Why, then, do T & D specialists ask learners to evaluate instructional technology? The proper and relevant questions concern learnings, and the learners' perceptions of those learnings.

Then there is the issue of timing. Perceptual data should be gathered at all phases of the learning—not at the end of the program when the real pressures are to get home, back to the office, or back to the shop.

The most useful perceptions come during the learning and when the learnings are being applied on the job. At end of learnings the "I can/I cannot meet the objectives" inquiry is especially useful. Coupled with the actual terminal test data, it gives T & D management cross-validated data on which to make the evaluation. On-the-job perceptions should focus on application of the new learnings.

A useful follow-up instrument asks learners to tally or estimate how often they have used the new skill on the job. Since this is a perceptual approach, they may simply choose between alternatives like "always" or "often" or "now and then" or "seldom" or "never." When the cumulative totals are presented as the basis for evaluations, modes and medians can be located as the basis for evaluation.

Let's look at such an approach, applied to that Collection Letter-Writing program. You have surveyed the perceptions of the perseverence of the acquired skills. The compiled data look like this:

	Always	Often	Now & then	Seldom	Never
Directly ask for payment	43	13	1	—	—
Ask in question format	40	10	6	—	1
Use first-person pronouns	50	1	5	1	—
Avoid thanking in advance	51	3	3	—	—
Set specific deadlines	41	12	2	2	—
Use less than 13% long words	35	18	2	1	1

Such a record would produce a favorable evaluation of the program, indicating the general validity of the learning goals and their usefulness—as the graduates perceive them. Such perceptual data, coupled with the hard data about operating results (in this case, whether the letters are indeed collecting money!) can give a very rich amount of data on which to base evaluation of T & D programs.

When post-training perceptions of applications reveal non-use of the new skills, the T & D consulting follow-up may reveal causes. As we've noted, those causes include such things as unreasonableness of the objective, irrelevance of the objective—and frequently, failure of the immediate boss to reinforce the new behavior. It is by such evaluation of an existing program that more than one T & D officer learns that the program started one level too low! The indicated action for that evaluative discovery is a training program for the bosses!

Post-training perceptual instruments can also make effective use of open questions. To get at perceptions, T & D evaluators like questions such as:

● If you were attending the same training today, what would you do differently?

● What objectives do feel should be expanded?

- What objectives would you condense?
- What objectives would you drop?
- What objectives would you add?
- What course activities would you expand?
- What course activities would you eliminate?
- What course activities would you condense?
- What would you like to tell us about this course and the way it has influenced you or the way you do your work?

SUMMARY

The thrust of effective evaluation is to make responsible judgments about important questions.

If an improved operation is what the T & D department wants to contribute, then the inquiry must focus on hard data—and the evaluation must indicate whether or not the problem has been eliminated or significantly diminished. It breaks down into these steps:

1. Identify an unbearably deficient performance.

2. Identify specific units which characterize the problem.

3. Count the number of unacceptable units to establish a baseline.

4. Establish quantitative goals—a post-program baseline objective.

5. Conduct the change program.

6. Count the satisfactory and unsatisfactory units after the program.

7. Evaluate. Is the number of satisfactory units equal to the objective established in step 4? In other words, did the program produce the desired results?

If the production of new behaviors is the extent of the T & D purpose, then the evaluation will focus on the *demonstrated* acquisition and the perseverance of those behaviors. The successive steps are:

1. Establish the performance (learning) objectives.

2. Establish a desired achievement quota (number of trainees divided into the number of behaviors acquired successfully.)

3. Conduct the training, or install the change program.

4. Test each trainee over each learning objective.

5. Compute the actual achievement quota.

6. Evaluate. Does the actual achievement quota equal or surpass the desired achievement quota?

When the mere acquisition isn't what the department wants to evaluate, there are additional steps which evaluate the on-the-job application of the new behaviors:

7. Wait until a predetermined time and retest the graduates on each of the learning objectives.

8. Compute the application quota: Divide the number of successful demonstrations by the number of graduates.

9. Evaluate. Do the retentions of the new behavior equal the goals established? (These goals would amount to a step 2a, with quotas established for both end-of-training and on-the-job evaluations.)

If the opinions of the organization and of the graduates are the major concern of the T & D deparment, then the process involves simpler steps:

1. Determine what opinions matter.

2. Develop a questionnaire or mechanism for graduates to express those opinions.

3. Establish quantitative goals—patterns of desirable responses by the graduates.

4. Administer the mechanism.

5. Count and classify the responses.

6. Evaluate. Did the profile of actual answers match the desired pattern?

Remember the noted psychologist and his remark, "We are all most talented as critics." The effective, precise evaluation of T & D programs challenges that by asking two questions: "Critics of what?" and "According to what criteria?" For answers, T & D officers who want to be relevant and accountable seek the hardest possible data from the widest possible range of representative sources.

CHAPTER 17

HOW DO YOU
SELECT AND
CARE FOR THE
T & D STAFF?

THE BAREFOOT T & D SPECIALISTS

You've heard, of course, about the shoemaker's children?

They went barefoot!

There are sometimes barefoot employees in T & D departments. They work for T & D officers, or for Directors of Human Resources Development, who develop the employees of every department except their own!

We cannot really call these people "neglected professionals," because their lack of expertise prevents them from ever becoming professional. Like the naked feet of the shoemaker's offspring, their missing competencies represent a pathetic and ironic training need: they do not practice T & D effectively because they do not know how.

This chapter examines methods for getting the right people into the human growth business—and for keeping them growing after selection.

SELECTING THE T & D STAFF

When T & D officers select people for their staffs, they should avoid some of the frequent traps.

Traps to avoid

The *good-worker* trap is the most common. Because Henry was the best salesman on the force, they made him Sales Trainer in the Northwest Region. Because Eloise was a flawless teller, the bank promoted her to the role of On-the-Job Trainer. In a few years Henry and Eloise will be the forgotten "professionals" in the T & D department. Somebody goofed. The selection process was faulty. Demonstrated excellence in one assigned task does not indicate potential excellence in another—especially when that other task is instruction. Doing the task is one thing; teaching others to do it is a dramatically different thing.

When organizations fall into the "good-worker" trap, they usually lose a good worker and gain a bad trainer. The truth is that they also multiply the number of bad workers. Why? Because inept or de-motivating instruction produces new generations who cannot do the job properly, or who have lost interest in doing so.

The *job knowledge* trap is very similar and equally dangerous. It is a particularly common error in selecting trainers. Now there is nothing wrong with knowing the subject, but since adult growth involves so much more than merely acquiring information, to study under a person who has nothing but subject matter expertise is a cloying and narrowing bore. (It would be unfair to call it an "experience," since sitting and listening is often the total fate permitted students of subject matter experts who pretend to teach.)

A very intelligent way to use the resources of subject matter experts: to make them members of the design team for training programs. These SME's are invaluable: they bring authenticity, reality, and thoroughness to the task analysis or course content. The SME role recognizes their real value; it avoids trying to make communicators out of people who, though highly knowledgeable, may not be articulate enough to explain what they know—much less help others learn it.

Replicating great teachers is a third trap. Here's how it works—to everyone's detriment. The T & D officer recalls with great affection and admiration some great instructor from a private past. Old Smith told great jokes, so the T & D officer decides that a sense of humor is the key ingredient of successful instruction—and develops a staff of comedians! Or Miss McGrath was so precise and careful. As a result, some T & D department is populated with an entire staff that thinks like accountants! The T & D officer remembers Professor Horner and the way he told things like they were. The result? Some T & D staff becomes a group of abrasive, rabblerousing malcontents; they undercut organizational goals and devastate the organizational image.

Why does this effort to draw analogies with great teachers work so badly? It isn't just that it results in a staff without variety. Another sad effect is that the T & D officer tends to mold the staff into the image of the revered "model." There is no organic growth for staff members. Whatever inventory the T & D staff originally had for effective performance goes unnoticed; it gets twisted into a standard, unnatural pattern. Learners are thus subjected to robots rather than human, facilitative instructors.

The fallacy is the one-dimensional nature of the selection and development process. There is no argument about the value of a sense of humor, or care or precision, or "telling it like it is." But none of these qualities in itself is a sufficient foundation for effective performance as a T & D specialist. The T & D officer must look for several dimensions when populating the T & D staff.

Trap number four is *wants out—not in* candidates. This merely means that some people will take T & D assignments not because they want T & D assignments, but because they want out of the position they're in.

This is an especially dangerous trap, because it's easy for such applicants to demonstrate great enthusiasm for the training function. They have read (or can easily imagine) all the standard, exciting things to say about how important it is to train and develop others. They can grow misty-eyed about the inspiration created by great teachers. Now they are not being dishonest; they mean it at the time because they so desperately want to escape their current assignment. So they legitimately tell how much they owe to a great teacher in their past . . . how exciting it must be to help others . . . how fulfilling!

Such testimonials are delusive, sweet songs to the ears of T & D officers. But when they select the singers of such sweet songs, they end up with a staff of temporary cheerleaders. That enthusiasm lasts just as long as the new T & D specialists are dazzled by their new responsibilities and position. As soon as they tire of it, they start looking. Once again they want out!

The *narrow-role* trap victimizes those who select a candidate who will excel greatly in just one role or very few of the many necessary skills. Such people may have little skill or interest in other facets of the total T & D spectrum. We recall the four major services: consultant, designer, instructor, and administrator; we recall the ASTD Competency Study with 15 roles and 31 competencies! Desire to perform, or competency in very few raises several potential problems.

First, the job may quickly become impoverished, focusing on such narrow tasks that the occupant becomes bored and disenchanted with the entire T & D process. Second, the T & D officer is unable to achieve necessary cross-utilization of the staff. If a sudden crisis or a new development requires a consultant's services, the "narrow-role" T & D specialist may be unqualified or uninterested. When selecting people for the T & D staff, it's wise to remember that, by definition, the department is concerned with growth. T & D officers are wise to select people who can grow with the department, and into more than one of the four roles which must be fulfilled by someone on the T & D staff.

The *personality* trap is the sixth and final pitfall. It is a two-dimensional snare: (1) the traits are hard to identify, and (2) they distract us from looking for identified skills.

We say we seek a person with "a good personality," whatever that means. We often mean gregarious, extroverted, pleasant, . . . all nice traits. But they don't reflect any specific, demonstrated competencies. Studies about the personality profiles of successful teachers, analysts, or administrators present little helpful data. One of the best is by Gagné: it mentions warmth, indirectness, cognitive organization, and enthusiasm. But when we really examine those "traits," they translate into behaviors rather than personality qualities.

"Warmth" boils down to establishing two-way communication, expressing concern for the learners and the learning process.

"Indirectness" involves skill in getting at things obliquely. It means not supplying answers, but answering questions with questions. It means referring the question back to the asker. It means using other learners as a resource for the answers . . . and for the learning.

"Cognitive organization" isn't the same as mastery of the subject, although it implies that. Rather, cognitive organization is skill in retrieving what is known . . . in showing learners where they can find answers . . . in establishing connections between several different parts of the learning inquiry.

"Enthusiasm" comes closest to being a trait. Yet even it is defined as "energy for the learner and learning goals." It is clearly distinguished from cheerleading and showmanship.

To understand the real problem encountered from falling into the personality trap, try to make a list of the traits you want in people who join your staff. There's patience, intelligence, flexibility, pleasing appearance, sense of humor, sympathy, empathy. It begins to sound like a recipe for divinity, doesn't it? Far more to the point are things like strong legs (to endure through the day) and questioning skills and the ability to count to ten when difficult students become abrasive.

The point is that these personality traits are hard to spot in other people, especially during the limited time available in interviews. Even if we have the aid of written tests (where they are still legal and perceived as valid!) we are unable to match the candidates' inventories with the tasks they will be performing as T & D specialists. At least we're not able to do so by examining traits. So what do we do instead?

Far better that we look for demonstrated abilities in the form of behaviors which we can watch for when we interview candidates. What are those skills we seek?

Skills to look for

The 31 competencies listed in McLagan's ASTD study include both skills and "understandings." The skills are:

Writing	Research
A/V	Computer competence
Cost-benefit analysis	Counseling
Data reduction	Delegation
Facilities	Feedback
Futuring	Group process
Library	Model building
Negotiation	Objectives preparation
Performance observation	Presentation
Questioning	Records management
Competency identification	Intellectual versatility
Relationship versatility	

The "understandings" required include:

Adult learning	Career development
Personnel/HR field	Organization behavior
Industry	Organization
T & D field	T & D field

With all that variety, and with continuous research adding depth to each competency, no one expects to hire a master of all—or probably even to develop one! Yet certain behavioral patterns emerge to provide a checklist to use when selecting people for any T & D staff.

These questions get at many of the competencies, with special focus on things like intellectual and relationship versatility, or counseling and feedback skills. It comes close to combining a search for traits, behaviors, and competencies all at once.

First, *can they listen?* They'll need to do a great deal of it, so it's good technique to give them a chance to listen while being interviewed. This doesn't mean that the interviewer does all the talking. The usual advice is correct: the candidate should do most of the talking. Most—but not all.

Since T & D specialists will need to listen for feelings as well as content, it's also a good idea to see how they handle some emotional things as well as some technical data and some intellectual content. Check to see if applicants pick up the little cues you give them about your feelings; find out how they handle process analysis by sharing some of your feelings about how the interview is going. Reflect what they have said, then check their response to that reflection. Double-check their listening by asking something which requires recall of facts you've already supplied. Find out if they "pick up on" questions arising out of a topic you've only sketchily described.

Next, do they *probe for feelings?* When they ask you about the work, do they inquire about the human responses associated with doing the tasks? Do they wonder about the qualms their students might feel at learning to do old things in new ways? Do they sense the feelings associated with acquiring brand new behaviors? Listening for feelings represents one essential skill; *probing* for them goes a step beyond (and ahead!) of mere listening. Beyond these, a third level of listening skill is needed.

Do they *respond constructively to feelings?* When you revealed something of your own emotions during the interview, how did the applicant react? Change the subject? . . . Blush? . . . Awkward silence? Or did you get further inquiry? Reflection? As Carl Rogers points out, the effective facilitator of learning will be as responsive to students' feelings as to their ideas.

Can they *deal with conflict?* For mature ideas to be examined in mature, dynamic ways, T & D specialists will need to handle conflict. When consulting they will face sharp differences about the nature, causes, and impact of performance problems. As designers, they will experience conflict about the appropriateness of a method, or about the receiving department's readiness for certain learning methodology. Instructors face sharp disagreement about theories, policies, and procedures. Administrators resolve conflict on their staff and they resolve conflicts with and between client-managers.

Can they *change their opinions?* Somewhere between total lack of conviction and plain bullheadedness is the degree of flexibility needed in effective T & D specialists. Perhaps it boils down to this for consultants, designers, and instructors: Does new evidence produce an amendment in their original opinions? For administrators this is a major mental skill. Without it there is no evidence that the T & D specialist can grow. If T & D specialists cannot grow, they will have great difficulty in stimulating growth in others.

This issue of mental flexibility ("intellectual versatility" in the ASTD Competency Study) again raises the issue of how important subject knowledge is to the instructor role. In Morris West's 1976 novel *The Navigator*, dealing with the subject of leadership, one of West's characters comments, "You've got to have secrets that everybody else needs and nobody else knows." The credibility of the instructor is important if the objective of the training is to *expand* the experience of the learner. As West puts it, "All his effort, all his planning had been dedicated to the dissemination of knowledge, the sharing of skills, so that in the event of death or casualty, the skill and knowledge would still reside in the community. Now a gossiping old woman had shown him that he was committed to a fallacy. The identity and the security of the community depended upon the existence and the exercise of power. Knowledge was an instrument of power. It must be preserved, but it must be reserved also . . . ."

As the leader in West's novel continues his self-discovery, he reasons that ". . . In an aircraft you don't have people running up to the cockpit to tell the captain what to do—not even if they're pilots themselves. He doesn't tell them what he's doing either. His job is private, secret . . ."

It must therefore be apparent that the instructor is more concerned with mental processes than with mental inventory. It must also be apparent that if instructors are selected just because they know the subject they will teach, the training program is headed for trouble. To be master or mistress of a technology is a comforting position—but that very comfort can be the source of failure in the dynamics of the classroom, or when the technology changes. Thus the importance of selecting instructors who can evaluate information . . . people who can change their minds when new information requires new opinions.

Do they *ask a lot of questions?* Questioning skills are important in the repertory of people performing in any one of the four T & D roles. A propensity to use questions can reveal itself during the interview. Later on, as part of their upgrading, the T & D officer can see that they learn the proper use of open, directive, and reflective types of questions. At the selection stages, one just wants to measure the quantity of their questions . . . their comfort with the interrogative mode." As good T & D specialists they'll be there a lot!

Is there a *high energy level* as they communicate? As we have already noted, this is enthusiasm—not showmanship. It is certainly a vastly different thing from public speaking skills. In fact, platform skills can be counterproductive to effective instruction. Why? Ego and speaking skills can tempt the trainer to send signals rather than to indulge in the two-way communication needed to create learning and to test what learners are learning. Speaking skills tempt trainers to feel that the job has been done well if the lesson has been "said" well. The focus gets onto presentation rather than on learning.

High energy levels, however, are important to the T & D specialist for a number of reasons:

- Days are long. The analysis of performance problems can mean arduous, taxing efforts which must be plowed through to completion—now! The analysis doesn't end just because the normal workday is over.

• Leadership is hard work. It's physically taxing. At the end of counseling, instructing, or consulting, both the body and the spirit can easily be "all achin' and racked with pain."

• Designing requires creativity—and creation (as many have noted) is part perspiration and part concentration. At any rate, it can be exhausting—and usually is!

• Conference or class leadership requires more than normal vocal and physical outputs. The instructor will need energy in great quantities at moments when the group must be "centered" around a single concept, task, topic, or issue. Group and individual attentions must be redirected every now and then; it requires great concentration, moving more purposefully, and talking louder.

• Above all, the instructor is always "living the learning" of every person in the group. That demands fantastically high energy levels.

Can the candidates *express themselves effectively?* Verbal skills play a heavy part in success for all four of the T & D roles. This does not mean a big vocabulary or impeccable English grammar. Rather, it means a vocabulary which responds to leaners' vocabularies. It means a vocabulary which blends the concrete and the abstract so concepts can become realities—and so immediate realities can lead to insights about principles. It means sentences which make sense the first time learners hear them. It means taking the trouble to communicate the transitions between ideas . . . linking them, contrasting them, showing parallels. It means letting people know when you move up or down the ladder of abstraction on which words and ideas exist. It means checking for clarity and stimulating the learner's imagination—simultaneously!

Can the applicant *reinforce?* Be careful of this one. It certainly doesn't mean, "Are they agreeable?" Far from it. All one needs on the T & D staff is a mollycoddle Pollyanna or an obsequious Caspar Milquetoast!

However, the ability to give positive reinforcement is extremely important in probing, in resolving conflict, in teaching. Especially in teaching! Positive reinforcement is vitally helpful in aiding learners as they reach learning goals, particularly difficult learning goals. Effective instructors find the element that is correct or appropriate in each learner-response. Then they reinforce that correct element positively. The ability to give this reinforcement can be observed during the initial interview; it can be strengthened as one of the first lessons in the further training of the T & D specialist. (That learning can begin during the interview if the T & D officer effectively reinforces worthwhile behaviors and responses from the candidate!)

The complexity and depth of the dynamics revealed in Dr. Schmidt's analysis may explain the long list of things instructors need to learn to do in order to become growing and growth-creating members of the T & D staff. Let's look at that list, considering first those things needed for classroom instructors and later the list for those who will do on-the-job training.

If the T & D Specialist Will Do Classroom Teaching and If the T & D Specialist Will Do Conference Leading

Then the initial upgrading should make them able to	*And later follow-up training can make them able to*
Follow lesson plans designed by others	Select media
Comprehend the intent and structure of behaviorally stated learning objectives	Design visual aids for display and/or projection
Write behaviorally stated learning objectives for tasks in all departments which will supply trainees to their classes or conferences	Conduct such special case methods as action mazes, incident process or critical incidents
Identify complete learning objectives	Design on-the-spot cases and tasks so buzzgroups or entire classes can solve identified but unanticipated job-related or learning problems
Develop performance standards	Conduct such special roleplaying formats as reversal, rotation, or doubling
Comprehend and apply stimulus-response theory	Create "hot roleplays" for dealing with class dynamics issues
Use dynamic listening skills	
Use questioning skills	Experience T-groups and become able to function as observer for T-groups
Probe for feelings	
Respond appropriately to feelings	Function in an LCI (open classroom) environment
Lead discussions	
Conduct workshops using buzz groups and team tasks	Speak before such large groups as management meetings and professional societies
Administer and review tests and quizzes	
Administer performance tryouts	
Design performance tryouts	
Conduct job-instruction training (JIT)	
Demonstrate how to do specific tasks	
Conduct structured case studies	
Conduct structured games and simulations	
Administer in-baskets	
Reinforce successive approximations of desired behaviors	

That's clearly an extensive list . . . a big order! All the lists shown here will be like that. Why? Because we want to show the full range of skills the T & D professional will use; and our use of the word "professional" doesn't apply to those who get "stranded" in the T & D Department.

Our professionals are those who can use a wide technology. The list shows the widest technology possible! To do their work well, single-person T & D Departments will need to select carefully, searching out those skills which will be used most frequently—and balancing the self-development program so they prepare themselves to function in as many of the four T & D roles as possible.

If the T & D Specialists Will Do On-the-Job Training

Then initial training should make them able to	And later follow-up training can make them able to
Conduct job-instruction training	Develop performance standards
Comprehend the intent and structure of behaviorally stated learning objectives	Design visual aids for display and/or projection
Write behaviorally stated learning objectives for the skills in their own department	Lecture
Comprehend the structure and intent of performance standards	Lead discussions
Do task analysis	Create "real things" as visual aids (actual or facsimile objects for trainees to handle while learning)
Demonstrate proper performance of tasks in their department	
Comprehend and apply stimulus-response theory	Follow lesson plans which call for experience-based methods
Reinforce successive approximations of desired student behaviors	
Use effective listening skills	
Use questioning skills	
Test achievement of learners	
Provide feedback of learning achievements	
Respond appropriately to feelings	
Probe for feelings	

As we know, there are at least four major roles to be filled in the T & D department. Designers of learning systems need special skills.

If T & D Specialists Will Design Learning

Their initial training should make them able to	*And later follow-up training can make them able to*
Create logical outlines	Design LCI (open classroom) systems
Do task analysis	Develop structures for special discussion formats as brainstorms, fishbowls, polling, collages, force-field analysis
Develop performance standards	
Write behaviorally stated learning objectives	Develop entire modules based on experiential methods
Apply learning theory (especially positive reinforcement) in lesson plans	Prepare scripts for motion picture or videotape filming
Include effective questions in lessons	Design new formats for lesson plans
Provide outlines and materials for job-instruction training	
Produce lesson plans in formats approved or required by client organizations	
Select appropriate media	
Design visual aids for display, projection, or handling	
Locate case studies, roleplays and exercises in standard sources	
Design case studies	
Design roleplays	
Create storyboards and scripts for A/V presentations	
Design behavior-maintenance systems and routinely include them in all training designs	
Design programmed instruction	
Provide mechanisms to test learner accomplishments of each objective	

Not all T & D specialists are concerned to cause learning, or to administer its processes. Before the decision is made to do any training, a great deal of performance analysis occurs . . . by T & D staff people serving as consultants to the organization. What does their expertise include?

When T & D Specialists Serve as Consultants Who Identify and Solve Performance Problems

Initial training should enable them to	*Follow-up training should add competencies so they can also*
Question clients	Conduct and design conferences
Conduct performance audits (analysis)	Conduct ongoing organization development, implying skill in:
Do task analysis	

When T & D Specialists Serve as Consultants Who Identify and Solve Performance Problems (*Continued*)

Initial training should enable them to	*Follow-up training should add competencies so they can also*
Do cost-analysis of performance problems	Process analysis
Analyze cost-effectiveness of solutions	Structured data gathering
Probe for facts and feelings	"Hot" data gathering such as:
Empathize and respond appropriately to facts and feelings	Organization mirroring
Verify perceptual data	T-Shirting
Help write performance standards	The Library
Use rational systems for problem solving	Lead discussions, using fishbowls, brainstorms, confrontation, case studies, valuing exercises
Comprehend a job-engineering project	Speak before large groups within the organization
Assist in installing a job-engineering project	Conduct research and present the results to client-management and/or professional societies
Install feedback mechanisms	Implement a changed-contingencies system
Help maintain behaviors acquired in any change program	Help install re-engineered jobs
Do contingency analysis	
Write investigative reports with recommended solutions for performance problems	
Present oral proposals to small groups	
Create behaviorally oriented learning objectives	
Do statistical analysis of raw data	

When we consider the skills required of the T & D officer, we are of course examining a list which looks like the behaviors of any manager—plus some important special considerations. Our chart will examine just those special things; we will assume that all the other administrative and managerial skills are part of the inventory the T & D officer brings to the position—or acquires immediately after the first day on the job! (If that's a hasty assumption, then the typical Management Education curriculum must be added to the top of the chart!)

The Administrator of the T & D Function, in Addition To a Full Inventory of Standard Management Skills, Will Need To Be Able To

Initially	*As later growth*
Plan the T & D mission	Conduct process analysis and T-groups
Establish position descriptions	

Initially	*As later growth*
Write a T & D policy statement	Lead organization development interventions, implying all the consultative, data-gathering, and problem-solving skills listed for T & D consultants
Select a T & D staff on specific criteria	
Organize T & D resources to meet the departmental goals	
Provide for ongoing growth for the T & D staff	Respond constructively to new directions required for the development and re-direction of the T & D department as a responsive subsystem in the total organization
Control the ongoing T & D activities	
Budget for T & D activities	
Write effective (results-getting) proposals	Design and help install and monitor job re-engineering
Lead discussions	
Speak before classes, conferences, workshops, management, and professional gatherings	
Practice positive reinforcement	
Explain learning theory, including andragogy and facilitation	
Comprehend all skills employed by other, subordinate T & D staff members	
Use dynamic listening skills	
Use all forms of questioning	
Write behaviorally oriented learning objectives	
Assist in writing performance standards for all departments	
Determine actual performance standards for the T & D department	
Complete and install contingency changes	
Design and install feedback systems	

Then there's *control of the situation.* Perhaps this is nothing more than asking that candidates be themselves. A significant trend in adult education and training is the need for instructors to be real people, not actors impersonating plaster saints. As Kohl says in *The Open Classroom,* "A teacher has as much right to be angry, frustrated, impatient, distrustful as students have and should let them know that . . . Only when a teacher emerges as another person in the classroom can a free environment evolve." (p. 81) This in no way implies that T & D specialists can be undisciplined, totally spontaneous creatures who lose their tempers or speak their minds whenever the spirit moves them to do so. But it does mean that they don't fall apart at the seams when their own humanity spills out. They are able to handle that; they are in control of the situation.

One might argue that the T & D officer who finds these behaviors or skills in candidates has really measured the personality traits of those candidates. If so, so be it. The important thing is that looking for demonstrated skill in listening, questioning, reinforcing, communicating, and being congruent assures the T & D officer that candidates can *do* something . . . that they already have in their inventory some of the things they will have to do when they become T & D specialists.

Granted, the nature of the initial T & D assignments makes a difference. T & D specialists who will analyze performance problems need somewhat different proficiencies from those who will instruct. Even within the instructor's role we expect different skills from classroom instructors, conference leaders and on-the-job trainers. But as already noted, the enriched T & D placement moves incumbents through more than one of the four T & D roles. Besides, there are some skills which are equally important to successful performance in *every* one of the roles.

THE CARE AND DEVELOPMENT OF T & D SPECIALISTS

Now that you have them, how do you care for them?

Growth and change are the output of the T & D function. Strangely enough, they are also the processes by which that change is achieved. But rather than wrestle with the involutions of such thinking, let's just look at a plan for the development of the T & D staff.

The development plan for T & D staff amounts to meeting a series of micro training needs, using any or all of the methods that solve any individual training need: independent study, coaching, seminars and workshops, membership in professional associations. The list is long.

This growth for T & D specialists is a form of job training, so the "Tell, Show, Do, and Review" stages are important—with special emphasis on *doing* some work as soon as possible. Designing or presenting short modules of existing programs is effective; so is membership in professional societies. Young T & D staff members make introducers, moderators, chairpersons, and chapter officers . . . each an excellent way to develop several competencies.

In what role will the specialist perform? We need to offer different training to different people, depending upon what they will do while serving in the T & D department.

Let's look first at the most familiar role, that of the instructor. To do so, we might well borrow an approach shared by Dr. Warren Schmidt of UCLA at a gathering of training officers in 1974. Dr. Schmidt pointed out that effective performance as an instructor varies with the mission. If trainees are "*expanding* their experience," one set of expectations about instructors applies. If they are "*organizing or reorganizing* their experience," another set applies. A summary of Dr. Schmidt's beliefs looks like this:

	If the learning expands experience	*If the learning organizes experience*
The instructor's role is primarily	To identify the real problems and concerns of the learner	To set a climate
	To clarify goals and their relevance	To put the learners' experience into perspective
	To describe the process by which learners will acquire new behaviors	To give feedback on the possible consequences of past behavior
		To help learners generalize from their past experience
Success depends upon	Clarity with which the new material is presented	Extent to which the climate is free from threat
	Learners' respect for the instructor's competence	Learners feel need to find new approaches to old problems
	Learners' perception of relevance of the new material	Learners' willingness to risk exposure to weakness
The climate should be	Exciting Absorbing	Not rushed Thoughtful
Problems to anticipate	Learner may feel inadequate	Learner may feel nothing has been learned
	Instructor may overestimate or underestimate the learner's inventory	Learners may reject analysis or theory which disagrees with their preconceptions

ROTATION POLICIES

"We have two kinds of people on our training staff," said the training manager sadly. "Promotable young people and the professionals."

That's rather common. The instructor position is often used as an educational experience for employees who are "going someplace" in the management of the organization. These "promotables" rotate through a year or three in the T & D department.

There's much to be said for such a system. T & D experience, early in the rotation program, gives high-potential employees a wide and steadily growing perspective of the entire organization: T & D offers great opportunities to work with lots of people from lots of departments . . . with people who have sharply differing motivations, needs, viewpoints, and value systems. Furthermore, if the assignment in T & D includes instruction, design, consultation, and administration, the "cadets" gain experience in sharply contrasted skills.

Then why would that training manager feel such sadness when commenting on the promotable young people and the "professionals"? Let's listen a bit more: "It's policy around here to keep people in training three years, then to move them on to higher jobs in management. But some of our people have been here for ten or twelve years! They just don't seem to make it."

And that's what's to be said against the system of "rotating through" T & D as an education for major management assignments. Not everybody "makes it"—and unfortunately the ones who don't make it usually become the "professionals." It's a quintessential expression of George Bernard Shaw's acidic comment, "Those who can, do; those who can't, teach." Only in this case, those who can't teach keep on doing so. Then as balm to the organizational conscience, they are informally referred to as "the professionals." The fact is that they are often lousy instructors who continue to inflict their amateur incompetence on helpless learners!

All apart from the organizational awkwardness such failures represent, there is the considerable pain for the individuals and T & D officers on whose "island" they tend to get stranded. Further conversation with the training manager we've been quoting revealed yet another dimension to the tragedy: "In fact I was supposed to rotate out of here myself. They brought me in here, and I didn't know anything about training. My three years were up last August—but I see no sign of getting out!"

This is a real situation—and not an unusual one. What does it teach us? That rotation through T & D assignments can be a good thing or a bad thing, depending upon how we manage such a system. If we use T & D as a springboard to other management assignments, we need to take certain precautions:

1. The selection process needs to be precise, uncovering skills which will indicate probable success as a T & D specialist. Seat-of-the-pants hunches that prospective T & D staff members look bright, or that they "have a knack for training"—these are no longer adequate.

2. If service in T & D is indeed to provide education for its incumbents, the T & D officer must establish and maintain precise programs for their continued growth. Normal budget ratios may be inadequate; higher percentages of staff time must be invested in staff training. T & D specialists need continuous acquisition of new technology in analyzing performance problems, in designing and implementing learning designs, and in general management practices. Remember the shoemaker's children? They were barefoot! Thorough plans to put professional shoes on "cadets in the T & D department" are vital. As much as 10 percent of the total work-time may go to professional upgrading for new T & D specialists.

3. Systematic, binding contracts for "re-entry" to the line organization need to be executed from the very start. The contingencies for successful tours within the T & D department need to be positively rewarding for the "tourists."

4. "Escape routes" must be established for cadets who perform badly in their early T & D projects. It doesn't follow that these marginal performances should purge such cadets from the "promotables program"—but it does follow that frank career counseling is in order. (Such escape routes and frank counseling are imperative whenever T & D specialists do badly in early assignments. If coaching cannot correct the problems, then reassignment should be considered a useful action. Nothing will be gained for the individual, the T & D department, or the total organization by permissively letting marginal T & D specialists establish reputations as second-raters!)

Many T & D departments regard themselves as professional, career placements. Thus rotation is not an established mechanism, and they have no "launching pad" responsibilities. Yet in actual practice, most departments turn out to have both temporary and permanent T & D specialists on the staff. Effective T & D specialists are attractive (and attracted) to other managerial assignments. When they make such moves, the T & D officer should analyze the pattern of movement out of the department: Where do these ex-T & D specialists go? To lateral placements? . . . to demoted positions? . . . to promotions? Unless the pattern is toward better positions, the T & D department is breeding "shoemakers' children." It is making a lie of the theory that training, education, and development enhance human resources. When placement within the T & D department does not lead to happy external placement, or expanded responsibilities within, the T & D officer needs to get busy with a solid plan for developing the T & D staff.

Let's stress one point that might—but shouldn't—get lost in that last paragraph. Unless the good T & D specialists assume increasing responsibility *within* the T & D department, then the good people don't become the "professionals." Even if there is no rotation policy—but particularly when there is such a system—the "old-timers" on the T & D staff should be the most professional as well as the most senior.

SUMMARY

Those lists of requisite skills seem a long way from Shaw's judgment that those who can, do—and those who can't, teach! It is also a long way from those forgotten "professionals" who never successfully rotated through a T & D assignment . . . or who performed marginally and became incompetent incumbents. Perhaps their lonely obsolescence came about because no one cared . . . specifically because no one cared for their continued professional development.

Why is that list of requisite skills so long? Well, it may be too long for some organizations . . . unrealistic as a picture of what technology most T & D staffs really master. But it is also a long list because we've come a long way since Shaw first deprecated the teacher. In fact, we've learned that the T & D department does a lot more than just teach.

It isn't just that the T & D department is no longer perceived as starting and ending with training. In addition, behaviorist psychology, facilitative learning theories, performance analysis technologies—all these have accounted for growth in our perception of the T & D function.

With that growth has come the concept of accountability. And one big accountability is for T & D specialists to serve as performance problem problem-solvers. To do that there is the inevitable added accountability of selecting and developing the right people to identify important problems and to solve them effectively.

The impact of that challenge is more apparent when we stop to think that every behavior by a T & D specialist or a T & D officer impacts geometrically upon the organization. A successful class changes the performance of everyone who attends; a wise decision about how to solve a performance problem produces changed working conditions for entire populations . . . for incumbents and for employees yet to be hired.

All the more reason for the careful selection and relentless energy in the continued growth of people on the T & D staff!

WHERE DOES
IT ALL END?

DISCUSSION

Where does it all end? It doesn't.

Training and development is by nature a cyclic thing: a problem requires solutions which bring progress which brings growth which brings problems which engender solutions which bring growth which brings . . . .

These inevitable phases of the T & D cycle are like the seasons: they cause each other, yet each in itself is an exciting, worthy experience.

If our look at the training and development function has seemed to be an endless succession of goals, standards, and problems; of objectives, learning, and feedback; of growth, stimulus, and response—well, that's correct! That's what T & D is all about. That's the relentlessness of it. That's the wonderfulness of it!

If an organization has no mission, it has no reason for existing. If it has no standards, it has no way of knowing how to achieve its mission. But its standards won't always be met; there will be performance problems.

The job of training and development is solutions to performance problems. Now solutions mean change, and change means new problems . . . just as new technology, new employees, new frontiers mean new problems. Perhaps it will all fit together into one concrete, constructive cycle if we "put it all together" this way:

- Organizations get established because someone finds a mission which cannot be achieved by one person working alone.
- Some output (product or service) is defined, but unattainable through the efforts of just one person.
- Distinct tasks are identified for the people needed to produce the product or service.
- Standards are set for each task. These standards involve units of work, time, and materials. These standards also involve levels of excellence . . . how the tasks must be performed to maintain an acceptable product or service.

So an organization gets born, and it takes people, technology, time, and material. Let's summarize the process in pictorial form (Fig. 18.1). That thin horizontal line at the center of the chart shows why training and development is a continuous activity. Remember how people have always said that woman's work is never done? Well . . . in one sense the T & D officer is like that—the behavioral housekeeper of the organization. And the work is never done!

That fact of life can be burdensome—the source of despair, of a sense of endlessness.

It can also be a joyous, encouraging thing . . . a security blanket. It means that there will always be full employment for those T & D officers who stay aware of the goals of their organization, and sensitive to the performance of the people who make that organization successful.

Adding zest and dimension to the business of being in the "change business" is that exciting volume of change that's going on within the "change business"! Growth is all about the T & D staff! Their mission involves producing growth in people and in organizations; their vitality and usefulness depends upon continuous growth in themselves.

Speaking of continuous growth, here is some.

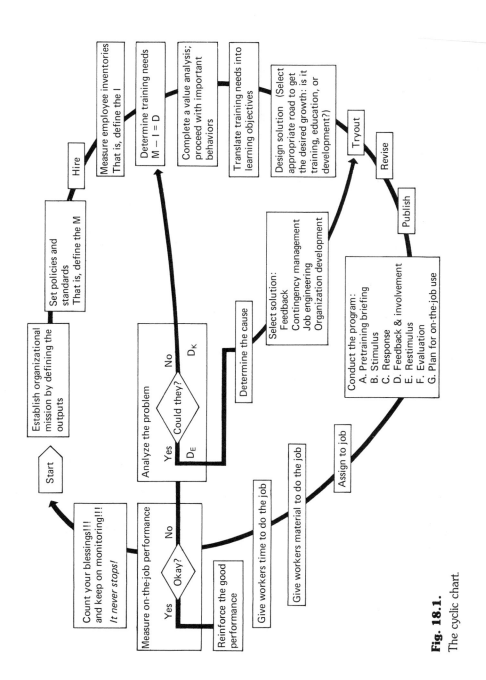

Fig. 18.1.
The cyclic chart.

MORE READING

Books

Anderson, Ronald H., *Selecting and Developing Media for Instruction,* New York: Van Nostrand Reinhold, 1976.

Baird, Lloyd S., Craig Eric Schneier, and Dugan Laird (eds.), *The Training and Development Source Book,* Amherst, MA: Human Resource Development Press, 1983.

Behaviordelia (Malott, Richard W., *et al.*) *CONtingency MANagement in Education and Other Exciting Places,* Kalamazoo, MI: Behaviordelia, 1972.

Bloom, Benjamin (ed.), *Taxonomy of Educational Objectives: The Cognitive Domain,* New York: David McKay, 1956.

Bloom, Benjamin (ed.), *Taxonomy of Educational Objectives: The Affective Domain,* New York: David McKay, 1964.

Broadwell, Martin M., *The Supervisor and On-the-Job Training,* 2nd ed., Reading, MA: Addison-Wesley, 1975.

Broadwell, Martin M., *The Supervisor as an Instructor,* 4th ed., Reading, MA: Addison-Wesley, 1984.

Canfield, Jack, and Harold C. Wells, *100 Ways to Enhance Self-Concept in the Classroom,* Englewood Cliffs, NJ: Prentice-Hall, 1976.

Cornish, Edward (ed.), *Careers Tomorrow,* Bethesda, MD: World Future Society, 1983.

Craig, Robert L. (ed.), *The Training and Development Handbook,* 2nd ed., New York: McGraw-Hill, 1976 (sponsored by the American Society for Training and Development).

Davis, Larry Nolan, and Earl McCollon, *Planning, Conducting and Evaluating Workshops,* Austin: Learning Concepts, 1974.

Dobson, James, *Dare to Discipline,* Wheaton, IL: Tyndale House, 1971.

Finkel, Coleman, *Professional Guide to Successful Meetings,* Philadelphia, PA: Successful Meetings, 1976.

Fluegelman, Andrew (ed.), *The New Games Book,* New York: Doubleday, 1976.

Fordyce, Jack K., and Raymond Weil, *Managing with People,* Reading MA: Addison-Wesley, 1971.

Gagné, Robert, *The Conditions of Learning,* New York: Holt, Rinehart and Winston, 1965.

Greenberg, Ira C., *Psychodrama, Theory and Therapy,* Beverly Hills, CA: Behavioral Studies Press, 1974.

Hart, Lois B., *Learning From Conflict,* Reading, MA: Addison-Wesley, 1981.

Horn, Robert, and David W. Zuckerman, *The Guide to Simulation/Games for Education and Training,* Lexington, MA: Information Resources, 1976.

Kirkpatrick, Donald L. (ed.), *Evaluating Training Programs,* Madison, Wis.: American Society for Training and Development, 1975.

Kirkpatrick, Donald L., *A Practical Guide for Supervisory Training and Development,* 2nd ed., Reading, MA: Addison-Wesley, 1983.

Knowles, Malcolm S., *The Adult Learner: A Neglected Species,* Houston: Gulf, 1973.

Knowles, Malcolm S., *The Modern Practice of Adult Education,* New York: Association Press, 1970.

Kohl, Herbert, R., *The Open Classroom,* New York: Vintage Books, a Division of Random House, 1969.

Kolb, David A., Irwin M. Rubin, and James M. McIntyre, (eds.) *Organizational Psychology: A Book of Readings,* Englewood Cliffs, NJ: Prentice-Hall, 1971.

Laird, Dugan, and Ruth House, *Interactive Classroom Instruction,* Glenview, IL: Scott Foresman, 1983.

Laird, Dugan, and Ruth House, *Training Today's Employees,* Glenview, IL: Scott Foresman, 1984. (Originally published, Boston: CBI, 1983.)

Lord, Kenniston W., Jr., *The Design of the Industrial Classroom,* Reading MA: Addison-Wesley, 1977.

Mager, Robert F., *Developing Attitudes Toward Instruction,* Palo Alto, CA: Fearon, 1968.

Mager, Robert F., *Goal Analysis,* Belmont, CA: Fearon, 1972.

Mager, Robert F., *Measuring Instructional Intent,* Belmont, CA: Fearon, 1973.

Mager, Robert F., *Preparing Instructional Objectives* (2nd ed.), Belmont, CA: Fearon, 1975.

Mager, Robert F., and Kenneth M. Beach, *Developing Vocational Instruction,* Belmont, CA: Fearon, 1967.

Mager, Robert F., and Peter Pipe, *Analyzing Performance Problems,* Belmont, CA: Fearon, 1970.

Margolis, Frederick H., and Chip Bell, *Managing the Learning Process,* Minneapolis: Training Books, Lakewood Publications, 1984.

McLagan, Patricia A., *Getting Results Through Learning,* St. Paul, MN: M & A Press, 1983.

McLagan, Patricia A., *Helping Others Learn,* Reading, MA: Addison-Wesley, 1978.

McKeachie, Wilbert J., *Teaching Tips: A Guidebook for the Beginning College Teacher,* Lexington, MA: D.C. Heath, 1969.

McVey, G. F., *Sensory Factors in the School Learning Environment,* Washington, DC: National Education Association, 1971.

Morrisey, George, *Management by Objectives and Results,* Reading, MA: Addison-Wesley, 1970.

Nadler, Leonard, *Developing Human Resources,* Houston: Gulf, 1970 (supported by the National Society for Training and Development).

The Audio-Visual Equipment Directory, Fairfax, VA: The National Audio-Visual Association (Annual).

Pfeiffer, J. William, and John E. Jones, *Structured Experiences for Human Relations Training,* LaJolla, CA: University Associates Press, 1969.

Pfeiffer, J. William, and John E. Jones, *Handbook for Group Facilitators,* LaJolla, CA: University Associates Press, 1972 ff.

Rigg, Robinson P., *Audio-Visual Aids and Techniques,* London: Hamisch Hamilton, Ltd., 1969. (Distributed in the United States by Olympic Film Service, 161 West 22nd Street, New York City, NY 10011.)

Rogers, Carl R., *Freedom to Learn,* Columbus, OH: Charles E. Merrill, 1969.

Skinner, B. F., *About Behaviorism,* New York: Alfred A. Knopf, 1974.

Skinner, B. F., *The Technology of Teaching,* New York: Appleton-Century-Crofts, 1968.

Tiger, Lionel, and Robin Fox, *The Imperial Animal,* New York: Holt, Rinehart and Winston, 1971.

U.S. Civil Service Commission, *A Training Cost Model,* Washington, DC: Bureau of Training, Training Management Division (CST 100-0001), 1972.

Warren, Malcolm W., *Training for Results,* Reading, MA: Addison-Wesley, 1969.

Booklets

Gilbert, Thomas F., *Levels and Structure of Performance Analysis*, Morristown, NJ: Praxis, 1974.

Harless, J.H., *An Ounce of Analysis (Is Worth a Pound of Objectives)*, Falls Church, VA: Harless Educational Technologists, 1970, 1971.

Harless, J.H., *Behavior Analysis and Management*, Champaign, IL: Stipes Publishing Company. (Original copyright by Harless Educational Technologists, 1968 and 1970).

Laird, Dugan, *A User's Look At The Audio-Visual World*, 2nd ed., Fairfax, VA: The National Audio-Visual Association, 1974.

Miller, Lawrence, M., *Behavior Management*, Atlanta, GA: Human Behavior Institute, 1974. (A self-study workbook designed to accompany a multimedia self-instructional learning system for supervisory personnel.)

Magazine articles

Asimov, Issac, "Life in the 21st Century," *Modern Maturity*, February-March 1984, pp. 36–42.

Brethower, Karen S., and Geary A. Rummler, "Evaluating Training," *Improving Human Performance Quarterly*, **5,** 3–4, Fall-Winter 1976, p. 103.

Broadwell, Martin M., "How To Improve the Next Batch of Course Objectives You Write," *Training*, May 1975, p. 50.

Broadwell, Martin M., "The Use and Misuse of A-V," *Training*, October 1970, p. 40.

Campbell, Donald T., interviewed in "The Experimenting Society," *Psychology Today*, September 1975, p. 46 (with Carol Tarvis).

Craven, Keith, "The Psychological Significance of Color," *New Dimensions*, **1,** 2, 1974, p. 4.

Cherry, Laurence, "On the Real Benefits of Eustress," (Interview with Hans Selye), *Psychology Today*, March 1978, pp. 60–70.

Davies, I.K., "Some Aspects of Measurement in Educational Technology," from *Aspects of Educational Technology III*, Chicago, IL: Educational Media, 1969 (out of print).

Davis, James, and John Hagman, "What's Right—And Wrong—With Your Training Room Environment?" *Training*, July 1976, p. 28.

Gilbert, Tom, "Praxeonomy: A Systematic Approach to Identifying Training

Needs," *The Management of Personnel Quarterly,* **6,** 3, Fall 1967 (Graduate School of Business Administration, University of Michigan, Ann Arbor, MI).

Haines, Frederick J., "Coping with Color: Easy When You Know How," *Video Systems,* July/August 1976, p. 24.

Hampe, Barry, "What's The Real Cost of a Ten Minute Film?" *Training,* July 1976, p. 19.

Harrison, Roger, "Self-Directed Learning: A Radical Approach to Educational Design," *Simulation and Games,* **8,** 1, March 1977, p. 73.

Kael, Pauline, "Annals of Architecture: A Better Sound," *The New Yorker,* November 8, 1976, pp. 51–145.

Main, Jeremy, "New Ways To Teach Workers What's New," *Fortune,* October 1, 1984.

Reed, J. D., reviewing *The Second Self: Computers and the Human Spirit,* by Sherry Turkle, *Time,* August 27, 1984, p. 58.

Schleger, Peter R., "Don't Sing the First-time Video Blues," *Training and Development Journal,* December 1983, pp 63–66.

Schleger, Peter R., "What, Me Produce Video?" *Training and Development Journal,* October 1984, pp. 40–48.

Schleger, Peter R., "A Guide for People Who Use Your Video Program," *Training and Development Journal,* December 1984, pp. 32–34.

Suessmuth, Patrick, "Training Small Groups: How To Structure Them for Better Results," *Training,* June 1976, p. 21 ff.

Wolfe, Tom, "The Me Decade, and the Third Great Awakening," *New West,* August 30, 1976, pp. 27–48.

INDEX